# The Concept of Liberty
## in the Age of the
## American Revolution

# The Concept of Liberty in the Age of the American Revolution

## John Phillip Reid

The University of Chicago Press
Chicago and London

John Phillip Reid is professor of law at the New York University School of Law. He has published extensively on legal and constitutional history, including the multi-volume *Constitutional History of the American Revolution*, of which two volumes—*The Authority of Rights* (1986) and *The Authority to Tax* (1987)—have appeared.

The University of Chicago Press, Chicago 60637
The University of Chicago Press, Ltd., London
© 1988 by The University of Chicago
All rights reserved. Published 1988
Printed in the United States of America

97 96 95 94 93 92 91 90 89 88    5 4 3 2 1

Library of Congress Cataloging-in-Publication Data

Reid, John Phillip.
  The concept of liberty in the age of the
American Revolution.

  Bibliography: p. 163.
  Includes index.
    1. United States—Constitutional history.
  2. Rule of Law—United States—History.   3. Liberty—
History.   I. Title.
KF4541.R45   1988      323.44'09      87–14971
  ISBN 0–226–70896–9

for the

Reverend Joseph T. Durkin, S.J.

of Georgetown

# Contents

# Introduction

Liberty was the most cherished right possessed by English-speaking people in the eighteenth century. It was both an ideal for the guidance of governors and a standard with which to measure the constitutionality of government; both a cause of the American Revolution and a purpose for drafting the United States Constitution; both an inheritance from Great Britain and a reason republican common lawyers continued to study the law of England.

That most treasured right, liberty in the age of the American Revolution, is the subject of this study, and it is important at the outset to recognize the boundaries of our quest. It will not do to look for questions that are not asked or answers that are not sought. This is not a constitutional history of the American Revolution. It is concerned with the concept of "liberty," not with the constitutional issues that led to rebellion from Great Britain. In other words, this study does not consider the American defense of such constitutional rights as the right to jury trial, the right of taxation by consent, or even those rights that the eighteenth-century legal mind associated most closely with the concept of liberty: the right to property, the right to security, and the right to isonomy (in the eighteenth century, the equality of political rights). [1] Rather, if this study were given a generic description it would not be "constitutional" history or "legal" history but "jurisprudential" history—which is, of course, intellectual history or that specialized area of intellectual history concerned with law and legal theory. It is eighteenth-century jurisprudence that we seek, "legal" and "constitutional" thought, true enough, but thought in the abstract more than in its application.

1

There are strengths to jurisprudential history. Because of its points of interest and purpose it permits us to concentrate on concepts, ideas, and even on semantic usage. There are also disadvantages, especially for those not familiar with its discipline. For readers seeking the broader thrust of general history, several objections may be raised. One might be that more comparisons could be drawn to the twentieth century, that the concept of liberty in the age of the American Revolution would be better understood if put in the context of today's values and definitions. That task could have been undertaken, but there would have been risks. Twentieth-century notions of liberty should not be allowed to intrude on eighteenth-century notions. The gap may be too great to be bridged. Depending on one's prejudices, today's emphasis on liberty, when compared to the eighteenth century's, can be labeled either "individualistic" or "permissive." Liberty in this age may not yet mean economic equality, but it is now closer to meaning individual autonomy than it was during the years of the American revolutionary controversy or the years of American constitution making. Focus today is on the liberty of the individual, on the person being allowed to do "his thing," on slogans proclaiming that the citizen has a right to "her own body."

In the meaning of liberty during the age of the American Revolution the equation was plural, not singular. Liberty meant that individuals had rights, true enough, but so did society. In the twentieth century the rhetoric of liberty leads to individual rights with which the state is forbidden to interfere. In the eighteenth century the word "right" was balanced by the word "duty." If people had rights they also had duties, owed less to the state than to society—to their fellow members living under the social contract—but the emphasis was still as much on duties owed as rights possessed.

For readers who are not familiar with legal literature or with how lawyers think, a second objection could be that some of the material in this book appears to lack a sense of time and place. To the degree that this discussion is about law and constitutional principle, the isolation of the concept "liberty" from social and economic considerations is both inevitable and a manifestation of reality. Even in the twentieth century common lawyers do not view law as anchored in time. A constitutional rule promulgated by the courts but yesterday is thought of by lawyers as always having been the "law."

They do not regard it as historians would, as the "latest" interpretation of the text or of the framers' intentions, but as the "right" interpretation. Previous interpretations are not only discarded as law, they are said to be "wrong," and, as law, they are "wrong."[2] To an even greater extent legal theory in the seventeenth and eighteenth centuries was a discipline adrift on a timeless sea. Law was an abstraction—an Anglo-Saxon inheritance, turned toward arbitrariness by the Norman Conquest and Tudor absolutism, but always returning to the pure stream of original principles, heedless of economic circumstances or political philosophies. It was not only common lawyers, but much of the educated public who thought of the legal past in this way. They conceptualized a timeless liberty, ever striving to be restored to the intemporal vigor of the ancient constitution. The perspective is well appreciated by lawyers, but frequently misinterpreted by historians.[3] The timelessness attributed to the ancient constitution was not an instance of lawyers misunderstanding historical dynamics. It was, rather, a matter of constitutional advocacy, of defending liberty as the status quo under an unwritten, customary constitution; in other words, of forensic history.

Eighteenth-century constitutional theorists knew that over the centuries of English and British experience, liberty had been the subject of continual historical ebb and flow. It was the concept of liberty, not liberty's historical experience, they thought "timeless," because, if it was not timeless but willed, or created, or granted it might be changed, amended, or revoked by the same will, creator, or grantor.

This lawyer's way of thinking should be kept in mind, for to the extent "liberty" was a legal or constitutional concept—and it is the argument of this study that liberty in the eighteenth century was a concept of constitutional law—it is best to approach and explain it more in the abstract than in the concrete. That certainly was how the eighteenth century envisioned liberty. Interest in the topic of liberty did not have to be triggered by specific events. It was, instead, a never-ending dialogue both in America where, as Forrest McDonald observes, "political discourse was an ongoing public forum on the meaning of liberty,"[4] and in Great Britain where, according to Bernard Bailyn, no political writer "could afford to neglect the theme of British liberty."[5]

It is for that reason—that eighteenth-century "liberty" was a

concrete concept, but it was becoming idea

concept generally evaluated in abstract terms rather than related to concrete events—that this study will not concentrate attention on the political struggles and partisan movements that incited discussions of liberty. It may, nevertheless, be useful to mention some of the political and constitutional controversies that, during their duration, increased the volume and intensity of the rhetoric of liberty. These included the excise crisis of 1733;[6] the cider and perry excise of 1763,[7] raising constitutional objections exactly the same as would two years later be raised against the Stamp Act;[8] the scheme of the attorney general to substitute informations for grand jury indictments;[9] the general–search warrant controversy[10] and the Middlesex election controversy,[11] both involving John Wilkes; the arrest of printers and officials of the City of London for violating parliamentary privilege;[12] the king's refusal to receive certain petitions, diminishing the appearance of an ancient English liberty-preserving right and consequently diminishing the procedure (though perhaps not the substance) of British liberty;[13] the growing realization that Parliament had acquired arbitrary power to alter what customarily had been perceived as fundamental liberties,[14] a change manifested by passage of the East India Bill, confiscating "property" that had been thought securely protected,[15] and by passage of the Quebec Act, authorizing for the first time the governance of a British colony without the right of representation or the right to trial by jury;[16] and, of course, the American revolutionary controversy itself—a controversy, it should be remembered, producing an outpouring of liberty rhetoric in the mother country as great as that in the colonies.

To treat the eighteenth-century concept of liberty as a legal and constitutional doctrine means that perceptions about liberty must be more tightly drawn than they would have to be had liberty been exclusively a political concept. A recent observation by Forrest McDonald provides an example of the problem. "Liberty, like property," he wrote, "was not a right but a congeries of rights—liberties, not liberty—that were derived from civil society and ultimately from the sovereign." "Liberties, in this sense," McDonald added, "consisted in limitations upon the powers of the sovereign and in a sharing, enjoyed by freemen, in the exercise of those powers."[17] No eighteenth-century constitutional theorist would have said what McDonald says, that liberties could both be "derived from the sovereign" and limit "the powers of the sov-

ereign." For the legal mind of the eighteenth century, the concept
of liberty, if it was to be a normative, viable, determinative concept, had to be a "possession," "inherited" at birth, independent
of sovereign caprice. Surely, it could not be a grant, whether
revocable or irrevocable.

A similar imprecision, separating our way of thinking from the
thought of eighteenth-century constitutionalism, is the notion
often stated by students of the American Revolution, that colonial
whigs equated "liberty with property."[18] Put another way, the idea
is that to have liberty one had to have property, that liberty could
not exist without property. If that association were true, if liberty
depended on material goods, the preservation of liberty would have
required the redistribution of wealth. No one in the eighteenth
century advocated such measures because then property was not
thought to be liberty and liberty was not confused with property.
The security of property, not property itself, was what ensured
British liberty.[19] Material possessions, especially hereditary
landed estates, bolstered liberty by making individuals independent of government. In a mixed, balanced monarchy, a certain
number of independent, propertied persons were essential to
maintaining the balance against arbitrary power. For that reason,
those who possessed property had to possess it absolutely, secured
from government interference.[20]

A second consequence of treating liberty primarily as a legal
concept in the eighteenth century is to see that we may have been
searching for its origins in the wrong directions. In recent years
those origins have been traced to such sources as classical republicanism, civic humanism, commonwealthism, and the country-
court dichotomy dividing English political society. One need not
quarrel with any of these supposed explanations for the eighteenth-
century concept of liberty to wonder whether the debate has
become so intense that exponents of one theory or the other have
been concentrating too much attention on differences, forgetting
similarities.[21] Our danger is that the search for exotic explanations
may make us overlook English and British liberty's most obvious
source: common-law constitutionalism.

A historian has recently written that the *Answer to the Nineteen
Propositions*, a constitutional declaration promulgated by Charles I
in 1642, presented "a classical republic." From the perspective of a
seventeenth-century common lawyer it would seem more accurate

to describe the *Answer* as a reformulation of the constitutional theory espoused by the parliamentary attorneys who had opposed Charles in 1628.[22]

Joyce Appleby has contrasted the liberty of "classical republicanism" with another, a different type of liberty; a liberty that comes remarkably close to being a restatement of common-law constitutionalism.

> Liberty in the classical republican paradigm and liberty in the historic rights tradition are distinct and potentially contradictory concepts. The classical liberty of freemen to participate in political decisions celebrates the public arena and the disinterestedness of civic virtue. The liberty of secure possession protects private, personal enjoyments—liberties that become vested interests. There is no suggestion of limiting the power of government in the classical tradition as long as that power serves the common good, whereas the particular liberties of citizens or subjects secured by law limits the scope of public authority. Classical republican liberty is a lofty ideal; the liberty of legal rights pertains to the mundane and everyday aspects of living.[23]

It was the second liberty, the liberty Appleby called the "historic rights tradition," that J. H. Hexter contrasted to the liberty of civic humanism brought into the debate over the origins of liberty by J. G. A. Pocock. That second liberty, unlike Pocock's liberty, did not focus on citizen participation, but was a liberty, Hexter contends, that could be possessed without political activity. And "possessed," a legal term with legal meaning, was the right word to use when conceptualizing why and how the English enjoyed that second style of liberty, for the "key words of its vocabulary" were "property," "law," "custom," "ancestors," and "inheritance." Put another way, Hexter adds, "the indispensable elements" of the second "kind of liberty" are "property and the rule of law."[24]

Of the various definitions of liberty recently advanced by historians of the eighteenth century, Bernard Bailyn's best fits the conclusions of this study.

> [P]olitical liberty, as opposed to the theoretical liberty that existed in a state of nature, was traditionally known to be "a

natural power of doing or not doing whatever we have a mind" so long as that doing was "consistent with the rules of virtue and the established laws of the society to which we belong"; it was a "power of acting agreeable to the laws which are made and enacted by the consent of the PEOPLE, and in no ways inconsistent with the natural rights of a single person, or the good of the society." Liberty, that is, was the capacity to exercise "natural rights" within limits set not by the mere will or desire of men in power but by non-arbitrary law—law enacted by legislatures containing within them the proper balance of forces.[25]

It does not detract from the basic validity of Bailyn's definition to call attention to two flaws, one minor, the second serious. Few in the eighteenth century would have said, as Bailyn says, that "non-arbitrary law" was statutory law. It would have been difficult then to have found students of liberty able to contemplate the idea that legislative promulgation could be, per se, "non-arbitrary law." When eighteenth-century constitutionalists thought of law balancing governmental, political, or constitutional forces, they thought of customary law.

The second flaw in Bailyn's definition bears directly on one of the central conclusions of this study. All of the sources that Bailyn cited were colonial, hardly objectionable as he was defining the American concept of liberty. It is, rather, the historical stirps to which Bailyn traces his definition that raises problems. His lineage is narrowly conceived. Professor Bailyn's reading of "the ideological origins of the [American] Revolution" led him to the conclusion that

the effective, triggering convictions that lay behind the Revolution were derived not from common Lockean generalities[26] but from the specific fears and formulations of the radical publicists and opposition politicians of early eighteenth-century England who carried forward into the age of Walpole the peculiar strain of anti-authoritarianism bred in the upheaval of the English Civil War. . . . More important still, it became clear that these ideas, which would become the Revolutionary ideology, had acquired in the mid-eighteenth-century colonies an importance in public life they did not have, and never would have, in England itself.[27]

Whatever substance this thesis may have had for general American political ideology, it has little substance for explaining the origins of Anglo-American constitutional ideology or the eighteenth-century Anglo-American concept of liberty.[28] What is demonstrable is that in the 1760s and 1770s, British radicals and American whigs alike turned to the same constitutional solutions to preserve their liberty against the emerging sovereignty of the parliamentary majority: they turned not to democracy or republicanism but to the discarded prerogatives of the Crown, asking King George to take actions he no longer felt empowered to take, to veto legislation and, on his own discretion, to dismiss the House of Commons.[29]

That British radicals and American whigs adopted similar constitutional strategies does not prove one the inspiration of the other. In truth, the sources for the American concept of liberty were not drawn primarily from British opposition theory. They came, rather, from what Jack P. Greene calls "mainstream" thought.[30] The fundamental definition of liberty held by American whigs may have differed somewhat in tone from the definition of the parliamentary majority that adhered to the leadership of Lord North, but it did not differ in legal or constitutional substance. It was in the application of principle, not in the rhetoric of liberty, that they differed. As Greene argues,

> both opposition thinkers and mainstream thinkers were proud of "the liberty-preserving" constitution of Britain and "agreed on the moral qualities necessary to preserve a free government." The crucial distinction between them was that the latter "spoke mainly with pride of the constitutional and political achievements of Georgian England," while the former viewed contemporary Britain "with alarm, 'stressed the dangers to England's ancient heritage and the loss of pristine virtue,' studied the processes of decay, and dwelt endlessly on the evidences of corruption they saw about them and the dark future the malignant signs portended."[31]

Even more to the point were the concerns that motivated and guided them in the ways that, in political practice, they applied the principles of liberty. Ministerial whigs worried about the threat to constitutional liberty from the anarchy of dissent. American whigs and British radicals worried about the loss of constitutional liberty from unchecked governmental power. Practice and application were what separated the schools of thought. Theory and vocabulary were the same, a fact that should not be surprising, since both were rooted in common-law ideology and all parties gave their loyalty to the liberty of the revered British constitution. "The primary aim, therefore, of all well-framed Constitutions," according to an American loyalist, reaching a conclusion as dear to colonial whigs as to ministerial servants, "is, to place man, as it were, out of the reach of his own power, and also out of the power of others as weak as himself, by placing him under the power of law."[32] It was the definition of law in this context, not disagreement about the meaning of liberty, that produced the constitutional crisis of 1776.[33]

Many objections have been raised to historical accounts that depict a "mainstream" to eighteenth-century political thought. Semantic meanings varied widely, we are told, and shades of differences must be taken into account. To ignore distinctions and stress superficial similiarities, "can only lead to the illogical and anachronistic error of viewing the [American] loyalists within the same ideological context as the patriots."[34] That contention may be true if we compound the application of constitutional principle with the principle itself. No one would deny that loyalist and colonial whig, British opposition and government supporter, disagreed about what coercive measures constituted a threat to liberty and what defensive measures were justified to protect liberty. To that extent and in that context they did not agree about the definition or conditions of liberty. But what they did agree on was the rhetoric of liberty and that the rhetoric of liberty both reflected eighteenth-century thought and motivated eighteenth-century actions. That fact becomes apparent when we compare the appeals to liberty by Lord North with the appeals of the pro-American opposition in the House of Commons, or the writings of the champion of liberty, Richard Price, with the commentaries of the conservative jurist Sir William Blackstone.[35] They used the same slogans because they thought similiar constitutional thoughts and shared common political values.

The language of eighteenth-century students of liberty was more effective with their contemporaries than it would be with us, because it was a taught, familiar language, full of inferences and suggestions from the common law. It was not only political rhetoric but also legal rhetoric that underlies the shared values of eighteenth-century colonial whig and eighteenth-century "king's friend." Perhaps in the earlier years of the century, old whigs had been hard pressed to reconcile their adherence to liberty with appeals for blind obedience to government against the threat of the Jacobites. By the age of the American Revolution there was less difficulty. The concept of liberty was only then becoming less an ideal restraining power and more an attribute of government. Although sometimes still confused with license, liberty was order because liberty was law.[36]

A final historical objection may be that the eighteenth-century concept of timeless liberty depicted on these pages is old-fashioned "whig history" resurrected in a new disguise. That criticism may be valid to the extent that labeling concepts as "neo-whig" or "super-whig" proves a negative point, but before it can be accepted there is a question that should be researched. To what extent, it must be asked, are the political ideas that nineteenth-century historians came to call "whig" nothing more or less than common-law principles carried from the legal to the political sphere of argument? We have long known that concepts once attributed to John Locke were part and parcel of the common lawyer's constitution decades before Locke wrote; that the principles of the American revolutionaries and of the framers of the federal Constitution, once identified as Lockean, would more accurately be described as Cokean and traced back through Chief Justice Fortesque to the English legal doctrine, valid in all ages until the nineteenth century, that power without restraint is not legitimate. Our error may be not that we dismiss the "whig," but that we use a term that has lost its charm to dismiss concepts that stand on better ground. To explore the legal in the eighteenth century may be to rediscover one of the main currents of whig or "republican" theory.

# 1

# A Word We Know

The topic of "the concept of liberty" may appear too narrow for a monograph but in fact problems may be with the other extreme: the material may be too rich. Liberty fascinated eighteenth-century English-speaking people as much as an abstraction as a practical constitutional principle. Many of the quotations below may appear taken out of context. They could not be. The extent to which eighteenth-century legal, constitutional, and political commentators discussed liberty in the abstract is simply amazing. Generally speaking, there is no context out of which to lift quotations. Even more remarkable was the utility of the abstraction. In the eighteenth-century vocabulary of Anglo-American politics and law, no term invoked more emotion than liberty. "There is not a word," Richard Price insisted, "which expresses so much of what is important and excellent."[1] It was a term on everyone's lips, flowing from everyone's pen, and appealed to by supporters of every political position. On the western side of the Atlantic both parties to the revolutionary controversy could use the word "liberty" in the same yet opposite ways—one invoking American liberty, the other British liberty—to support opposing causes. Whig committees of enforcement, on one hand, employed the expression "an enemy to *American* liberty" to stigmatize a violator of the nonimportation agreements. On the other hand, the New York loyalist printer, James Rivington, seeking to avoid the same stigma, protested that his conduct had "always been conformable to the ideas which he entertained of *English* liberty."[2] It was even possible for each side to use the word in the same way, one intending to disparage, the other to defend. The commander of the Royal Navy in American waters reported whigs "tumultuously assembling in the Cause of Liberty," and Virginia's House of Burgesses told the colony's governor that "[n]ext to the possession of liberty," reconciliation with the mother country would be "the greatest of all human blessings."[3]

In Great Britain the same vocabulary dominated opposition politics. Two slogans stirring the heat of public affairs during the 1760s were "Liberty, Property, and no Excise" and "Wilkes and Liberty." As a candidate for Parliament in 1768, John Wilkes stood on liberty and little else. There was no need to build a broader platform. To be asked to vote for liberty was enough for his supporters. "The chief merit with you," he told the liverymen of London, "I know to be a sacred love of Liberty."[4]

### A WORD TO LOVE

"Liberty" may well have been the most trenchant word in the eighteenth-century English language. "There is," a British writer observed in 1776, "an enchantment in the sound of *liberty, free, self-governed*, and the like." That same year, Henry Goodricke evaluated two of those enchanting sounds—"liberty" and "freedom"—contrasting them with their opposites, "slavery" and "servitude." These terms, he contended, raise "instantaneous feelings of approbation or indignation, in a degree proportionatable to the circumstances of the case." Not only British politicians but also New England clergymen knew what he meant. They constantly sought to invoke those "instantaneous feelings." Passage of the Stamp Act, Rhode Island's Elisha Fish preached, had caused the "unexpected *eclipse* of our darling Sun of Liberty," producing a "dark day, when the Sun of our *Liberty* set in a gloomy cloud, which, for a season, boded perpetual night." The darkness was dispelled when the Stamp Act was repealed, announced Henry Cumings to a congregation in Billerica, Massachusetts: "[T]he dismal dreary clouds flee away, the heavens recover their wonted serenity, . . . [and] reviving liberty, . . . with height[e]ned lustre and beauty, flies to our longing bosoms, while slavery, that brat of satan, vanishes out of sight."[5]

On either side of the Atlantic few metaphors were thought too farfetched for the praise of liberty. To a Massachusetts clergyman liberty was mankind's "crown and diadem"; to a barrister of Gray's Inn it was "the most precious jewel under the sun." The word most commonly used to describe liberty was much less worldly. It was "blessing." Preaching to Connecticut's Assembly, Judah Champion called liberty "one of heaven's choicest blessings to mankind." Preaching to Great Britain's House of Commons, Samuel Hallifax called it "the choicest of earthly blessings," "the most invaluable of blessings."[6] More than a blessing itself, liberty was "the foundation of almost every temporal blessing," "requisite to the growth of every good seed in a commonwealth." Put in those terms, liberty was a plant, "spread like a vine from this country to the colonies," a seed that "was first planted under the genius of the constitution; it has grown up into a verdant and flourishing tree; and should any severe strokes be aimed at the branches, and fate reduced it to the bare stock, it would only take deeper root, and spring out again more hardy and durable than before."[7]

More frequently than as a plant, liberty was depicted as a human, often a child—"that darling child," "the fair Child of Liberty"— whose cradle was the common law of England. The "darling of generous and noble souls," that is, of Englishmen, liberty had some enemies and many friends. Learning, knowledge, and virtue were its best friends, and liberty, in turn, was the best friend of mankind.[8] Whether a child or a friend, liberty was always female: "the great Goddess LIBERTY," ever ready to "indulge the Prayers of her several Petitioners," possessing both feminine weakness— "so delicate and modest, as not to sit long in the proud lap *of presumption and security*"—and feminine fortitude—a fighter against tyranny and arbitrary government, who "has been for a *while* suppressed, but like the sun she has again rose, with *double force*, and *double lustre*."[9]

It was well that liberty had strength, for she not only was constantly fighting, she was often on the move. Centuries earlier, "[L]iberty, being driven out of the best part of the world by the Roman arms, took refuge on the further side of the Rhine; . . . where, in the fastnesses of woods and morasses, sometimes on the defensive, and sometimes making courageous sallies, she combatted five hundred years together, against tyranny and all her train." Later, "the northern Parts of *Europe* became the Seat of Liberty," especially England, until the era of the Stuarts when, "for a season," liberty "deserted the British isles, and set up her standard in the wilds of America." Although eventually returning to the mother country, liberty probably felt at home in the colonies until the Stamp Act crisis, when a tory (fearful of mob rule) asked, "O Liberty whither art tho' fled?," and a whig (fearful of an arbitrary Parliament) "saw *fair Liberty* so suddenly fled from her former delightful abodes."[10]

## THE BRITISHNESS OF LIBERTY

It may have been difficult for many people during the eighteenth century to contemplate the possibility that liberty was fleeing Britain. Where else could she find a home? "O Britannia, divine region of liberty," one observer exclaimed, knowing as did everyone else that Great Britain was "a land, wherein liberty is supposed to have fixed her favourite residence." It was not only "the peculiar lot of Great Britain to have liberty, and the blessings deriving from it, to take up their abode with her," but "the History of England" was "the History of *Liberty*" and "civil liberty" was "the second nature of Englishmen." Indeed, Great Britain was "truly stiled, *the land of liberty*. Its subjects, from the mildness of its laws and the happiness of its religion, are blest beyond any other nation."[11]

The point was hardly subtle. The British were not only blessed, they were best, and it was because they were blessed that they were best. In their own estimation the British were the finest people on earth, the most honest, cheerful, compassionate, and hearty; eating the best roast beef, drinking the best water, and living the best lives. Their soldiers were invincible, their sailors "the bravest and honestest the World can boast of." They were also the least oppressed, perhaps the only nation that did not know tyranny, living under a government "*founded on the* Principles of Liberty, by a WISE, a FREE, and a BRAVE PEOPLE."[12]

The British were not vain about their race. They did not claim that they were naturally the world's best people, that they possessed inherent qualities that other nationalities lacked. It was liberty that made them best. Because the argument is no longer familiar, it is worth quoting a typical instance of the boast so that its range and extent will not be underestimated.

> [T]he *English* Character has acquired a vigour and a manliness from the Constitution. The consequence of

which every *Englishman* feels to belong to him as such, and the sense he entertains of the value of those important rights and privileges which he enjoys as his birthright, endue him with firmness and magnanimity, and inspire him with a sense of honour, and a dread of disgrace;— while his disposition, formed under the mild and genial influence of legal, orderly, and salutary Freedom, is as open, humane, and generous, as it is bold and brave. Every species of cruelty is repugnant to his nature; he is as ready to forgive and succor as to fight; and he will no more hurt or even insult a vanquished foe, than he will yield the palm of victory while he has strength to dispute it. Nor is there a People in the world so distinguished for their benevolent bounty as the *English*. Munificence and Charity are here displayed beyond all example and without ostentation; and Woe, which by the laws of Nature, is ever attendant upon the condition of Humanity, is sure among us to attract pity and relief. [13]

The explanation why liberty helped to make the British the finest specimen of human stock is best deferred to a later chapter when the concept of slavery is discussed. The point to be made here is that liberty not only made the British the best people, but also blessed them with the best liberty, the key factor contributing to their being the best. Great Britain was "the freest nation that ever existed," enjoying "the most perfect System of Liberty ever known to mankind." British "lives and liberties" were preserved "in a degree of security known to no other nation," and the kingdom was "distinguished from all others by the Liberty it enjoys." The Swiss constitutionalist, J. L. De Lolme, even asserted that because of liberty, "no true comparison can be made between it and the government of any other state," and the reason, according to those willing to make the most extreme claim, was that "*Britain* is the only kingdom, and *Britons* the only people who can truly say, we are free." [14]

There were two legal certainties about which everyone, Americans as well as Britons, agreed. The first was that, due to liberty, Great Britain and its constitution were "the Admiration and Envy of the World." [15] The second was that the colonies shared all the blessings of British liberty. [16] How else, asked John Witherspoon, could one explain the fact "that the British settlements have been improved in a proportion far beyond the settlements of other European nations." It could not be due "to the people for they are a mixture of all nations. It must therefore be resolved singly into the degree of British liberty which they brought from home."[17]

That very fact that they enjoyed so much British liberty complicated the American whig case against the mother country during the revolutionary controversy. There were two consequences to the enjoyment of perfect liberty making colonial charges of British oppression less persuasive, if not outright unbelievable. The first was that a people such as the British, "the Patrons of Liberty," who "stand foremost in the annals of fame, as having shaken off the fetters which hung upon the human mind," could never be guilty of oppression. "To talk of oppression from a free and generous people, [from] the mildest government under the sun," was unthinkable. "We are a free, generous, and brave people, and cannot enslave or oppress others. . . . [I]f every American would lay his hand upon his heart, and conscientiously and dispassionately consider, he must confess that we have the most admirable system of government the world ever beheld, and that our laws are wonderfully calculated to support liberty, and to prevent lawless oppression from individuals." What should be understood is that most Americans agreed with these boasts, for they, like their fellow Britons at home, could conveniently overlook the fact that generous, benevolent Great Britain was the ruler of Ireland.[18]

There was a second consequence flowing from British pride in British liberty. In addition to making less believable American whig charges of oppression, British pride gave to those charges a subversive coloring. It was not just that the British and the colonists enjoyed so much liberty. If, as was often asserted, "the freedom of the subject in England is now arrived at the highest degree of perfection consistent with the nature of civil government," or "the nature of society will admit of no greater degree of liberty," it followed that government could not be improved, that liberty could not be expanded with safety. Sir Francis Nethersole had made the point a century and a half earlier. "There is not any government in the world like ours," he told the petition-of-right Parliament. "The King's prerogative such as it were not good for the subject to have it less nor the King to have it bigger. So the liberty of the subject such as it were not fit to have it less, and dangerous to make it bigger."[19]

Change and cries of oppression not only were suspect; they had to be resisted in the name of liberty. There was rather a positive duty upon every citizen "to contribute all in his power, to the support and preservation of a system of laws which afford such ample protection and liberty." The doctrinal truism that the British had a monopoly on liberty, and that their liberty was perfect, was argued not just as a theme for legitimating the existing social and constitutional order, but for preserving it inviolate. Merely on grounds that "Britain is the seat of Liberty," Americans were urged "to pay a just obedience to the Laws, and a loyal respect to the King." No matter what complaint they might have, Britons were told, they should let well enough alone and glory in their liberty. "Yes, poor of England," a London publication exclaimed, "though riches, honours, palaces, equipages, are not your's, LIBERTY is; O preserve it inviolate! Loath, abhor, shun the wretches, who would wrest the valuable treasure from you." British liberty, incapable of improvement, should have been enough for anyone. Nothing else was needed. Knowing that they possessed that liberty, American colonists, like the poor of Britain, should have been content with their lot.[20]

# 2

# The Importance of Liberty

There may have been nothing good, honorable, or rewarding that someone, somewhere on either side of the Atlantic, did not at some time in the eighteenth century attribute to liberty. "Liberty" was both "the Soul of Commerce" and "that delicious and wholesome fruit on which the British nation hath fed for so many ages." It was "the foundation of all honour, and the chief privilege and glory of our nature," "the Corner Stones of the *Welfare* of a People or Government; without which they will never arrive to any thing great, either in Labour or Learning, in War, or Peace." The belief, as stated by Thomas Gordon, was that "all Civil Virtue and Happiness, every moral Excellency, all Politeness, all good Arts and Sciences, are produced by Liberty." The pastor of Weatherfield, Connecticut, preaching to the colonial Assembly, rounded out the theme by making liberty

> the source and spring of almost every Thing, that is excellent & valuable upon Earth—the Nurse of Arts and Sciences, the Parent of Diligence & Industry, the Procurer of Wealth and Riches, & needful to the unmolested Profession and Practice of Christianity it self: it adds Chearfulness, Ease and Alacrity to the Mind—Sweetens & endears the Social Life, and heightens the Relish of all the common Enjoyments of Time. [1]

It was this proclivity for propagating everything worth having that made liberty "the most valuable of blessings in the world," "the supreme object of all men's desires," "the highest and most

valuable *temporal* object of Englishmen." Again it must be empha-
sized that this boast was made on both sides of the Atlantic. Liberty
was the most "desirable" temporal blessing to the *New York
Gazette* in 1765, "the first and most valuable of all human
possessions" to the archbishop of York in 1777, and "the greatest of
all human blessings" to a Massachusetts clergyman a year later.[2]

In fact, if you sought the ultimate measure, English-speaking
people of the eighteenth century would have told you liberty was
worth even more than life. "What signify riches, what signifies
health, or life itself without Liberty?" someone asked. "*Life
without Liberty*," it was answered more than once, was "the most
arrant Trifle, the most insignificant Enjoyment in the World."[3]

## The Motivation of Liberty

Three aspects of the eighteenth-century concept of liberty con-
verged on one point—the fact that it was the most important possession of civilized people, the fact that its existence was precarious,[4]
and the fact that it had to be defended or it surely would be lost.[5]
These aspects all contributed to making the concept of liberty a
motivating force in eighteenth-century British politics and law.
People professed to act for reasons of liberty or, by their arguments
on behalf of liberty, implied that English, Scots, and Americans
could be persuaded to act on grounds of liberty. "The love of liberty
is natural to all," a Rhode Island loyalist wrote. "It appears the first,
operates the most forcibly, and is extinguished the last of any of our
passions." "Men love Freedom," a London pamphleteer agreed
four years later, "and Liberty is an *Ætna* which burns in the breasts
of Englishmen, with an extreme hatred towards those who oppose
it." Americans, the *Boston Gazette* said, "have a warm sense of
liberty." That fact, a reviewer for the *London Magazine* warned,
meant "[t]he genius, temper, and circumstances of the Americans,
should be . . . attended to. No people in the world have higher
notions of liberty. It would be impossible to eradicate them."[6]

That Americans could not be separated voluntarily from liberty
was significant if one agreed with John Wilkes that "the sacred ideas
of liberty" not only "warm the hearts" but "inspire the actions of my
countrymen."[7] Liberty was credited with being a directing force in
public affairs. Although suppressed "by the exorbitance of regal and
of aristocratical power," an English clergyman preached to the

Durham Assize, liberty "still retained enough of life and vigour to
be able to exert itself effectively, as occasion offered." Liberty, a
New England clergyman preached to the Connecticut Assembly,
"inspires the human breast with the noblest sentiments." We may
think these boasts mere gasconades. Eighteenth-century politicians did not. They were forever calling on liberty to arouse those
noble sentiments. William Pitt furnished an example when he
warned his fellow Britons that "if liberty be not countenanced in
America it will sicken, fade and die in this country."[8]

The concept of liberty in the eighteenth century was an
abstraction that was both a standard and an objective goal, a
concept so charged with content that it had utility. "[I]n a Free
State like this," Thomas Bernard said when speaking in support
of the Quebec bill, "it is not to be wondered, if the sound of that
single word, '*Liberty*,' should be equal to an army of other words;
for arguments in favour of Liberty are, and ought to be, heard
with avidity in this assembly;—they merit and they receive
favour in our courts of law." Bernard's words take on additional
impetus when it is realized that he was opposing the "liberty"
side of the issue. Knowing that liberty was the most potent
concept with which he had to contend, Bernard conceded its
force as he distinguished it away. England's attorney general
contemplated the same persuasive force when confronted with
the refusal of Virginia's judiciary to issue writs of assistance. "[I]t
seems strange indeed," he mused, "that any judge in the
colonies should think the laws of the mother [country] too harsh
for the temper of American Liberty." A legal debate very similar
to the colonies' writ-of-assistance controversy had recently been
waged in Great Britain over the question of private papers seized
by government authority without a warrant identifying the
person whose property was to be seized. "Is it LAW?" a
pamphleteer asked. "Is it LIBERTY? Is it GOVERNMENT? Or
is it TYRANNY and OPPRESSION? If it is LAW, where is
LIBERTY? If it is NOT LAW, where is the VOICE OF
LIBERTY?" Eighteen pages later he answered the question,
writing of liberty as though it were an independent, animated
entity—an entity that, merely by its existence, provided
solutions to legal questions. "The expectations of LIBERTY," he
wrote, "are, that if the late most extraordinary, and, as is
thought, unprecedented and illegal *seizure of papers*, produces a

legal trial, it will be found to have been manifestly AGAINST LAW." If, in fact, precedents affirming the legality of general search warrants were discovered, "[t]hey must at the name of LIBERTY shrink back into the gloomy caverns of tyranny, where vulcanian thunder bolts only could be forged."[9]

In the dynamics of forensic as well as political debate, therefore, liberty was a word appealed to. In the colonies a Boston newspaper praised a book by saying it "breathes a true Spirit of Liberty." In London a writer praised a judge by observing that he had been "educated in the broadest principles of liberty." Of course, the word could be abused. It flowed too freely from John Wilkes's pen, and an American loyalist had a valid complaint against "those ambitious spirits who . . . made a notable stalking horse of the word LIBERTY." But even writers who protested the imprecision and demagogy of "liberty," "freedom," "slavery," and "servitude" conceded that these words not only had force during the eighteenth century, they also could motivate people to take actions or to support policies. "[B]y bestowing them liberally on any things we choose to support or vilify," Henry Goodricke complained, bias could be aroused "merely by a dextrous application of those names."[10]

In addition to being a word appealed to, "liberty" in the eighteenth century was a test applied. One could measure the worth of an action by evaluating it in terms of liberty. A proposal to conduct what would have been Great Britain's first census could be denounced in the House of Commons as "subversive of the last remains of English liberty." The tendency of judicial institutions to replace trial by jury with trial by attachment, a tendency perceived to be increasing, was condemned as "unfavourable to liberty" and "odious to every idea of Liberty."[11] The converse was also common. Just as writers invoked liberty to prevent action, they invoked it to urge action. Calling upon the government to increase circulating money, one author asserted that without more specie people could not be "in a comfortable enjoyment of liberty." Indeed, liberty might even be cited as an excuse to do nothing: a pamphlet on the general warrants controversy concluded that perhaps it would be best not to press the matter to a definitive legal formula. "There must be in every complex Government," the author explained, "certain points which it is for the interest of liberty to leave undecided."[12]

# 3

# Sources of Liberty

Historians of politics and political theory would wish to explore such questions as how various uses or definitions of liberty in the eighteenth century fit with notions of classical republicanism or within the country-court dichotomy. The historian of law and of legal theory is less concerned with putting labels on arguments about liberty than with learning in what ways those arguments contributed to public affairs. Interesting questions can be asked about what the commonwealth tradition or classical republicanism meant by liberty, but those questions would be our questions more than eighteenth-century questions.[1] The historian of law, jurisprudence, and the constitution must ask about eighteenth-century arrangements and eighteenth-century usages. Distinctions must be made similar to those drawn by Sir Robert Phelips and Sir Dudley Digges during the seventeenth-century debate as to whether Charles I's practice of prerogative imprisonments violated individual liberty. "I do believe there are such restraints to the prerogative as no man would diminish it," Phelips told the Commons. "But we are now for liberty. 1, the thing itself; 2ly, the right; 3ly, the violation." Although not disagreeing with Phelips that "the thing" had to be defined, the right established, and the violation condemned, Digges was not persuaded that "liberty" was the correct word. "In the business for the subject," he said in the same debate, "I would leave out 'liberty' and call it 'justice,' which is a claim more pertinent for both the subject to ask and the King to grant."[2]

Phelips and Digges were thinking of what today would be called "liberties" or "civil rights"—of procedures that protected rights and of remedies that vindicated them—more than of the abstract concept "liberty." It is important that the distinction be kept in mind. It is not quite true that a semantic change occurred and that "liberty" in the singular replaced "liberties" in the plural in common usage.[3] As Phelips's argument indicates, the concept of "liberty" as an abstraction strengthening specific liberties was in vogue in 1628. And as Digges remarked, it would have been constitutionally perilous to petition for liberty or to suggest that the king could grant it. Better to ask the king for justice—for the processes by which liberty could be vindicated when violated by government power.

During the revolutionary controversy, American whigs, whether complaining of grievances or asserting rights, were claiming liberties—that is, civil rights. These rights were postulated and defended on several legal grounds: custom, original contract, constitutional principle, ownership, inheritance, migration, and, to a minor extent, natural law.[4] One of the most frequently cited, though far from being among the most important, grounds upon which claims to particular civil rights were based was the abstraction of liberty. It is a basic jurisprudential fact that has been often noted, but seldom explored, by students of the American Revolution. But there is an additional issue to be resolved. If the right to liberty was one of the secondary sources or authorities for specific civil rights, what was the legal source or authority for claiming a right to abstract liberty? The answer to that question is less concrete than we might like. The eighteenth-century legal mind did not feel compelled to treat an abstraction as less than abstract.

## OWNERSHIP OF LIBERTY

The question being addressed is not about the definition or usages of the concept of liberty, but about what eighteenth-century English-speaking people believed was the jurisprudential source or legal authority for their claim to the right to liberty. We are concerned only with the authority for liberty, not with the authority for rights in general or for such rights as the right to property, the right to security, or the right to constitutional government.[5] Two additional points to bear in mind are that the authority for liberty was not different from the authority for rights in general and that the right to liberty was itself a minor, although frequently cited, authority for other rights.

During the eighteenth century it was widely understood in both Great Britain and her American colonies that the right to liberty could be established as a matter of legal principle. One source (to be developed below) was the constitution. To say that liberty was a constitutional right was to assert a constitutional claim. One feature of that claim was the premise that the right to liberty was, at least in part, based on custom or prescription. Another legal source sometimes cited for liberty was the theory that civil liberty was "immediately derived from human compact."[6] The original compact, not the social compact, was meant; the contract of government between the ruler and the ruled, not the contract by which people agreed to enter into a society.[7]

The preferred basis for claiming liberty was that people held it in fee. They had acquired it in various ways: it had been bequeathed to them as an inheritance; their ancestors or they had fought for and won it; their ancestors or they had obtained it by prescription; or—a claim favored by Americans—their ancestors had earned it by clearing a wilderness. The legal principle was ownership and the favorite words describing that ownership were "birthright" and "inherit." Liberty, to which "all men are equally originally proprietors," was "the birth-right of human kind," "the natural birthright of mankind." Everyone seems to have used the expression. Americans living in London told Parliament that liberty was their "dearest birthright," and John Wilkes, released from prison, spoke of being "restored to my birth-right, to the noble liberties and privileges of an Englishman." The thought was most often expressed by saying that the British, or more particularly the English, were "born to Liberty," that liberty was "inherited from our fathers."[8]

There was nothing unique to the assertion that liberty was irrevocable property. That was precisely the legal theory upon which the British based most of their civil rights, including trial by jury, the right of petition, and the privilege of being bound only by legislation to which consent had been given.[9] "These first principles of our constitution," Stephen Sayre explained in a pamphlet published in both London and New York, "are our birthright, and just inheritance."[10] This was a constitutional theory expounded and defended on both sides of the Atlantic, and summarized many times but perhaps never better than by a correspondent of the *Boston News-Letter* in 1766. "*English* Liberty," he wrote, "is a propriety attached to the individuals of the community, founded on the original frame or constitution of our Government."[11]

The principle was so simple that there is no need to develop it further. A basic authority for the right of British people to liberty was that they possessed the right as inherited or purchased property. There is, however, a historical consideration that has not been understood or at least not properly appreciated. The fact that liberty, as well as other civil rights, was property helps to explain why eighteenth-century British constitutional law accorded such high priority to the right to property. The defense of property meant the defense of liberty, not merely the preservation of material possessions.

## NATURALISM OF LIBERTY

Another source for liberty, less frequently cited than birthright, was God's gift. "All Men are born free," John Trenchard explained. "Liberty is a Gift which they receive from God himself." After all, James Duchal observed, as God "hath endowed us with free-wills, and a power of acting from choice," it is evidence that God "intended we should be free."[12]

Duchal's proof of God's gift—that humans have free wills, hence it must have been intended that they be free—is an argument close to natural law. All one has to do is omit God as the source, and what is proven is a principle of natural law: by their nature humans have free wills, hence liberty is their natural condition. Indeed, revelation and natural law were often associated in the eighteenth century, sometimes mentioned together and probably seen as sharing a common origin. Liberty, Capel Lofft asserted, was derived "from God, from the nature of man, and the nature and ends of society." Not everyone, however, thought a connection necessary. Natural law could stand on its own as authority, and, as a perceived source of liberty, was probably cited more frequently than any other—with the exception of ownership in fee. Who gave people liberty? Lord Bolingbroke asked. "No man gave it to me," he answered, "liberty is the natural right of every human creature. He is born to the Exercise of it as soon as he has attained to that of his reason." A common way to express the theory was to say that "every man has a natural right to LIBERTY," a right found in "the charter of our nature. It is the franchise of our soil; it impregnates our climate."[13]

The theory seldom was given concrete expression, at least not in significant areas of applicable law. Just about the only lawyer or politician on either side of the Atlantic to identify specific principles attributable to the natural right of liberty and present them as rules for legal conduct was Lord Camden. Opposing passage of the 1766 Declaratory Act that asserted Parliament's supremacy over the American colonies, Camden told the House of Lords that the proposed legislation "is illegal, absolutely illegal, contrary to the fundamental laws of nature, contrary to the fundamental laws of this constitution. A constitution grounded on the eternal and immutable laws of nature; a constitution whose foundation and centre is liberty, which sends liberty to every subject, that is or may happen to be within any part of its ample circumference." This statement may have been the most extreme claim for natural law made during the revolutionary era; certainly it is the most extreme for natural liberty. Impressive as the words may have been when delivered in the Lords, Camden must have known they were little more than rhetoric; his liberty was an abstraction not capable of being formulated into a concrete program. It was one thing to say that humans had a natural right to liberty and hold that maxim up as a standard for legislative or executive action. It was quite another thing to test positive laws by standards of natural liberty. In the eighteenth century the abstraction was simply too abstract. By just about every definition, natural liberty meant liberty in the state of nature, not in a state of society, the state for which programs of actions were needed. "[E]ach Man has an inherent Right to make a free Use of his Reason and Understanding, and to chuse that Action which he thinks he can give the best Account of," a Boston newspaper explained in 1756. "This is Liberty in the *State of Nature;* by which every Man has the sole Power over his own Actions, and the sole Right to the Fruit of all his own Labor." Expressed in other terms, natural liberty "was an unlimited power to use our abilities, according as will did prompt," or "in being free to act according to the Law of *Nature* and *Reason;* whose instructive Dictates are such, as, if properly regarded, will direct every Man to conduct himself in the Pursuit of his own particular Advantages, so as never to interrupt or injure another in the same Pursuit."[14]

## THE EXTREMES OF LIBERTY

It would be premature to define liberty as the word was understood in the age of the American Revolution. There is much more evidence deserving elaboration. What can now be said is that during the eighteenth century liberty was defined much as Henry de Bracton once defined freedom. "Freedom," according to Bracton, "is the natural power of every man to do what he pleases, unless forbidden by law or force."[15] Bracton wrote five centuries before the American Revolution and the era of constitution making, yet what he said was identical to the definition used by people on both sides of the Atlantic during the last half of the eighteenth century, when people still thought of government as limited by law and thought of force as constitutional when employed as "right" not "power" (except that many would have omitted the word "natural," and some might have said "right" rather than "power"). Richard Hey was one of the very few contemporaries to disagree. Writing a decade after the conclusion of the American Revolution, he defined liberty as "freedom from the Restraints of civil laws." Hey's definition was extreme, yet it is worth dwelling upon as its very extremeness helps demarcate the mean. Consider for purposes of comparison two definitions as extreme as Hey's. "Liberty," the law writer and future judge, William Jones, maintained in 1768, "signifies simply, power unrestrained." Second is the claim that "[t]he liberty or freedom of man . . . consists in the power of doing, or forbearing to do, any action at his pleasure. If there be any impediment, either to his doing, or not any action, he is in such case not free."[16] These definitions might have been accepted in the eighteenth century as descriptions of physical liberty, but they were unique for political liberty. Even among those few writers who tended to interpret liberty without restraints, it was usual to add some qualifications. The author of *Americans Against Liberty*, for example, was said to fix "the limits of genuine freedom at that point where the power of voluntary action may be exercised by each individual, without violating the happiness of others." Somewhat similarly it was asserted that "the liberty of the subject extendeth just as far to authorise him to choose evil for himself, but not to force it upon another."[17]

On the basis of evidence to be presented in the following chapters, it could be concluded that few people, certainly few writers in the eighteenth century, believed that natural liberty had any significance except as a theoretical explanation as to why people were entitled to liberty. There were few who did not agree with the author of a 1734 pamphlet who pointed out "that all Peace, all Order in Society is maintain'd by some Restrictions on natural Liberty, and that the Anarchy of natural Liberty wholly unrestrain'd, would be as great an Evil as the Slavery of no Liberty at all allow'd." To agree that natural liberty could not exist in social reality, however, did not mean that the theoretical notion was given up.[18]

One explanation of why the concept of natural liberty was cited and discussed as a reality in the eighteenth century was that it always retained some utility. Edward Wynne, for example, used it to explain international law. "Societies are still, with respect to each other, in a state of nature," Wynne pointed out, "and as jealous of liberty and independence, as individuals are."[19] More significantly, the notion of natural liberty—liberty outside society—could be employed as a measure for liberty within society. The most extreme theory, one enunciated by the Connecticut clergyman Elisha Williams, was that upon entering society from the state of nature people gave up "no more natural Liberty" than was "necessary for the Preservation of Person and Property," a standard to be used to judge the constitutionality of government decrees restricting action.[20]

Williams's notion can be evaluated from opposite perspectives. It was important because it was widely shared by English-speaking writers in the eighteenth century, and, therefore, may have been thought of as providing a standard for action. It was unimportant because it had no application in positive law and as a test was ideal, not practical. Just about the only positive-law principle that seems to have been elucidated from natural liberty was the maxim that, due to the residue of natural liberty retained even after a state of society becomes operative, "no Man can make himself a Slave."[21] Aside from that doctrine, the notion of natural liberty reserved in the state of society does not seem to have been rendered into specifics by eighteenth-century British legal theorists. At most it was stated in terms of vague general concepts, generalities that seem always to have been drawn from current definitions of British *constitutional* liberty and current apprehensions of *constitutional* perils.

Close attention should be paid to the manner in which people such as Elisha Williams used the word "natural" in the 1760s and 1770s. We may think that natural liberty is being appealed to and that the argument is one of natural law. But if the writer equates natural liberty with constitutional liberty, and understands that natural rights correspond to constitutional rights, we should be suspicious of the appeal. What looks like an attribution to the authority of natural law may be chiefly rhetorical. This rule is true even for New England clergymen delivering homilies. In the eighteenth century, the word "natural," although charged with enchantment, was an appellation of form with less substance than has been suspected. Again, it would be premature to develop the argument at this point. More evidence must be presented to alleviate the shock of intellectual heresy. The thesis can be summarized by considering the words of one Rhode Island minister, speaking at the conclusion of the Stamp-Act crisis. "It is," D. S. Rowland boasted, "our happiness under English government to enjoy whatever we have a natural right to."[22] Consider Rowland's meaning from the point of view of positive law, not of historical speculation. A natural right was a right existing "under English government"; that is, a right established and recognized under the British constitution or English law. What exists under the British constitution is natural, and it is natural because it exists.

## UNNATURALNESS OF LIBERTY

The argument is not that we should dismiss the natural origins of liberty. Rather, what must be done is to separate the rhetorical vocabulary from arguments of substance. Eighteenth-century people using the word "natural" generally did not mean that nature provided definitions or was the source of liberty independent of other factors. Just as natural law almost always proved to be positive law in the eighteenth century, so natural liberty was a curiously exact mirror of positive liberty. We should expect nothing else. Natural liberty as understood in the sense of extreme or perfect liberty—liberty without restraint—simply was not conceived to exist outside of the state of nature, even if there. Certainly it could not exist in the state of society. "Any attempts to reconcile perfect *Liberty* with *Government* must ever fail," Henry Goodricke insisted, and there is little doubt that his contemporaries agreed. Thomas Rutherforth, in a study entitled *Institutes of Natural Law*, gave "liberty" a definition similar to Bracton's, several centuries before. Liberty, he said, is "the power, which a man has to act as he thinks fit, where no law restrains him." Legal restraint was the probative concept converting theory into practicality, for liberty, rather than being the absence of restraint, could not exist without restraint. Liberty from restraint could exist only if there were laws restraining the liberty of others.[23]

The conclusion is simple, yet it bears iteration to be certain that it is fully appreciated: natural liberty may have been a vague model against which to measure the standards of freedom in civil society, but it was not perceived to be a reality. As Edmund Burke told the sheriffs of Bristol, "Liberty, too, must be limited in order to be possessed."[24]

The controlling proposition, stated in the language of the eighteenth century, was that natural liberty could not exist once human beings formed societies. "Is it not therefore absolutely necessary," an assize preacher asked in 1766, "to give up a part of this self-destroying privilege of nature, and exchange it for that more secure species of liberty, which is guarded by the Civil Power?" Many years earlier, Algernon Sydney had articulated the theory most generally accepted. "[L]iberty without restraint," he wrote, "being inconsistent with any government, and the good which man naturally desires for himself, children, and friends, we find no place in the world where the inhabitants do not enter into some kind of society or government to restrain it." If the premise seems a paradox—that to preserve liberty people entered into government to restrain liberty—the paradox was not apparent in the eighteenth century. Rather, the logic of the conclusion appeared inescapable. "For hereby each one becomes secured of the protection and united force and counsel of the whole state, whereby life, property and every thing else that is valuable, is almost infinitely better secured, than in a state of natural liberty."[25]

A governor of Rhode Island was only one of many eighteenth-century commentators to assert that "[a]bsolute liberty is, perhaps, incompatible with any kind of government."[26] The better theory may even have been that government was created to escape from natural liberty.[27] For legal theorists who started with the notion that there could be natural liberty, it was possible to end with the notion that government could be defined as coercion. "Right is Liberty, but Law, is a Fetter," it was explained in 1764. "It is not Liberty, unless we can act as we please. Whatsoever, therefore, is a Law or Restraint to it, must needs be superinduced upon it." "Every law," a critic of the Declaration of Independence insisted, "is an abridgement of man's liberty."[28] John Lind, a pamphleteer in the pay of Lord North's government, defined natural liberty as "clearly nothing more nor less than the absence of coercion." Civil liberty "means only a partial absence of coercion." Even if there were such an entity as the law of nature it had to be "alienated in a State of Society." After all, the "law which secures *my* property, is a restraint upon *you;* the law which secures *your* property, is a restraint upon *me*."[29]

We may be surprised at the conclusion but should not resist it: natural liberty in the eighteenth century was not perceived to be a practical factor in the lives of humans. No matter what it meant in the ideal, in the real world of civil society natural liberty was less than liberty, because it was liberty too much. "Liberty, like the Wind, may be too much, or too little. Too much may drive our shattered Bark on some Quicksand or fatal Rock: Too little checks us in our fairest Course, and keeps us toiling to a slender Purpose on the Sea of Life."[30] Precious as was any liberty, too much could be  as undesirable as too little.

# 4

# The Bane of Liberty

To speak of restraints upon personal freedom and yet call the political condition that was restrained "liberty" was to speak of what in the eighteenth century was known as "civil liberty." Civil liberty may best be described as a civic process, a process that balanced the coercive power of the state against the anarchy of an unchecked populace.[1] Government was not merely a matter of restraint; it was the exercise of restraint for certain communal purposes, one of which was to guarantee liberty by curbing its excesses. "Civil Government," Thomas Gordon explained in a 1721 book read by most American whigs, "is only a partial Restraint put by the Laws of Agreements and Society upon natural and absolute liberty, which might otherwise grow licentious."[2] That was the point: restraint was compatible with liberty when the purpose of restraint was to keep liberty from turning into licentiousness. And licentiousness had to be avoided, or it could prove the end of liberty.

We must give close attention to the concept of licentiousness if we are to understand the eighteenth-century concept of liberty. Licentiousness was one of three concepts helping to define liberty by describing what liberty was not and by identifying potential licentious actions to be avoided if liberty was to survive. Licentiousness was the nether side of liberty and, together with slavery and the arbitrary exercise of government power, was one of the opposites of liberty.

## THE DARKER SIDE OF LIBERTY

Unlike liberty, "licentiousness" is a word we no longer know, at least in its eighteenth-century connotations. Then, the word was almost as important as "liberty" to those who wrote about contemporary politics and law. It was a marvelously prodigal term, applied both loosely and effectively to just about any event, movement, or person someone wanted to criticize. In his official letters to London, Thomas Gage, commander-in-chief of the imperial army stationed in North America, was continually describing the colonial whigs as "licentious." When a correspondent to James Rivington's newspaper in New York signed himself "Anti-Licentiousness," loyalists recognized a fellow sufferer. Most commonly, the noun "licentiousness" was matched with the noun "liberty." Addressing Middlesex juries, a common-law judge assured the British that they enjoyed "true, amiable, delightful Liberty, without Licentiousness." Licentiousness was called "the bane of liberty" and liberty's "worst Effect," and was even thought of as having the same sex as liberty. "There is," an Irishman hypothesized,

> a certain Personage upon Earth who picks all People up just where Liberty drops them. . . . She is, indeed, as like to Liberty, as the Twins who came out of *Laeda's* Egg, were to each other, She assumes the same Features, Garb, Mein, and Deportment; She affects the same Expressions, though with somewhat of greater Clamour, to enflame her Votaries. In short the Resemblance is so perfect as to deceive the very Elect. But, in the Universe . . . no two Things can differ more essentially from Each-other. Yet She, also, is called LIBERTY by herself and her Adherents; but in Heaven She is called LUST, and by the Discerning upon Earth She is called LICENTIOUS-NESS.[3]

The writer's warning was familiar. It was common knowledge in the eighteenth century that licentiousness frequently masqueraded as liberty. "[L]et us never mistake licentiousness for liberty," a Massachusetts clergyman urged. "There is a very essential difference between liberty and licentiousness," a Georgia clergyman agreed, "and it is highly criminal under pretence of the one to indulge the other." Yet that, a dissenting British clergyman explained, was what frequently happened. "Under the pretext of liberty, *licentiousness* has been introduced." There were two causes: carelessness and deliberate design. "Licentiousness," the anonymous author of *Licentious Unmask'd* claimed, "too often passes upon the world for liberty; yet the licentious are the greatest enemies and disturbers of liberty, though at the same time they cry loudest for it." As a result, John Shebbeare thought, "dissolute Licentiousness . . . is constantly mistaken" for liberty. Even worse, Peter Peckard mourned in a sermon delivered to Cambridge University, "of late the terms Liberty and Licentiousness have by some persons been industriously confounded, as if they were in fact the same thing, differing only in degree."[4]

The danger posed by licentiousness came less from the enemies of liberty than from those too fond of liberty. People in the eighteenth century had to "check the progress of Licentiousness arising from an insatiable appetite for Liberty." The British especially had to be watchful "lest our love of liberty degenerate into licentiousness."[5] After all, Lord North was reported as pointing out, licentiousness was liberty "carried beyond the bounds within which the interest of civil society requires it to be confined," which meant that "every man who has liberty, has at the same time a power of abusing it; which power, if put into execution, is called licentiousness."[6]

## THE BONDAGE OF LICENTIOUSNESS

We must be careful not to simplify. It would be wrong to think of licentiousness as liberty's peril. When people in the eighteenth century contrasted licentiousness to liberty they were less interested in describing licentiousness than defining liberty. Indeed, there was no need to contrast licentiousness with liberty if one cared to take an extreme position and think of extreme liberty, or liberty in the state of nature. "[A]n *unlimited Indulgence* of Appetite, which in the *savage* State is called *natural Liberty*, in the *social* State is stiled *Licentiousness*."[7]

A second perspective from which to approach licentiousness was the social state. "Licentiousness in the people," a 1763 pamphlet insisted, "is as surely subversive to the constitution, as tyranny in the crown." Richard Price thought it more useful to equate licentiousness with governmental tyranny than with liberty. "Licentiousness, which has been commonly mentioned, as an extreme of liberty, is indeed its opposite," he argued. "It is government by the will of rapacious individuals, in opposition to the will of the community, made known and declared in the laws."[8] Few eighteenth-century writers agreed with Price. The word "licentiousness" was generally not associated with governmental power.[9] Abuse of authority was termed "tyranny" or "arbitrary," not licentiousness. Licentiousness originated not from authority but from those disdainful of authority. To preserve liberty, both tyranny and licentiousness had to be avoided. Arguments could be framed to imply that they were equally dangerous, but beyond doubt licentiousness was a more serious threat to liberty than tyranny, especially because licentiousness was so often and so easily confused with liberty it might have become established either by error or carelessness.[10]

Again the point should be made that arguments on both sides of the Atlantic taught a single lesson. Scotland's Thomas Blacklock warned that "licentiousness naturally resolves into anarchy, and the general result of anarchy is despotism." In Massachusetts, the pastor of Dartmouth was even more succinct. "[W]here licentiousness begins," Samuel West told the colony's legislators, "liberty ends." The conclusion was that people had as great a duty to oppose licentiousness as to defend liberty. In fact, the two actions went together according to Ireland's Henry Brooke, who thought that efforts "to restore LIBERTY to Man, have been successfull, so far, only as they were able to suppress or controul LICENTIOUS-NESS," and, Sir William Blackstone, who believed that the surest way to "maintain the liberty, of the press" was "to censure" its licentiousness. The task, according to Sir William Meredith, was as much "to check that Spirit of Licentiousness, which raises the Hand of Power; as to stop that Hand . . . from striking through the Front of Licentiousness at the Vitals of Liberty."[11]

## LICENTIOUSNESS AND REVOLUTION

If licentiousness was a peculiarly British concern in the eighteenth century, there were many who thought it a peculiarly American trait. In fact, how people perceived the threats to liberty often signaled how they reacted to the American Revolution. In the colonies it was not unusual for a loyalist to be a person who felt that the major danger to liberty was posed by the licentious mob, and for a whig to be a person more concerned with the danger of unchecked government power. Comments by two Massachusetts lawyers delineate the difference. The true patriot, loyalist Jonathan Sewall thought, "will think it eligible that *small* tho' *real* evils in government should subsist for a while, rather than by an over hasty attempt to eradicate them, to run the hazard of subverting a *good constitution.*" The whig Josiah Quincy, Jr., viewed the question from the opposite legal perspective. "It is much easier," he contended, "to restrain liberty from running into licentiousness than power from swelling into tyranny and oppression."[12]

Loyalists, fearful of anarchy, called American whigs "the violent sons of licentiousness," and charged that, far from preserving liberty, they were introducing "the worst species of tyranny, and the most dangerous kind of slavery that any country had ever experienced." Rejecting the Continental Association created by the first Continental Congress, the inhabitants of a Connecticut town voted to "disapprove of and protest against said Congress and the measures by them directed, as unconstitutional, and subversive of our liberties, and as tending to licentiousness."[13] Warning the lower house of the New York General Assembly against the same Congress, Isaac Wilkins argued that the whigs had carried their opposition to Parliament too far, degenerating from a defense of liberty into licentiousness. "Liberty and licentiousness are nearly allied to each other; like wit and madness, there is but a thin partition between them." Licentiousness, he warned, "invariably leads to slavery. . . . I fear from the present licentious conduct, we are much nearer to a state of slavery and oppression than we seem to be aware of."[14]

A point of extreme importance for understanding the intellectual atmosphere of the American Revolution is that across the Atlantic events were appraised from a similar perspective. The government of the rebelling colonies was described as "Licentiousness without Liberty, Power without Authority, Subjection without Allegiance or Security, Government without Law."[15] All of which was true accepting eighteenth-century legal and political semantics.

Whigs comprehended and occasionally expressed respect for the tory fear of anarchy through licentiousness. The tory apprehension was not rejected so much as said to be irrelevant to the imperial crisis. Indeed, whigs even agreed that "a spirit of licentiousness . . . is the reproach of true liberty, and has been the overthrow of free governments," and that one of their major concerns must be to insure "that, while we are contending for liberty, we may avoid running into licentiousness." They, however, feared unchecked government more than potential anarchy and agreed with Richard Price that between licentiousness and tyranny, licentiousness was "the least to be dreaded, and has done the least mischief . . . that if licentiousness has destroyed its thousands, despotism has destroyed its millions."[16]

The dichotomy between liberty and licentiousness was a vital reality in the constitutional struggles of the eighteenth century. It helped to form the vision of people, and how they saw events in terms of that division could determine both the action they took and what side they supported. Samuel Cooke was one of many participants in the American revolutionary controversy who realized this fact and sought to mobilize it. Long before the fighting commenced he had urged his fellow colonists not to allow their fears of anarchy to mislead them. The concept of liberty was not a grant but an inherent right possessed by the people, Cooke reminded the Massachusetts General Court in 1770. "And tho', possibly, under a just administration, it may degenerate into licentiousness, which in its extreme, is subversive of all government; yet the history of past ages, and of our nation, shews, that the greatest dangers have arisen from lawless power."[17]

# 5

# The Opposite of Liberty

In the parlance of eighteenth-century politics and law, licentiousness was not the opposite of liberty. Slavery was. There were some writers, not many, who may have thought that licentiousness, rather than liberty, was the opposite of slavery. Liberty was sometimes depicted as precariously perched between the two, threatened from opposite ends—liberty in this scenario becoming "a sort of middle point, between the two extremes of slavery and licentiousness."[1] In the overwhelming number of cases, however, the division was dual, not triparitite, with liberty not between two but one of two, the counterpart of slavery, the reverse of slavery, the concept that slavery helped to define by putting into sharper focus. "Oh Liberty! Oh Servitude!," Thomas Gordon exclaimed, "how amiable, how detestable, are the different Sounds! Liberty is Salvation in Politicks, as Slavery is Reprobation."[2]

Aside from "liberty" (its opposite) and "arbitrary power" (its most closely related concept), "slavery" was the word most appealed to in eighteenth-century legal and political literature. Just as liberty was the goal to seek, slavery was the hazard to shun. It was the "worst of evils," a condition "worse than death." No accusation was more charged with disparagement and anger than to say that someone favored principles of slavery. Governor Stephen Hopkins intended to abase Martin Howard when he asserted that Howard's defense of Parliament's authority to impose the Stamp Act demonstrated a "desire of enslaving the colonies." All throughout the revolutionary controversy slavery was employed as a motivating concept. To avoid it, American whigs justified civil war.[3]

## ENGLISH BACKGROUNDS

It is necessary to look again across the Atlantic, this time to see how the term "slavery" was used in the British Isles. The excursion might have been less necessary than others taken in this book, had not a prestigious journal recently provided space to an attack upon a school labeled "establishment historians," in which the author contended that Americans using the word "slavery" in the revolutionary controversy were recoiling from visions of chattel slavery, from the domestic slavery of Africans. "A careful persual of the relevant literature can only lead to this conclusion," it was argued, "that the thought of the colonials, when they spoke of slavery, was keyed directly to their own experience and observation of black bondage. The American patriots, when they used the rhetoric of 'slavery,' were expressing their fear that England [*i.e.*, Great Britain] actually intended to subjugate and reduce them to the status of chattel slaves." It is the author's thesis "that the rhetoric of the American pamphleteers makes sense as soon as it is realized that their predicament, shortly after the Seven Years War, bore a striking resemblance to that of the black slaves in their midst," that "[t]he outrage of the colonials stemmed from their conviction that only black people in America were deserving of servile status."[4]

It is difficult to imagine a more blatant example of historical presentism. The truth is that American whigs used the word "slavery" precisely as it was used by their British contemporaries in the mother country, and all of them inherited that usage from the political and legal vocabulary of their English ancestors.

It is not necessary to go far back in time, to Richard Marshal, earl of Pembroke, for example, telling Henry III that to obey the king unconditionally would be to behave as a slave. Our survey can start with the shipmoney controversy, when English barristers made the same arguments and employed the word "slavery" in the same way that American whigs would use it against the Stamp Act 130 years later. "That Judgment of Ship-money," Charles I's prosecutor, John Cook insisted, "did, upon the matter, formalize the people absolute slaves." The radical lawyer and antiroyalist pamphleteer Henry Parker called shipmoney "unnatural slavery."[5] When Parliament impeached Sir Robert Berkeley for his judgment upholding the legality of shipmoney, William Pierrepont told the Lords on behalf of the Commons that "The Judge will not allow us our Knowledge, or any Reason: he will have our Minds, our Souls Slaves."[6] Similarly, addressing the upper house in the impeachment of Chief Justice Lord Finch, Lord Falkland charged that the shipmoney decision would "have made even your Lordships and your posterity but Right Honourable Slaves."[7] After the Civil War began the two houses of Parliament used the same word to explain why they had to continue fighting. If the king did not return to the confidence of the people, everyone would know that his advisors intended "to make *us Slaves*."[8]

Following the defeat of Charles I, the Levellers asked the Commons to abolish the House of Lords "or else tell us, That it is reasonable wee should be slaves." At the Putney debates the Levellers' leader, John Lilburne, complained that English laws had always been laws of slavery; the radical John Wildman argued that a proposed constitutional arrangement did not contain enough safeguards for "[By it] the foundation of slavery was riveted more strongly than before;" and Thomas Rainborough, protesting that there were too many safeguards around property to the depredation of liberty, asked "what the soldier hath fought for all this while? He hath fought to enslave himself, to give power to men of riches, men of estates, to make him a perpetual slave."[9]

People in eighteenth-century Britain and America remembered the English Civil War as a time when their ancestors secured "themselves and their Posterities from Slavery and Oppression." It was a triumph of liberty that colonial whigs made their model in the struggle against Parliament. "Slavery, my dear mother, we cannot think of," *Betvannus Americanus* told Great Britain. "We boast of our freedom, and we have your example for it. We talk the language we have always heard you speak. Britons will never be slaves."[10]

John Locke described the next English rebellion, that of 1688, in his own time, as one to save "the Nation when it was on the very brink of Slavery and Ruine." Locke was intent on criticizing Filmer's *Patriarcha* because it would "perswade all Men, that they are Slaves." "Slavery," Locke scolded, "is so vile and miserable an Estate of Man, and so directly opposite to the generous Temper and Courage of our Nation; that 'tis hardly to be conceived that an *Englishman*, much less a *Gentleman*, should plead for 't."[11]

In England in 1689 a writer referred to the reign of James II as the "former *Slavery*" of Englishmen. New Englanders during that reign had spoken of "being sold for slaves." Staging their own "glorious revolution," Bostonians justified it on the same grounds that their fellow citizens in old England had justified their rebellion. "[T]he people in *New-England* were all *Slaves*," it was explained, adding (in one of the few references to chattel slavery in the literature) that "the only difference between them and *Slaves* is their not being bought and sold."[12]

During the early decades of the eighteenth century, references in British political and legal literature to slavery were even more common than they had been during the Stuart age. In their *Cato's Letters*, John Trenchard and Thomas Gordon constantly employed the word, warning not only of the Crown's prerogative power but of ministers seeking "to make the People poor, and themselves rich; well knowing that Dominion follows Property," and that "Poverty dejects the Mind, fashions it to Slavery, and renders it unequal to any generous Undertaking, and incapable of opposing any bold Usurpation." Although the *London Journal* of 1733 boasted that Great Britain was for the first time enjoying liberty, having escaped from "absolute slavery," the excise crisis opened people's eyes to new dangers. "I am convinced that our constitution is already gone," William Pulteney lamented in 1735, "and that the people are already in effect slaves." What worried him was the same threat that would make American whigs apprehensive of slavery, "unconstitutional" taxation.[13]

## BRITISH CONTEMPORARIES

To know that Great Britain was the best country in the world in the age of the American Revolution was to know that the British were not slaves. "Britons are unacquainted with slavery," it was boasted, "and all attempts of reducing them to it have ever proved abortive." Just about every other nation, certainly any Catholic nation, was in "a state of *slavery*." One was Ireland, of which it was said in 1769 that "the little shadow of liberty . . . left to this unhappy country, is on the very brink of annihilation; and . . . the shackles of abject slavery will be our future fate."[14]

The cider excise enacted in 1763 aroused doubts about British liberty identical to those that two years later the Stamp Act would arouse in the colonies. "[T]he exposing private houses to be entered into, and searched, at pleasure, by persons unknown, will be a badge of slavery upon your people," officials of London told the king. "Badge of slavery" was a frequently used expression. The

cider excise was a "badge of slavery on the shoulders of every land-
holder in Great Britain who grows Cyder." The reason was the
authority vested in excise men to enter private houses—unquestion-
ably "a slavery to a people, who have forgot the bondage of military
or feudal tenures." The issue was constitutionally close to one raised
by John Wilkes concerning the legality of general search warrants.
When Wilkes won his case in court a lawyer and former admiralty
judge of Ireland observed that "[h]ad the General Warrants been
found to be legal, we should next day been greater slaves than they
are in *France*."[15]

It would be both tedious and impossible to catalogue all the
uses to which the concept "slavery" was put in Great Britain
during the age of the American Revolution. It is enough to note
that there is absolutely no evidence that the British living in the
mother country were apprehensive of chattel slavery, yet they
employed the word exactly as it was employed in the colonies.
Certainly it can not be supposed that the British were thinking of
race relations. Eighteenth-century thoughts were not always our
thoughts, and it is misusing history to force our prejudices back
two hundred years and to quote yesterday's idioms to reinforce
twentieth-century arguments.

We also must be careful not to make wrong assumptions about
former institutions. One assumption too often found in the historical literature is that the doctrine of parliamentary supremacy and
the legal principle of sovereignty were understood to mean what
they do today: that law is command and what Parliament says is
law.[16] That doctrine was not yet accepted in the 1770s. In eighteenth-century Great Britain, as well as in her American colonies,
law was still defined as "right" rather than "power," and government was explained in terms of restraint.[17] Thomas Rutherforth
summarized the constitutional theory when he maintained that "a
state will cease, if all the members of it are brought into perfect
servitude. The social compact is destroyed by the slavery of the
parties in it: because the obligations of slavery are inconsistent with
the obligation of this compact." Traditionally the doctrine of restraint had been applied against the authority of the Crown. In
1743, for example, a writer warned against conceding the king the
power to dismiss people from office without cause and explained his
reasoning in terms of slavery. The power would be "of the very
worst Sort of corrupt Influence, because it is founded upon Fear,

which debases the Minds of the Persons influenced, and makes them *of all Slaves the most slavish.*"[18]

Lessons taught by the Interregnum had long before made constitutional theorists aware of the potential power of Parliament. The ministerial rule of Sir Robert Walpole had made them aware of the potential of the administration to direct that power. Events of the 1760s—Parliament's proceedings against printers and its American legislation, for example, as well as apprehension about the influence of Lord Bute and the supposed emergence of an "inner" cabinet—produced writings reflecting increased concern about both these potentials. Parliaments, the bishop of Salisbury warned, "when once they become appendages of administration, must open the widest door to slavery." Should the House of Commons "fall in with the factions of a vicious and despotic ministry," an anonymous pamphleteer agreed, "then this nation will find those liberties, the boasted glory and inheritance of Britons, enveloped in obscurity, and subverted into slavery." For some people in Britain and many in America the theoretical potential became an alarming constitutional reality when the Commons not only refused to admit into its membership John Wilkes following his election, but seated in his place a man whom he had outpolled by a wide margin. "We see ourselves," the voters of Middlesex told the king, "deprived even of the Franchises of Englishmen, reduced to the most abject State of Slavery."[19]

The Middlesex petition expressed a principle of liberty widely held, one that would contribute to the coming of the American Revolution and to the framing of most American constitutions: that liberty depended upon representation. "[T]hey, who have *no* Voice nor Vote in the electing of *Representatives, do not enjoy* Liberty," a broadside circulated to London around 1775 announced, "but are absolutely *enslaved* to those who *have* Votes, and to their Representatives: For, to be enslaved, is to have Governors whom *other Men have set over us*, and to be subject to laws *made by the Representatives of Others.*"[20] The legal writer Capel Lofft took the conclusion one step further. "A people governed, or to speak more properly governing, by the representatives of their choice, is enslaved if their will is one, and that of their representatives another," he contended. Colonial whigs were saying exactly the same when they protested their potential enslavement should Parliament's pretensions of supremacy be constitutionally established. The many

legal theorists in Great Britain who went further and argued that
representation alone was not sufficient for liberty have generally
been ignored by students of the American Revolution. "The voice
of the people is the voice of the constituents, as well as of the representatives," it was said in 1763. "If there was no other voice but that
of the representatives, the people would be absolute slaves; such as
they are in France, and other despotic countries."[21] Not just Americans, but also British radicals, readily applied the "slavery" predicament to the unrepresented colonists over whom Parliament
claimed the authority to legislate. "But *many* of you have a voice in
parliament: *None* of them have," Richard Price reminded his fellow
Britons, comparing their condition to that of the Americans. "*All*
your freehold is represented: But not one foot of *their* land is represented. At worst, therefore, you can be only enslaved *partially.*—
They would be enslaved *totally.*"[22]

Three months before the battle of Lexington a political
newspaper began publication in London. Its motto was, "*Liberty*
with *Danger, preferable* to SERVITUDE, with SECURITY." Its
message was alarming: "all the Horrors of SLAVERY, now stare us
in the Face." The point to notice is that the newspaper used the
word slavery just as the Americans were using it, and applied it to
the same institution of government that Americans believed was
enslaving them. Just as revealing is the fact that the eighteenth-
century British, when they applied the word "slavery" to North
America, usually did not think of the colonies as a land of chattel
slavery. Many people in the mother country, when comparing the
colonies to Great Britain, saw America as a land of liberty.
"[W]henever the liberties of this country shall be destroyed, one
hope, perhaps, may still remain to us," Britons were advised in
1768. "The extensive regions of America, even at that time, may
afford a secure asylum to those, who prefer a state of independency
in a foreign land, to slavery and misery in our own."[23]

Once the Revolutionary War had commenced, the British began
to apprehend the possibility of American slavery if the colonists
were to win. Again, it was not chattel slavery that was feared, but the
slavery of people who had lost their civil liberty. An American
victory, it was surmised, "is most likely to put down the best form of
government under which any subjects ever lived, and erect in its
place a combination of petty tyrants, and keep the provinces of
America in Venetian slavery for ages to come."[24]

## ANALOGY OF CHATTEL SLAVERY

Of course people were aware of chattel slavery. The argument is not that the subject was never mentioned. The topic was on people's minds, and it is likely that when persons spoke of slavery as the opposite of liberty they had thoughts of chattel slavery.[25] A direct connection, however, was seldom drawn between chattel slavery and the slavery that Americans feared. Voters of Danbury, Connecticut, were among the few to do so when they praised a proposal "to import no more Negro Slaves." "[W]e cannot but think it a palapable absurdity," they resolved, "to complain of attempts to enslave us, while we are actually enslaving others." Looking from the opposite perspective, an anonymous London pamphleteer condemned an act of Parliament banning American boats from the North Atlantic fisheries, saying that the asserted authority, if legal, would mean that Parliament could dispose of colonial property, and "Americans would be to the Parliament of Great Britain, what the Negro Slaves are to the Planters in the West-Indies."[26]

It is not germane to speculate as to how eighteenth-century Americans could warn about slavery being introduced into the colonies, when they were already surrounded by chattel slavery in terms of black and Indian involuntary servitude. Whatever the reason, the fact is that most commentators of the eighteenth century thought slavery the opposite of liberty without equating it with chattel slavery. As a result of this amaurosis, some arguments warning American whites of their impending slavery were truly wondrous. Jonathan Mayhew, for example, even suggested that "our bought Negro slaves apparently shared in the common distress" felt in the colonies following passage of the Stamp Act. "For which one cannot easily account, except by supposing that some of them saw, that if *the act* took place, their masters might soon be too poor to provide them suitable food and raiment; and thought it would be more ignominious and wretched to be *servants of servants*, than of *free-men*."[27]

Perhaps we should not be surprised that the type of slavery that was the opposite of liberty was not equated with chattel slavery during the eighteenth century. What may prove surprising, however, is the fact that chattel slavery was not necessarily considered the worse of the two. It was even contended by more than one writer on the subject that political slavery, the slavery that was the opposite of liberty, was harsher than the chattel slavery of blacks.[28]

The concept may strike us as farfetched, but in the eighteenth century chattel slavery and liberty were not incompatible. Thomas Gordon, writing in London, counted as one of "the Blessings of Liberty" the fact that, by purchasing British manufactures, "*English* Planters in *America,* besides maintaining themselves and ten times as many *Negroes,* maintain likewise great Numbers of their Countrymen in *England.*" Several decades later, during the revolutionary crisis, a South Carolinian urged his readers to support a boycott of British products by wearing "the same garb your slaves hitherto have done." They should do so, he wrote, to keep slavery out of South Carolina, a home of liberty. Liberty, the writer explained, had "found an asylum" in North America. "Learning, liberty, and every thing that ennobles the human mind, have constantly been traveling westward. I never can believe, that in this sacred land slavery shall be soon permitted to erect her throne on the ruins of freedom."[29] It is doubtful if persons reading these words in the eighteenth century thought their author a hypocrite. There were more chattel slaves than free people in South Carolina, yet South Carolina was a land of liberty and would become a land of slavery only if Parliament made good its claim to legislate for the colonies.

# 6

# The Concept of Slavery

One reason why eighteenth-century English-speaking people so often referred to slavery was not that they were guilt-stricken about chattel slavery, but that they used the concept of the other type of slavery—political slavery—to define the concept of liberty. Slavery itself was most often defined by contrast to liberty. "In general," Richard Price explained, "to be *free* is to be guided by one's own will; and to be guided by the will of another is the characteristic of *Servitude*."[1] That definition, of course, could apply to chattel slavery as well as to the type of slavery that was the opposite of liberty. It is therefore necessary to define the second type of slavery, and to ask why it is certain that when people in the eighteenth century spoke of slavery they were not always referring to chattel slavery.

It is significant that eighteenth-century Britons, including Americans, applied the appellation "slave" to nations as well as to individuals. "Tyranny, despotism, and the like," Joseph Hawley, the leading whig lawyer in western Massachusetts, explained a month before Lexington, "are general abstract terms, expressive of a certain relation subsisting between different communities, or different parts of the same community, similar to that subsisting between a master and his servant, from which the term slavery, as applicable to States, probably took its rise."[2]

A second revealing point is that even though licentiousness and slavery were both perceived to be liberty's opposites in the eighteenth century, people did not think them the same. They were, however, closely linked in paradoxical ways, as well as related, sometimes inconsistently, to other concepts. An example is provided by the comparison regularly drawn between them and the concept of government restraint. If licentiousness was liberty unrestrained, slavery was licentiousness restrained. "There is," John Missing assured Lord Mansfield, "such a Thing as Constitutional Liberty which Englishmen are intitled to; that when carried beyond its true Point it degenerates into Licentiousness, and tends to Anarchy; and when too much restrained and narrowed, it loses the Name of Liberty, and verges towards Slavery." Yet the opposite was also true. "The unrestrained LICENTIOUSNESS of any one Person, in any one Nation," Henry Brooke pointed out, "infers the universal Slavery of that Nation." Either way, restrained or unrestrained, licentiousness, because it was the opposite of liberty, led to slavery.[3]

## THE MEANING OF SLAVERY

When we get to the question of the definition of liberty, we will learn that its primary meaning in the eighteenth century was contained in the rule of law. Similarly, slavery was the absence of law: law that protected the individual and law that limited the authority of both private masters and public rulers. "Only the Checks put upon Magistrates make Nations free; and only the Want of such Checks makes them Slaves," John Trenchard wrote of the rule of law. "They are free, where their Magistrates are confined within certain Bounds set them by the People, and act by Rules prescribed them by the People: And they are Slaves, where their magistrates choose their own Rules, and follow their Lust and Humours."[4]

Another eighteenth-century political concept, arbitrary power, will be introduced in the next chapter. It is mentioned here only to the extent that it helped to define the type of slavery that was the opposite of liberty. One form of arbitrary power was government free of the rule of law; that is, rule by unlimited discretion. This aspect of political arbitrariness was, in the eighteenth century, said to be slavery. "Power unlimited," according to the *Boston Gazette*, "would be absolute Slavery."[5] Montesquieu labeled "slaves" the subjects of despotic governments in which rule was not by law but by will and caprice.[6]

The most striking and persistent definition of slavery was the opposite of what below will be argued was the most commonly applied meaning of liberty: the British constitution. It was previously suggested that when eighteenth-century people abandoned generalities and explained the specifics of natural law, the definition invariably turned out to be a mirror of the British constitution or of English common law. The same is true of liberty. On close inspection, the eighteenth-century idea of liberty was the current constitution, and slavery was the opposite. Not only did the British "enjoy as great freedom, as it is possible any should enjoy under any form of government," but it followed that they could "never be enslaved without their consent, or a violation of the constitution."[7]

It is important for students of the American Revolution to study the language of slavery that colors the literature of the controversy. To object to eighteenth-century vocabulary could cause our failure to understand the polemic apparatus of eighteenth-century constitutional advocacy. To warn against slavery was the way Britons raised questions about constitutionality. There were, for example, few principles better established in eighteenth-century law than that a standing army was unconstitutional. Sir William Meredith translated that rule into a definition of slavery. "A people over whom a standing army is kept for the purpose of chastisement," he contended, "are in actual slavery." Caleb Evans did the same with other British constitutional guarantees. "Where an arbitrary tyrant can imprison whom he please, without even producing an accusation, or naming the accusers; where he can even deprive of life, merely to gratify his resentment and caprice; and where the property of his subjects is at *his* absolute disposal, not their own: what are such men, but poor, abject slaves."[8]

Given this polemical tradition of defending constitutional liberty by flying the red flag of its opposite, it should not be surprising that purported British violations of American constitutional rights were almost certain to be labeled slavery by someone. Taxation without representation meant that those taxed were "no longer the *subjects* but the slaves of government."[9] The same word described the condition of people for whom laws were made without consent. "[T]hey, who have *no* vote in the electing of representatives in parliament," John Cartwright argued, "are *not* freemen, but are truly and really slaves to the representatives of those who *have* votes." "A Government without the Consent of the Governed," someone else explained, "is with me the very Definition of Slavery."[10] Again the point should be made that the same thought was being articulated on both sides of the Atlantic. "What . . . is the definition of a slave," an Irish barrister asked Lord North during Ireland's volunteer movement. "Is it not where a man is bound by laws, to which he never assented, and lies at the mercy of a power over which he has no controul?" The Townshend duties and Parliament's claim of authority to bind the colonies, Philadelphia's grand jury presented, "have a manifest tendency to reduce Americans to the most abject slavery. For what slavery can be more compleat, more miserable, more disgraceful, than that of a people, where justice is administered, government carried on and a standing army maintained at the expence of the people, & yet without the least dependance upon them?"[11]

A final point: when the British and Americans thought of slavery they thought of other peoples, especially the French and Turks. Just about every nation was "enslaved," and the reason was that in just about every nation "the Good of the Governed is so far from entering into the Heart and Counsels of the Governors, that it is opposite to the Genius of their Politicks, either to do them Good, or to suffer them to acquire it for themselves." That way of thinking was why colonial whigs attacked supporters of parliamentary supremacy by saying that they were championing as constitutional law the principle "that we in the colonies are so far from being free Englishmen, that we are as errant slaves as any in France, or Spain, or any nation in Europe, not excepting Turkey it self."[12]

## The Blessings of Liberty

The time has come to elaborate a point referred to earlier. For it was the concept of slavery that taught the eighteenth century the blessings of liberty by delineating the opposites of those blessings. "LIBERTY is the glory of a community, and ensures its felicity so long as it is retained," Judah Champion told Connecticut legislators. "SLAVERY, on the other hand, debases the mind—clogs the finest movements of the soul; discourages industry, frugality, and every thing praise-worthy; introduces ignorance and poverty, with the most sordid vices, and universal misery. How striking the contrast!" And it was striking indeed, according to another New England clergyman, for under slavery, in contrast to liberty, "men . . . sink below the primitive standard of humanity. . . .

They become stupid, and debased in spirit, indolent and groveling, indifferent to all valuable improvement, and hardly capable of any."[13]

The study discussed earlier has catalogued the traits attributed by American whigs to slaves—"cowardice, ignorance, weakness, barbarism, depressed spirits, and a heritage of shame"—and has concluded that "[o]nly an Afrophobic colonial would have offered the world this unflattering evaluation of slaves." American whigs were concealing their "antiblack prejudices by distorting historical realities," pretending that they were referring to political rather than chattel slavery. Whatever support this thesis might muster when tested only by American evidence, it does not survive the test of comparative historical data. Again we encounter an inherited way of writing and a view of the world that colonists shared with the British, a view with roots in traditional English political and legal thought.[14]

To list the characteristics that American colonists attributed to slaves is to list the characteristics that the British attributed to slaves. One was cowardice, alluded to frequently by writers and speakers who had never left the British Isles and could hardly have been thinking of colonial blacks. John Pym referred to it in 1642 when insisting that "[t]hose who are brought into the condition of slaves will easily grow to a slavish disposition, who, having nothing to lose, doe commonly shew more boldnesse in disturbing than of defending a kingdome." Clearly speaking of political, not chattel slavery, Thomas Gordon made the same point as Pym. "Men eternally cowed and oppressed by haughty and insolent Governors," he wrote in 1721, "want Spirit and Souls to meet in the Field Freemen, who scorn Oppressors, and are their own Governors, or at least measure and direct the Power of their Governors."

Direct evidence that the cowardice eighteenth-century people associated with slavery was the cowardice begot by political oppression, not cowardice attributed to race, was furnished by an anonymous British pamphleteer who reminded his readers that the white people of England experienced the cowardice of slavery. Praising "the Courage and Industry which Liberty begets," he warned that the "more Liberties are encroached upon, the more the People will be rendered cowardly and poor, as may be plain enough seen by comparing the Valour and Riches of this Nation in Queen *Elizabeth's* Days, with what hath been of late Days."[15]

Another characteristic trait of slavery was stunted education. Just as the "slavery of a people is generally founded in ignorance," so by contrast "knowledge and learning may well be considered as most essentially requisite to a free, righteous government."[16]

A third slavery trait was insensitivity to liberty. Because most people in the known world were in political bondage, it followed that most humans demonstrated "a strange propensity to *slavery and submission.*" The mind as well as the spirit was deadened by the status. "A sense both of political and civil slavery makes a man think meanly of himself," Joseph Priestley explained, "and, in fact, renders him that poor abject creature, which he fancies himself to be." People who thought that liberty had already slipped out of contemporary Britain—that the British were already enslaved—had an explanation why citizens in the mother country were insensitive to American cries of parliamentary oppression. "In short," a Londoner wrote to Philadelphia, "your cause is not a favourite cause in this Kingdom. . . . Having submitted, in some degree, to slavery ourselves, we do not so fully feel the distress it may occasion in others."[17]

The contrast that eighteenth-century legal and political theorists drew between liberty and slavery is today truly startling. Recall that everything good in the world, even religion, was credited to liberty. By the same reasoning, everything bad was due to slavery. "Slavery," John Arbuthnot stated in a typical appraisal, "turneth the fruitful Plains into a Desart; whereas Liberty, like the Dew from Heaven, fructifieth the barren Mountains." Slavery was the cause of every evil—ignorance, error, poverty, wretchedness, immorality, irreligion, vice, and, of course, political tyranny.[18]

## THE MOTIVATION OF SLAVERY

There was one other aspect in which the concept of slavery was the opposite of the concept of liberty. Like liberty, slavery motivated people to action, warning them of events, policies, and programs to avoid.[19] The warnings were a vital core of eighteenth-century constitutional theory, for it was universally assumed that the only ways slavery could become established in a free country were by corruption, by deteriorations produced by the passage of time, by "defects of political constitutions," or by people not being on their constitutional guard.[20]

Because the word "slavery" has not been taken as seriously as it should be, students of the American Revolution have overlooked the important role that the motivation to avoid slavery played in providing the eighteenth century with a program of political, social, and legal action. We may be certain the colonists appreciated its significance. After all, they boasted that their forefathers had left the mother country for the sake of liberty, that they had chosen "rather to trust themselves with beasts and savages, than with Englishmen who had resigned themselves to slavery." Even for those Britons whose ancestors had not fled Europe, the literature of the day was replete with warnings to be watchful, to maintain a vigilance against those in power, to be motivated not only for liberty but against slavery.[21]

There were no limits to the vigilance, for there were no limits to the danger. One warning pertinent to the American revolutionary controversy was to be concerned about the political condition of fellow subjects: to allow part of the nation to be enslaved would put one's own liberty at risk. "Slaves are always for extending slavery," David Williams reminded the readers of a work on "political liberty" published in 1782. That widely accepted theorem either motivated people to support the American whig cause or was used as an excuse for doing so. The Intolerable Acts, passed by Parliament to punish Massachusetts for the Boston Tea Party, were greeted in the colonies with universal defiance. The rallying theme was inordinate: the threat of slavery to one colony threatened slavery to all. If their "Sister Colony of Massachusetts Bay is enslaved," people in Hanover County, Virginia, resolved, "we cannot long remain free." The same motivation spurred support for the colonial whigs among a few Britons who professed to be alarmed about the future of their own liberty. It explains the thought behind William Pitt's famous plea for the repeal of the Stamp Act. "I rejoice," Pitt told the Commons, "that America has resisted. Three millions of people so dead to all the feelings of liberty, as voluntarily to submit to be slaves, would have been fit instruments to make slaves of the rest."[22]

These warnings did not bestir many Britons, but on the colonial side of the Atlantic a remarkable number of Americans were aroused to action. The Massachusetts Council and House claimed that they would not have participated in the most important constitutional debate of the revolutionary era, had they not feared that failure to answer Governor Thomas Hutchinson's defense of parliamentary supremacy would have been "construed into an acquiescence with the doctrines contained in it, which would have been an implicit acknowledgment, that the province was in a state of subjection, differing very little from slavery." Even Lord North professed to understand the motivation, telling the Commons that "he hoped the Americans were too brave and worthy of their glorious ancestors, to hesitate a moment in their choice between slavery or war, between ignominy and death; but in the present instance there was no question of slavery."[23]

American whigs disagreed with North. Believing that a very clear question of slavery was posed by recent parliamentary statutes, they cited the danger as a motivation for action. In the small Maine seaport of York, shortly after the Boston Tea Party, the voters resolved "to give all assistance" to the colonial opposition of parliamentary taxation. "[A] Dread of being Enslav'd ourselves and of Transmitting the Chains to our Posterity," they explained, "is the Principal Inducement of these Measures." Farther south, in the much larger seaport of New York, the same justification was pleaded. "Persuaded, that the Salvation of the Rights and Liberties of *America*, depends, under God, on the firm Union of its inhabitants," a whig association announced. "We the Freemen, Freeholders, and Inhabitants of the City and County of *New-York* . . . DO, in the most solemn Manner resolve, never to become Slaves."[24]

# 7

# The Antithesis of Liberty

The clearest definition of slaves in the eighteenth century was people living under arbitrary rule. "In arbitrary governments," Joseph Towers pointed out, "all are equally slaves." Everyone commenting on the matter, whether in Great Britain or her American colonies, seems to have agreed. According to eighteenth-century legal theory, there was no greater servitude than to be subject to will and pleasure. "[A] vague and indefinite obedience, to the fluctuating and arbitrary will of any superior, is the most abject and complete slavery."[1]

There was no concept more dynamic, more exegetic, or more useful for eighteenth-century politics and law than the concept of arbitrary power. The notion of arbitrariness appears in the polemical literature as frequently as any other concept except liberty, slavery, and constitution. For both constitutional law and nonconstitutional public law it was the most hermeneutic conception, serving more than any other to define law and set theoretical limits to governmental actions. There was no accusation against an official more serious than that he sought to impose arbitrary rule. It had been the first count in the attainder of the earl of Strafford, an article in the impeachment of the judges who rendered the shipmoney decision, one of the major charges justifying the execution of Charles I, and part of the indictment against George III in the American Declaration of Independence.

This is not the place to develop the significance in English, British, or American history of the concept of arbitrary power.[2] The question that concerns us is how the notion of arbitrary power related to and helped define the eighteenth-century concept of liberty. There may be no better summary of the relationship than that given by George Campbell, preaching in Aberdeen, Scotland, on the fast day commemorating the American rebellion.

> [W]hen men are governed by established laws which they know, or may know, if they will, and are not liable to be punished by their governors, unless when they transgress those laws, we say they are under a *legal government*. When the contrary takes place, and men are liable to be harrassed at the pleasure of their superiors, tho' guilty of no transgression of a known rule, we say properly they are under *arbitrary power*. These are the only distinctions I know between *free* and *slavish*, *legal* and *arbitrary*, as applied to governments.[3]

### LIBERTY AND ARBITRARY POWER

From what Campbell said, as well as from the evidence in this and the next chapter, it is apparent that people in the eighteenth century did not distinguish between what today is termed "positive liberty" and "negative liberty." As noted above, very few writers identified liberty with a freedom to do what one wished to do without restraint; on the contrary, that was precisely how James Otis defined the concept of "arbitrary." Rather, liberty in the eighteenth century was thought of much more in relation to "negative liberty"; that is, freedom *from*, not freedom *to*, freedom from a number of social and political evils, including arbitrary government power.[4]

Arbitrary power was not thought of as abuse of authority. Nor was it associated with any particular form of government, as it could exist under a democracy as much as under a monarchy, aristocracy, or oligarchy. Tyrannical power was abuse of power, arbitrary power was power without restraint. "[N]o liberty can subsist where there is such a power," Sydney wrote in the seventeenth century, and his words were echoed on both sides of the ocean in the age of the American Revolution, when the contrast was between arbitrariness and liberty. "The idea of an unlimited power is inconsistent with the genius of liberty," a South Carolinian observed. "For liberty cannot exist where oppression may be exercised without controul," a London pamphleteer explained. "[I]n a state where discretion begins, law, liberty, and safety end," the king was warned.[5]

As arbitrariness contrasted with liberty, it was, in eighteenth-century minds, associated with slavery. One as much as the other was believed to be a source of all the evils that make life miserable. "When *People* live under a tyrannical, arbitrary Government, nothing great or noble can be expected from them," Nathaniel Hunn told the Connecticut legislature. "Such a People must of Necessity become mean and low." Such a people, Thomas Gordon added, "grow daily thinner and their Misery greater."[6]

## ARBITRARY POWER AND REVOLUTION

In the coming of the American Revolution the fear of arbitrary power exerted an influence similar to that exerted by the love of liberty.[7] For opposite yet related reasons both concepts made the American whigs' claim of constitutional oppression less believable. Because the belief was prevalent that Great Britain was the special land of liberty, many people would not credit the charge that colonial freedom could be endangered by British constitutional policies. American whigs had to overcome a similar presumption about arbitrary rule. A self-evident truism, to which almost every eighteenth-century writer subscribed, was that the government of Great Britain could not be arbitrary. The British constitution, Stephen Johnson of Rhode Island asserted, "has amply guarded every avenue of slavery and arbitrary power, and strongly barred them out of the British dominions." Even the dean of Armagh, despite living in and writing of Ireland, boasted that "Our form of Government is happily placed between the two extremes of arbitrary Power and popular Licentiousness."[8]

There were a few murmurs of dissent—among, for example, people objecting to certain statutes or government agencies as arbitrary, such as the game laws, the Riot Act, the excise service, and the substitution of informations for indictments.[9] Even stronger objections came from writers shocked at discovering that in Great Britain Parliament had displaced law as sovereign, that the country was ruled by a power that, although "representative" in the eighteenth-century meaning of that word, was now arbitrary, as it was above the restraints of the rule of law. "For my part," Charles Francis Sheridan wrote in reaction to Blackstone's doctrine of parliamentary omnipotency, "I have ever had such inveterate prejudices in favour of Liberty, that I could never relish the Idea of an arbitrary despotic power's being lodged by our constitution in any person, persons, or different bodies of Men whatever." "No country," an anonymous writer explained, "can be called *free* which is governed by an absolute power; and it matters not whether it be an absolute royal power or an absolute legislative power, as the consequences will be the same to the people."[10]

No part of the British population was more troubled to learn of Parliament's newly-acquired arbitrariness than residents of the colonies. Jamaica's Assembly, for example, "with deep and silent sorrow, . . . lamented this unrestrained exercise of legislative power," saying they feared "that last and greatest of calamities, that of being reduced to an abject state of slavery, by having an arbitrary government established in the colonies, for the very attempting of which, a minister of your predecessor was impeached by a house of commons." The reference was to the earl of Strafford, but the thought was on Lord North. He was perceived to be a minister who, through control of Parliament, could impose his arbitrary will on imperial government. "If a boundless extent of continent," the famous Suffolk Resolves announced, "will tamely submit to live, move, and have their being at the arbitrary will of a licentious minister, they will basely yield to voluntary slavery, and future generations shall load their memories with incessant execrations."[11]

The exact same argument of law was made in the mother country. "As we would not suffer any man, or body of men to establish arbitrary power over us," the livery of London told George III, "we cannot acquiesce in any attempt to force it upon any part of our fellow subjects." Joseph Towers, addressing Samuel Johnson, spelled out several specifics he thought to be arbitrary impositions upon the colonies. "If the British parliament, in which the Americans have no representatives, can enact any laws of capital punishment respecting them, can *take away life, seize upon property*, and tax them at pleasure, are the Americans, in a political view, more free than the inhabitants of the empire of Morocco?"[12]

Americans had an additional list of grievances they thought were products of arbitrary power. The standing army was one, the Quebec Act a second, and the tea tax a third. Of the last the voters of Providence complained "That the express purpose for which the tax is levied on the Americans, namely, for the support of government, administration of justice, and defence of His Majesty's dominions, in America, has a direct tendency to render Assemblies useless, and to introduce arbitrary government and slavery." Arthur Lee, writing as *Junius Americanus*, cited the same legal values when accusing Governor Francis Bernard of preparing Massachusetts for arbitrary rule. "That you have attempted," Bernard was charged, "to subvert the constitution of the Province of *Massachuset's* Bay, and by devising schemes for removing the constitutional limitations, necessary to render Monarchy consistent with Liberty, have meditated the greatest mischief that can be brought on any people, the making the Crown arbitrary."[13] Lee was really thinking of parliamentary, not royal, arbitrariness. He mentioned the Crown due to the fashions of eighteenth-century constitutional polemics. The danger of arbitrariness was almost always discussed as a revival of Stuart prerogativism, not as the emergence of parliamentary sovereignty.[14] No matter the source, however, the menace was undisputed. The antithesis of liberty was arbitrary authority.[15]

# 8

# The Lawfulness of Liberty

Arbitrary power, like slavery and licentiousness, was the opposite of liberty. It was also the opposite of law, and in that fact lies the first ingredient in the positive definition of liberty. For just as people thought the "rule of law" the opposite of arbitrary power[1]—"Law and arbitrary power are at eternal hostility," Edmund Burke asserted[2]—so they thought of law as the central pillar of liberty.[3]

The frequent thought, seemingly on everyone's minds, was that the two concepts were inseverably linked. "We ought to set a due Value on Law and Liberty as the greatest of Earthly blessings," Bishop Gilbert Burnet urged in 1710. He was saying more than that the two were equally precious. The prevalent eighteenth-century perception was not that law and liberty were concepts supporting one another, but that liberty could not exist without law and that law was liberty.[4] A descriptive term, used occasionally, was "legal liberty," with unlimited liberty called "illegal liberty."

Before considering what specifics of law constituted liberty, attention should be paid to the concept of law as it was contemplated by eighteenth-century laymen and lawyers. Law per se—law as an abstract noun—was necessary before there could be liberty. "For supposing no Law, there can be no true Freedom," John Forster reminded the Northampton Assize. "Where there is no law there is no freedom," John Locke had said many years earlier, and Bolingbroke agreed. "I am free not from law, but by law," he wrote in his often reprinted *Freeholder's Catechism*. When the word "law" was used in this sense, it was generally thought of as an entity, a person, with a separate, distinct reality, much like liberty "herself." This concept of law, Sir William Meredith explained, "deals out her Dispensations by the single Rule and Measure of Equality; knows no Distinction of Persons, no Difference of Stations; is deaf to Intreaty, free from anger; insensible of Hatred and Affection, void of Prejudice. This Law allows no Honor, but what arises from Obedience to herself; and assumes no Dignity but what is consistent with her own Preservation. Where this Law prevails, *there* is Liberty."[5]

There were paradoxes to the dependence of liberty upon law, apparent contradictions that eighteenth-century writers continually mentioned but did not often analyze. There could be no civil liberty "without the *Government of Authority*," "no true liberty, where there is no subordination," liberty "cannot exist at all without" order and virtue, and "Liberty can exist no where, but by the protection of the laws."[6]

At first glance the idea may seem much like the balancing process referred to in the introduction to chapter 4. Just as humans could not live in a state of nature and therefore gave up some natural liberty, so law was a manifestation of the government they accepted, the equilibrium that guaranteed liberty by checking its excesses.

John Wesley was thinking of this balance when he defined civil liberty as the poise between individual initiative and governmental restraint. "Civil liberty, is, a liberty to dispose of our lives, persons and fortunes, according to our own choice and the laws of our country," Wesley wrote. "I add," he went on, "'according to the laws of our country:' For, although, if we violate these, we are liable to fines, imprisonment, or death; yet if, in other cases, we enjoy our life, liberty and goods, undisturbed, we are free, to all reasonable intents and purposes." The proposition was simple enough. Government, the guarantor of liberty, used law as its instrument to protect liberty. But behind that proposition lay the paradox that liberty was to be defined by constraints: liberty was to be understood in terms not of how far it extended but of how much it was confined. "What is the Civil Liberty of a *Nation* or *Community?*" a barrister enquired in 1776. He answered the question with a second. "What are the Civil Restraints by which a Community can be bound?"[7]

There was another implication. Not only could liberty not exist without law, but the restraints law placed upon natural liberty were themselves essential to the definition of true civil liberty. "In a sense," Edmund Burke noted, "the restraints on men, as well as their liberties, are to be reckoned among their rights."[8]

## THE PARTICULARITIES OF LAW

As with just about every other law-related topic in the eighteenth century, metaphors and slogans came readily to the minds of those describing liberty's dependence upon law. Liberty was called "the Child of Law" and was said to grow "under its shelter and protection," for law was "the ground of our liberty" and "the grand support of civil Liberty," "the surest foundation of true Liberty," "the very Basis & Foundation" of liberty, and "the only basis on which *real liberty* can stand." People had "to be *the servants of law*, in order to be truly free."[9]

Although poetry and imagery were more prevalent than specifics, it is evident that when legal theorists in the eighteenth century said that law was the foundation of liberty, their thought was on what today is called public law or constitutional law, not private law or natural law. In the next two chapters the question will be asked as to what constitutional principles were necessary for liberty to exist. Here the questions concern the nature of that law and how it contributed to liberty. An issue to be raised below, for example, is whether consent to law was necessary for liberty or whether it was enough that law be certain no matter how it was made, even by a single tyrant. What was not disputed was that there had to be certainty, a principle established well before Locke mentioned it. "The freedom of men under government," Locke was quoted as having written, "is to have a standing rule to live by, common to every one of the society, and made by the legislative power created in it."[10] Lord Carysfort provided one explanation as to why certainty of law is necessary for liberty: it helps to make people equal, for as long as every citizen "keeps within the bounds of law, there is an equality."[11]

Respect was a second attribute necessary for law to be the foundation of liberty. It had to be executed, that is, it had to be functioning law, and people had to respect it. The freeholders of Grenville County, North Carolina, applied this test when, during the revolutionary controversy, they were faced with the possibility that courts of law would be closed. "[A] Suspension of the Proceedings at Law is . . . dangerous," they resolved, "for where there is no Law, there is no Freedom, and that species of Liberty, which leaves the People unguarded by the judicial Power, and their Civil Institutions, is not worth contending for."[12]

Eighteenth-century legal theory was even confident enough to identify the trait most vital for law if it was to serve as liberty's underpinning. It was that law should not depend upon the will of a maker. "[I]n a government founded upon liberty, even the appearance of force is . . . unnecessary." Put more jurisprudentially, the prevailing thesis was that in a free government "law, and not will, is the measure of the executive Magistrate's power" and "the measure of the subject's obedience and submission." A "free government," therefore, "is a government *by law*, where every man knows the Law by which he is to be judged, and the security of any right does not depend upon the will of Judges, or upon a Law to be arbitrarily made by them."[13]

The law that the friends of liberty trusted to protect liberty was not a code of substantive rules or guiding principles. It was, rather, restraint upon arbitrary power—the old law, the folk law, the good law, the customary law of the community. Today we know that even in 1776 this notion of law was already superannuated. A point that must be repeated is that most legal theorists then were not aware of the change and still thought of law as sovereign, not as a manifestation of sovereignty. As a result, when they described law as the foundation of liberty, they meant the old law that was not the sovereign's command but the sovereign's restraint.[14]

This law that restrained the sovereign was sometimes said to emanate from the people to limit magistrates. The contention deserves scrunity as it may be easily misread. Eighteenth-century legal or political theorists who would have had magistrates subject to "the people" did not want the law that protected liberty to emanate from those people in the form of the arbitrary and capricious will of a majority. The law that was liberty's foundation checked the ruling majority as well as the aristocratic magistracy or the hereditary monarchy. "The primary aim, therefore, of all well-framed Constitutions," an American loyalist wrote, in words quoted earlier in this study, "is, to place man, as it were, out of the reach of his power, and also out of the power of others as weak as himself, by placing him under the power of law."[15]

Just what were the bounds confining magistrates was a topic seldom discussed in the eighteenth century. Generalities, not particularities, provided the norms for argument. Specific guarantees of individual rights characterizing twentieth-century legal theory seldom were mentioned in the age of the American Revolution. Rights recognized by law or expounded in theory were constitutional rights and termed "natural" primarily for embellishment. Indeed, eighteenth-century thought about liberty was so attuned to the existing constitution and so removed from the ideal that many rights recognized today were thought of then in opposite ways. Religious tolerance is an example. It was not just a matter that the concept of liberty did not require that Catholics be treated equally with Protestants. Rather, principles were so dependent on the current constitution that a proposal to allow Catholics to be candidates for public office in one of the ceded islands could be condemned as contrary to liberty. The possibility that Catholics might stand in elections was said to be "an outrageous violation of the laws of England, of the constitution of this colony, and of the liberty of the subject."[16]

Due to the emphasis upon generalities rather than specifics, most eighteenth-century discussion of the law of liberty dealt with sweeping principles rather than with individual privileges. Perhaps the closest writers then came to stating particularities was when the end of law was considered in terms that today might seem too broad to be a guide for governmental conduct. One example is Blackstone's maxim that the "first and primary end of human laws is to maintain and regulate these absolute rights of individuals." Another was Locke's frequently quoted principle that the "*end of Law is not to abolish or restrain, but to preserve and enlarge Freedom.*" In terms of constitutional theory, the principle could be stated as a limitation on government action with liberty defining the limits. In Great Britain in 1776, Henry Goodricke argued that "the end of Government is only to restrain an injurious exercise of private liberty, that is, licentiousness." In Massachusetts that same year, Samuel West told the General Court that "the end and design of civil government cannot be to deprive men of their liberty or take away their freedom; but, on the contrary, the true design of civil government is to protect men in the enjoyment of liberty."[17]

We would misinterpret the eighteenth-century legal mind were we to suppose that people at that time thought these sweeping maxims meaningless platitudes. William Blackstone believed he was stating a practical, substantive theorem when he claimed that "civil liberty is the natural liberty of mankind, so far restrained by human laws as is necessary for the good of society." This test—whether stated as "the good of society," "the good of the community," or "the enjoyment of liberty"—was the most particular and precise criterion stated in the eighteenth century for setting the limits of liberty. Applying that criterion, civil liberty was said to exist when a person was free "from all restraints except such as established law imposes, for the good of the community," or, as Blackstone observed in his *Commentaries*, "that system of laws, is alone calculated to maintain civil liberty, which leaves the subject entire master of his own conduct, except in those points wherein the public good requires some direction or restraint."[18]

## THE GOVERNANCE OF LAW

Blackstone's theorem was certainly clear: if liberty was to be secure, law should be for the good of society. But how was the good of society determined? It might be guessed that "good" would be determined by the utility of a particular rule or the benefit bestowed by that rule on the community—that is, that constitutional theorists would concentrate attention upon the limits of restraint and how it could safely be applied. Instead, the test of law's "goodness" in the eighteenth century was the degree to which it freed the individual from government direction, the very test that Blackstone set for "civil liberty." Put another way, the less a law restrained the citizen, and the more it restrained government, the better the law. Stated positively, the rule was that the "[s]ociety whose laws least restrain the words and actions of its members, is most free." Stated negatively it was that "every causeless or unnecessary restraint of the Will is an infringement of that political freedom, to which every member of society is entitled."[19]

The lesson being taught was more than the eighteenth-century political truism that "the Restraint of Government is the true *Liberty* and *Freedom* of the people." There was also the balance to be struck between that aspect of liberty that was the sum total of personal rights creating a restraint on government and that aspect of liberty that was law, the prime restraint on persons as well as government. The task for statesmen, Edmund Burke said, was to strike a balance—"to find out, by cautious experiments and rational, cool endeavours, with how little, not how much, of this restraint the community can subsist. For liberty is a good to be improved, and not an evil to be lessened."[20] The task of a free government, a government of liberty, was to strike that balance and, once that balance was struck, to maintain it. Bishop Burnet, in his sermon at the coronation of William and Mary, spoke of the government that balanced personal liberty with restraint by law as "a Just Government."[21] In the political language of the eighteenth century it became common to speak of an unbalanced government as no government at all. Rule by law not only defined liberty; it also defined government. "There is an essential difference betwixt government and tyranny," Jonathan Mayhew wrote. "The former consists in ruling according to law and equity; the latter, in ruling contrary to law and equity."[22] Either side of the balancing equation, if accorded undue weight, could destroy government. To have not enough restraint upon the people could be as fatal as to have not enough restraint on power. A "Maxim of Government," Jared Eliot told the Connecticut General Assembly, "is, *That where there is absolute Liberty, there is no Government.*" Conversely, government had to be restrained for there to be liberty because "*liberty* is to be met with only in moderate governments."[23]

A final point deserving attention is the contribution made to American constitutional theory by the concept of law as liberty and liberty as law. The idea was English, not colonial, but colonial whigs had inherited it as part of their political culture and had been prepared to defend it even before the revolutionary controversy began. It was stated as the operative definition of liberty many times before the American constitutional consciousness was awakened by passage of the Stamp Act. An example comes from 1762, when the Massachusetts House of Representatives instructed its agent in London to resist encroachments upon liberty.

> Our political or Civil Rights will be best understood by beginning at the Foundation. . . . "In General freedom of Men under Government, is to have standing fundamental Rules to live by, common to every one of that Society, and made by the legislative power erected in it; a Liberty to follow my own will in all things where that Rules prescribes not, and not to be subject to the inconstant, uncertain, unknown arbitrary will of another Man; as freedom of Nature is to be under no Restraint but the law of Nature." This

Liberty is not only the Right of Britons, and British Subjects, but the Right of all Men in Society, and is so inherent,
that they Can't give it up without becoming Slaves, by
which they forfeit even life itself. Civil Society great or
small, is but the Union of many, for the Mutual Preservation of Life, Liberty and Estate. [24]

# 9

# The Security of Liberty

When the Massachusetts legislators said that civil society existed for the "Mutual Preservation of Life, Liberty and Estate," they were expressing a fundamental tenet in British constitutional theory. Whether in or out of doors, few principles were more frequently stated during the eighteenth century. An example was provided by Joseph Moss when he reminded the Connecticut Assembly in 1715 that "Law is the great Bulwark to secure Religion, Life, Liberty and Property." A similar platitude had been expressed the year before in a neighboring colony. "The End of Law," the New York Assembly had been told, "is to Secure our Persons and Estates; the End of Government is to put the same in Execution."[1]

The concept deserving attention is not law, but security. Law was the foundation of liberty because it provided security. "The Law," a British pamphlet explained in 1740, "is the great Security we have for our Lives, our Liberties, and Properties." The theme would be repeated in the age of the American Revolution. "True political Liberty," a pamphlet observed, "consists in the protection, safety, and defence of every one in the peaceable enjoyment of his own rights, guarantee'd and secured to him by the laws, to which a full and exact obedience and submission is due."[2]

Security was the most absolute principle in eighteenth-century constitutional theory. "The great Ends of Society" were said to be to "secure Enjoyment of our Rights and Properties." The reason was that, "without liberty, and security of property, it is impossible any people can be happy." As true with most concepts, the proposition could be summarized as a legal theorem. The "established Rights of

68

[the] Constitution . . . reduced to their first principles," the earl of Abingdon explained, are "Security of Life, Liberty, Property, and Freedom in Trade."[3]

John Locke was often quoted in the eighteenth century for his aphorism that the "Reason why Men enter into Society, is the preservation of their Property; and the end why they chuse and authorize a Legislative, is, that there may be Laws made, and Rules set as Guards and Fences to the Properties of all the Members of the Society."[4] As with just about every other political and legal theory associated with Locke, this idea did not originate with him but had been enshrined in English constitutionalism long before. Liberty and security of property had always been linked in the thoughts and programs of the opponents to arbitrary power,[5] and was an especially gravid proposition during times of constitutional crisis, as when Charles I and his opponents quarreled, not about the principle, but about which side of the controversy better protected liberty by providing security for English lives and property.[6]

Eighteenth-century legal theorists, like the opponents of Charles I, utilized the concept of security to safeguard liberty. One reason why Britons boasted that their liberties were the best in the world was that their liberties were the most secured. As other nations enjoyed less security, so they enjoyed less liberty.[7] Although a few writers, such as Thomas Gordon and Richard Price, depicted security as a good that, like every other good, flowed from and owed its existence to liberty, most agreed with Thomas Hutchinson that the two concepts were mutually dependent, with people giving up some natural liberty to obtain "that Security in our Persons and Property which we could not have in a State of Nature."[8]

There is an apparent paradox to eighteenth-century constitutional thought about the security of rights. The prevalent legal theory seems to have been that abstract rights could be secured without procedural guarantees. Yet the rhetoric does not seem to match the constitutional reality. Aside from the two rights that everyone agreed had to be secured—the right to security of property and the right to security of person—the rights generally mentioned as being constitutionally secured in eighteenth-century British law were as much adjective as substantive. They were rights that secured other rights, making both property and person (and hence also liberty) secure—the right to impartial judges, the right to trial by jury, and the right to "good" criminal laws.[9]

Some dissenting Irish lords provided a revealing example of eighteenth-century legal thinking about how rights were to be secured when they attempted to preserve a secondary right in order to secure the primary right of property ownership. The lords were protesting passage of a bill permitting Quakers to use affirmations rather than to swear oaths. They did so not to maintain the sanctity of oaths but to secure property, the dissentients explained, "Because it being a great Security to all his Majesty's Subjects of this Kingdom, in the quiet Enjoyment of their private Fortunes, that no Man . . . can be deprived of his Property, but by Testimony given under Oath, which is the strongest Obligation that can be laid upon Conscience." The "Property of the King and his Subjects," they claimed, "is by this Act made less secure than it needed to have been."[10]

### THE PROPERTY OF SECURITY

Liberty and security were so interconnected in eighteenth-century political thought that today it is almost impossible to untangle them. Some political theorists even expressed themselves in such a way that they seemed to say that, instead of security being one of the props of liberty, liberty was the source, even the protection of security. "[O]ur lives, persons, and properties will be secure, in proportion as this generous principle [*i.e.*, liberty] prevails," Noah Welles told the Connecticut Assembly in 1764. "The safety of these is inseparably connected with civil liberty." John Dickinson was even more blunt. "[L]iberty," a Scots magazine reported him as saying, "is the great and only security of property."[11]

These words might be interpreted to say that liberty could exist independently of security, or that liberty was the means by which security was secured. What generally was meant, however, was not the primacy of liberty but the mutual dependence of the two concepts. Security of property was necessary for liberty, and the laws of liberty were necessary for property to be secure.

Preservation of liberty was essential, or property could lose its security; yet liberty was not to be measured by "the power" it provided individuals or classes, but by "the security they have for the preservation of their rights."[12] The proposition could be stated either way. Security could be explained as dependent upon or derivative of liberty.[13] Or, more frequently, liberty was depicted as needing security for survival. "Liberty, life, or property," Dickinson wrote, "can, with no consistency of words or ideas, be termed a *right* of the *possessors*, while *others* have a *right* of taking them away *at pleasure*." "If my property is at *their disposal*," Caleb Evans agreed, "and they have a right to take what *they please;*— what becomes of my *liberty?*"[14]

No matter how the proposition might be stated, everyone agreed with Evans's basic premise. The concept of security was vital to the enjoyment of liberty, and what mattered most was the security of property. Had eighteenth-century constitutional theorists been asked, they would have said that the interdependence was best expressed as one between liberty and the security of property. "*Liberty* and *Property* are not only join'd in common discourse," an anonymous writer told readers of the *Boston Gazette*, "but are in their own natures so nearly ally'd that we cannot be said to possess the one without the enjoyment of the other." Liberty and property were mutually dependent, even to the extent that whereas John Arbuthnot could say in 1733 that it was security of property that made him a freeman, Thomas Gordon said in 1721 that it was liberty that secured property. "[A]s Happiness is the Effect of Independency, and Independency the Effect of Property," Gordon explained, "so certain Property is the Effect of Liberty alone, and can only be secured by the Laws of Liberty; Laws which are made by Consent, and cannot be repealed without it."[15]

## THE LIBERTY OF PROPERTY

Two questions remain: What was meant by property that secured liberty, and why was property the security of liberty? The first has two contradictory answers. The type of property that secured liberty was both material and a mixture of the material with the ideal. It is apparent that some eighteenth-century constitutional theorists thought that security of physical possessions was sufficient to safeguard liberty.[16] That was not the better or majority view. The type of property securing liberty in the eighteenth century must not be narrowly defined. It was only to an extent material goods, and even then by no means in the sense that concept is understood today.

For one thing, property, even the concept of property as material accumulation, was not limited to the physical in the eighteenth century. It included constitutional rights that English people counted among the attributes of liberty.[17] In fact, a point that should not be forgotten is that liberty itself was property possessed.

A second factor is that even those political theorists who indisputably were talking about material possessions when describing the security of property, generally associated that security with the security of personal liberty. "Our persons and earnings are our own," was a common way of expressing the right of security. J. L. De Lolme, the Swiss constitutionalist, confined his definition of British liberty to securing the individual person and his material property. "Liberty," he explained, "consists in this, That *every man, while he respects the persons of others, and allows them quietly to enjoy the produce of their industry, be certain himself likewise to enjoy the produce of his own industry, and that his person be also secure.*" The three values, security itself as well as personal liberty and protection of property, were linked together as rights. "The absolute rights, or civil liberties of *Englishmen*," a writer told *Gentleman's Magazine*, "are principally three; the right of personal security, of personal liberty, and of private property."[18]

The third reason why the property that secured liberty should not be thought of merely as accumulated material goods is that it was not thought of in those terms during the eighteenth century. Today, private property is a means of survival, a standard of well-being, or a source of capital. Then, it was a means of survival and of well-being, but instead of being thought a source of capital it was valued as the source of liberty. Property was liberty because property secured independence. Material goods were valued less for their market worth, as a means of economic development, or as a capital resource, than as a guarantee of individual autonomy.

The condition or status that people hoped to obtain with property was not only affluence or social position but personal and political independence. Property was, in Sydney's words, "an appendage of liberty" because possession of property meant that its owner was, to the extent of that property, not dependent upon another person. "For eighteenth-century Americans," Edmund S. Morgan has observed, and he could have added for eighteenth-century Britons as well, "property and liberty were one and inseparable, because property was the only foundation yet conceived for security of life and liberty: without security for his property, it was thought, no man could live or be free except at the mercy of another."[19]

To be free, it was necessary to be secure, but you could not be free without property, and could not have property unless it was secure from arbitrary interference. It was security that made possible the enjoyment not only of physical property but also of liberty, and even life itself.[20] Security of property not only rendered its owner the opposite of a slave and encouraged industry, learning, and the arts, but also it was the last, the most essential element in the definition of liberty.[21] "The state of Liberty," Peter Peckard concluded in 1783, "is circumscribed on all sides, and supported by Laws calculated to prevent men from making, and secure them from suffering encroachments." Sixty years earlier, *Cato*, the eighteenth century's prolific champion of the concept of liberty, who persistently praised it as the most precious property human beings possessed, had defined liberty almost entirely in terms of material property and its security.

> By Liberty, I understand the Power which every Man has over his own Actions, and his Right to enjoy the Fruit of his Labour, Art, and Industry, as far as by it he hurts not the Society, or any members of it, by taking from any Member, or by hindering him from enjoying what he himself enjoys. The Fruits of a Man's honest Industry are the just Rewards of it, ascertained to him by natural and eternal Equity, as is his Title to use them in the Manner which he thinks fit: And thus, with the above Limitations, every Man is sole Lord and Arbiter of his own private Actions and Property.[22]

# 10

# The Constitutionality
# of Liberty

Eighteenth-century British subjects had a word to describe both the rule of law and the concept of security, the two elements underpinning political liberty. The word was "constitutional," or what today we call "constitutionalism."

Referring to themselves in the third person, inhabitants of New Jersey's Monmouth County resolved in 1774 that "They do highly esteem and prize the happiness of being governed, and having their liberty and property secured to them, by so excellent a system of laws as that of *Great Britain*, the best doubtless in the universe."[1] They meant not only that they lived under the security of certain laws, but that they lived under the British constitution, the very essence of liberty.

There were two general ways of looking at the association of liberty and constitutionalism. One was to think of the British constitution as saturated with liberty. The other was to seek the principles of liberty within the confines of constitutional government. "We have reason to rejoyce in the excellent form of government we live under," a Massachusetts clergyman wrote, "whereby we are delivered from oppression, slavery and tyranny, and are secured in the free unmolested enjoyment of our lives and property." The "form of government" to which he referred was the British constitution which, a Massachusetts lawyer explained, "has for its prium mobile, groundwork and leading principle, Liberty, civil and religious." It was a constitution that "preserveth liberty from invasion," and "does actually bestow upon its subjects higher degrees of Liberty than any other people are known to enjoy." "Such is the excellent nature of the British constitution," Caleb

Evans concluded, "that the voice of its laws is the voice of liberty. The *laws* of England are the laws of liberty."[2]

By "the very CONSTITUTION of the land," Evans wrote, "liberty is law, and law the charter of liberty."[3] He was stating a fact literate Britons both assumed to be true and took pride in, much as they took pride in the acknowledgment by Montesquieu that their country was the only one in the world "that has for the direct end of its constitution political liberty." Blackstone said much the same. "Liberty is the very End and Scope" of the constitution, he wrote, and New York's General Assembly claimed that the constitution's "direct end and aim is the liberty of the subject."[4]

People during the eighteenth century were so enraptured by the liberty of the constitution that they often mistated its premises and had to be corrected. Once during a parliamentary debate a speaker complained that the attorney general's discretionary authority to file informations in the place of indictments "is always exercised to restrain Liberty." Lord North objected to statements of this type. "I wish these Gentlemen would shew what power of Government is or can be directed to any other purpose," North replied.

> To restrain Liberty, is the very essence and end of all Government, which became necessary when a state of nature was improved into civil society, merely because it became necessary that natural Liberty should be restrained. It is by the restraint of natural Liberty that the weak are protected against the strong, that property is secured against the thief, and life against the assassin. There is, however, such a thing as civil Liberty, which, I believe, our bellowers against the powers of government are neither willing nor able to define.

North then defined civil liberty, and it is important to note that his definition was the same as the general eighteenth-century definition that has been discussed. The fact is indicative of how much supposedly antagonistic parties—the government and opposition, tory and whig, court and country—concurred on basic theoretical premises. Applications may have been different, but there was agreement about political and constitutional goals and values. Civil liberty, Lord North explained, "*subsists whenever natural Liberty is no farther restrained, than is absolutely necessary to secure the*

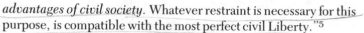
*advantages of civil society.* Whatever restraint is necessary for this purpose, is compatible with the most perfect civil Liberty."[5]

Contemporaries who bragged of the liberty of British constitutionalism did not necessarily disagree with Lord North. There was general acknowledgment that government consisted more of restraint than of liberty. What they were saying was that the British constitution gave the widest possible latitude to what North called "the most perfect civil liberty." The constitution was free not because the British people were free; there could be free people under an unfree constitution and free constitutions over unfree people.[6] Rather the British constitution was the charter of liberty because it provided for the rule of law and, in fact and in legal principle, was the rule of law, binding the rulers as well as the ruled to the security of law.[7]

## THE CONSTITUTIONAL FRAMES OF LIBERTY

Eighteenth-century legal literature is crowded with debate over the roots of the constitution of freedom. Most contemporaries thought of it as always having been in existence, a fixed constitution, containing immemorial principles of liberty extending back through Anglo-Saxon times, if not before. Another theory, much less frequently articulated, maintained that the reign of Charles I "was the first Period of Time, for the dawning of Liberty; it was the first Attempt of forming or new-modelling our ancient Constitution." A third view traced constitutional liberty to the Glorious Revolution and the Act of Settlement. "That Settlement," a group of dissenting peers contended, "was founded on liberty, and by the nature of things must be coeval with liberty."[8]

It is remarkable to contemplate, considering the sophisticated concepts of history in the eighteenth century, but few theorists thought the constitutional premises of liberty subject to political change or legal redefinition.[9] In that fact—in the concept of a timeless, unchanging constitution—may lie one explanation why the constitutional procedures upon which liberty depended in the eighteenth century were not as numerous as might be expected. The "essential" one, according to Edmund Burke, was control of the purse by "the people themselves" through Parliament. Others sometimes mentioned were free speech and the two essential ingredients of constitutional liberty discussed in the next two sections, balanced government and government by consent.[10] Aside from these "institutional" guarantees, just about the only rights enumerated by constitutional theorists had to do with restraints on arbitrary police power. A liberty that eighteenth-century Britons "are particularly blest with, is the Liberty of our Persons, or a Freedom from unlawful Arrests, Restraints, Confinement, and Imprisonment, that is, without just Cause and lawful Authority." All through the eighteenth century, the rights to indictment and to trial by jury remained vital elements of liberty in British constitutional theory, protections against arbitrary government which if ever lost would signal the end of liberty in Great Britain.[11]

## THE BALANCE OF LIBERTY

If the concerns of eighteenth-century Britons regarding liberty could be reduced to one single image it would be "power," one of the opposites of liberty. "Liberty and power," it was said, "are naturally as jealous of one another, as any two states can be of their several encroachments."[12] One could not get along without the other, yet by the nature of power they were more apt to be antagonistic than cooperative. "*Power* and *Liberty* are like *heat* and *moisture*," a 1774 pamphlet explained; "when they are well mixt, every thing goes on well; but when *not* so, they tend towards certain ruin and destruction." As Andrew Eliot told the political leaders of Massachusetts in the year of the Stamp Act, the problem for both those who were governors and those whom they governed was to know "where power ends and liberty begins."[13]

The challenge was to maintain a proper balance, and one difficulty was that there were various types of opposites to be balanced. Not only did competing aspects of government power, such as legislative power and monarchical power, have to be kept equal, so did the rights of government against the liberty of the individual. Until notions such as those of Thomas Paine gained currency, few writers suggested that liberty could be guaranteed by democracy alone. During the eighteenth century there was general agreement that liberty as well as power could be abused. Liberty needed the balance of power as much as power needed the balance of liberty. Few political truisms were more self-evident to the eighteenth-century constitutional mind than that no person or set of persons could be trusted with power. Power had to be restrained, and it was restrained by being divided and its divisions balanced.[14]

Again it is necessary to warn against the wrong assumption. It may be thought that such theories were looking to the future, to the constitutional balance of executive, legislative, and judicial powers. In fact, when liberty was discussed in the eighteenth century, writers often were not even thinking of the current balance of British theory between monarchy, aristocracy, and democracy. Rather, the danger to be guarded against was one we should expect had long since been eliminated from British constitutional fears—the royal prerogative.

Fear of the royal prerogative dominated the literature of constitutional theorists, and even of lawyers, in the age of the American Revolution. "The books of law are filled with the most absurd notions of prerogative," an English barrister complained in 1768.[15] He might also have said that they were filled with fears of prerogative, long after there was any practical possibility that prerogative law could obtain supremacy over parliamentary law.[16] In constitutional theory there was no problem older than the balance that had to be maintained between liberty and prerogativism. That balance had a complicated legal history, a history still influential during the age of the American Revolution, when pamphleteers continued to assume that prerogativism was the chief menace to liberty.[17] It was a time after the constitutional reforms when, according to Montesquieu, "The English to favour their liberty, have abolished the intermediate powers of which their monarchy was composed." The reforms supposedly had settled the constitutional imbalance in favor of liberty, yet attention continued to be paid to the conflict. "Liberty," one Briton wrote, "is so tenacious of her rights, that she will never suffer the ambition of princes, in this limited government, to subvert it into an absolute monarchy, by extending their prerogative beyond its bounds." "So long as personal security, personal liberty, and private property, remain inviolate," Blackstone was quoted in the *Boston Evening-Post*, "the subject is perfectly free—To preserve these from violation it is necessary that the constitution of Parliaments should be supported in its full vigor; and limits certainly known to be set to the royal prerogative."[18] Even American whigs, struggling against the claims of Parliament, not the pretensions of a king, expressed thoughts implying that liberty needed to be protected against prerogative.[19]

There are at least two questions that must be answered. Why did Britons and Americans in the age of the American Revolution continue to be concerned about the constitutional balance between liberty and prerogative power? Why did they still think of liberty in conflict with prerogativism long after prerogative power had ceased to be a threat to liberty?

One answer, perhaps the only one, is that they did so because of the manner in which they conceptualized liberty. They did not regard it as an ideal, or a goal, or even something to which they possessed a natural right. Rather, they looked upon it as an element encased in their constitution. Liberty was constitutional and its perimeters were set by established constitutional doctrine.

Historically in English constitutional law, the chief threat to liberty had come from prerogativism, and liberty's greatest constitutional triumphs had been achieved during struggles against the prerogative pretensions of Charles I and James II. Thinking of the constitution in historical terms, Britons and Americans continued, even in the age of the American Revolution, to envision liberty as constitutionally menaced by prerogativism.[20] As a consequence, when constitutional balance was mentioned in legal literature, liberty was set against prerogative power and not, as we might expect, against arbitrary power or licentiousness. There may be additional reasons why that was so. Prerogative power, after all, was arbitrary power in constitutional disguise, and, by implication, when jurists warned of prerogativism they included arbitrariness in that warning. Secondly, although liberty had run into licentiousness in the years immediately after 1642, that time, the era of Oliver Cromwell, was, in the second half of the eighteenth century, perceived to be the only period when the threat of licentiousness had become an actual, governmental reality. Prerogative power, by contrast, had been a frequent, recurring, always potential menace in English constitutional history.[21]

## THE LIBERTY OF CONSENT

If the existence of prerogative power was a test for determining the loss of liberty, the principle of consent was a test for determining the strength of liberty. In fact, the proposition may be carried further. Consent to government, especially consent to statutory law either in person or by representation, was the test for determining the existence of liberty most commonly stated by eighteenth-century political theorists. "Wherein" does liberty consist? Lord Boling-broke asked. "In Laws made by the consent of the people, and the due execution of those laws," he answered. [22]

This definition of liberty had long been part of English constitutional theory, going back beyond Locke and Sydney, both of whom repeated it in their writings. Even in Massachusetts during the 1770s the definition was not new. As early as 1637 a paper entitled "Libertye and the Weale Publick" asserted that liberty required "That the people may not be subjected to any lawe, or power, amonge themselves, *without theire consent:* whatsoever is more than this, is neither lawful nor durable, and instead of libertye, may prove bondage or licentiousnesse." [23]

Despite the simplicity of the concept, the principle of consent was by no means uniformly interpreted in the age of the American Revolution. There were two extreme arguments. A few writers, perhaps influenced by the Wilkes election controversy, insisted that people did not possess liberty unless they participated directly in the choice of their legislative representatives. [24] Others maintained that consent was not necessary in any form.

A dispute erupted in 1773 after Richard Price asserted that liberty was "too imperfectly defined when it is said to be 'a Government by LAWS, and not by MEN.' If the laws are made by one man, or a junto of men in a state, and not by COMMON CONSENT, a government by them does not differ from Slavery." [25] Few of Price's ideas were more roundly attacked by his critics than this, and what they had to say provided evidence of the degree to which British legal theorists in the age of the American Revolution continued to define liberty as the rule of law, and not to think of it in terms of democracy, representative government, or consent.

To be free, one of Price's critics asserted, was to live under "virtuous laws which secure liberty." A man could have a right to participate in legislation "and may exercise that right, and yet be a slave." Living under virtuous laws, however, "he may enjoy perfect freedom, without having the least right to assist in the framing the laws, or being at all consulted therein," Alexander Gerard agreed. "Wherever laws require only what is right, and forbid only what is wrong, there is liberty, by whomsoever the laws are made," he wrote. "British civil liberty," another critic asserted, did not mean that people "have an immediate share in the legislative power, but that they are under the government of wise and equal laws, and can do what they please, except in so far as they are restrained by such laws; and that by the wisdom of the constitution they are equally secured against the miseries of anarchy, and the terrors of despotism."[26]

Price's answer was less persuasive than it might have been had he been willing to admit that laws made by democratic consent could be oppressive toward liberty, or that laws made without consent could serve liberty. Replying to his critics, Price singled out the arguments of the archbishop of York, who had defined liberty as freedom from all restraints except such as established law imposed for the good of the community. Objecting that the archbishop's formula depended on nothing but the rule of law—"According to him, therefore, the supremacy of law must be liberty, whatever the law is, or whoever makes it"—Price asserted that the rule of law alone, without consent to that law, could never guarantee liberty. For, he wrote, the qualification that law be made for the good of the community "can make no difference of any consequence, as long as it is not specified *where* the power is lodged of judging what laws are for the good of the community. In countries where the *laws* are the *edicts* of absolute princes, the end professed is always the good of the community." As an anonymous writer had said in 1769, "To do what the laws of Turk[e]y permit, certainly is *not* liberty."[27]

The controversy was largely about the definition of liberty, and there is no doubt that a majority of contemporaries agreed with Price that the rule of law was not sufficient for liberty. Constitutional consent was also necessary. There were various explanations why consent was needed. One was very similar to why property had to be made secure. It was that, if people do not consent to the laws by which they are governed, "they become subjected to the will of others, instead of their own; and thus their property, liberty, and whatever beside is held dearest by mankind, is like a forlorn hope, submitted to the same will, and left entirely at the discretion and disposal of another." No one, it was suggested, would "call this a state of freedom." Government by consent, therefore, was a prop of liberty because it helped to secure property by restraining the conduct of officials, especially

legislators, who "are to transact for us Matters of vast Consequence relating to Life, Liberty, Property, Estate, and all those
other dear Rights, Privileges, and Blessings, which we have at
present the free Possession of."[28]

There is one important aspect of the definition of consent that
bears mentioning, as it played a major part in the controversy
leading up to the American Revolution. It is the doctrine of British
constitutional law that taxes could not be imposed without consent.
That rule could also be explained as one of liberty. It was, as the
Council and Burgesses of Virginia pointed out, "a fundamental
Principle of the British Constitution, without which, Freedom can
no where exist; that the People are not subject to any Taxes, but
such as are laid on them by their Consent, or by those who are
legally appointed to represent them."[29]

The principle was not controversial. Even the British minister
who attempted to tax the colonies did not deny that it was general
consitutional law. The disagreement contributing to the coming of
the revolution was whether Americans could be bound only by
taxes voted by elected delegates in the colonial assemblies, or
whether members of Parliament were their constitutional representatives, constitutionally authorized to bind them by consent.

## THE CONSTITUTION OF LIBERTY

Legal theorists in the eighteenth century had ways of expressing the
relationship between liberty and the British constitution. Sometimes they spoke of the constitution of liberty; more frequently the
term was the liberty of the constitution. Not only was liberty
perceived as embodying constitutional principles, but also the two
concepts, liberty and constitutionalism, were so closely associated
that to diminish one could diminish both.[30] The benefits were
reciprocal. The constitution was an instrument of liberty, and
liberty was the spirit, the soul, the essence of the constitution. A
barrister made perfect legal sense, at least by eighteenth-century
learned and professional semantics, when he said that to determine
the legality of informations and attachments for libel, he would
"consider them on constitutional principles, whether they breathe
the mild spirit of the laws of *England*, and of a congenial disposition;
or whether they are in their nature repugnant to the principles of
our free constitution."[31]

Of course there were occasions when writers used the standard of liberty to argue for an ideal constitution, to contend that liberty mandated certain reforms not then part of the British constitution, such as annual elections, an independent House of Commons, and even a future American constitutional principle that Great Britain never would adopt, "that government can only be pronounced FREE, in which the errors of those who administer it, can be rectified by an immediate interposition of the *judicial* powers."[32] But these arguments were rare. When eighteenth-century Britons identified the constitutional principles of liberty, they did not refer to the ideal or the "natural," but to the existing balanced constitution of consent and restraint.

The blend of liberty with constitutionality in eighteenth-century Great Britain was one reason why some theorists insisted that British liberty had reached so high a state it could not be improved upon. It was frequently asserted that, under the British constitution, "[n]othing further can be attained toward the Perfection of CIVIL LIBERTY."[33] J. Champion, for example, urged his readers not to jeopardize the constitution of liberty by experimenting with either the reforms of idealists or the misguided discontent of the colonists. "Happy under such a constitution," he asked, "would it not be folly, treason, and impiety, to sacrifice those inimitable advantages to the dreams of enthusiasts, or the projects of American rebels?" What Champion may not have realized was that the colonial whigs were making their stand on behalf of the same constitution of liberty which he professed to be defending. "The idea of liberty in the abstract is the same in one continent as another," the *London Magazine* had pointed out in 1766. So too was the concept of constitutionality. The liberty possessed by people in the colonies, Edmund Burke asserted, was "liberty according to English ideas, and on English principles," which meant constitutional principles.[34]

The conclusion had two parts. The first was that Americans shared equally with their fellow subjects in the mother country the liberty of the British constitution. The second was that because Americans participated in the constitution of liberty they were a free people. "It was wise and generous to give them the form and spirit of our own constitution," Jonathan Shipley wrote of the colonies in 1774, adding, "we gave them liberty."[35]

# 11

# Liberty and the Revolution

The constitution of liberty was lodestar of colonial whigs during the age of the American Revolution, taking them along contradictory paths by first guiding them to union with their mother country and then pointing them toward rebellion. "Had our Creator been pleased to give us existence in a land of slavery," the First Continental Congress told George III, "the sense of our condition might have been mitigated by ignorance and habit. But thanks be to his adorable goodness, we were born the *heirs of freedom.*" They were born the heirs of freedom, Americans knew, because they had been born under the constitution of liberty and by their legacy owned a share in the enjoyment of the liberty of the constitution.[1]

Opponents of American independence living in Great Britain did not quarrel with either the colonial whig definition of the liberty of the constitution or with the claim that it existed on both sides of the Atlantic. In truth, one of the difficulties eventually leading to civil war was that most writers and government officials who insisted on resistance to American whig demands acted on principles of law and order, which led them to oppose the colonists in the spirit of the constitution of liberty. Many Britons, including barristers, argued that the very fact that the consitution spread the blessings of liberty throughout the colonies, as much as in the mother country, was precisely why Great Britain had to uphold Parliament's supremacy over America.[2] The issue considered in this chapter is why American whigs rejected this argument. They continued to associate "true liberty" with "legitimate government," and to define liberty as government under the rule of law. But considering that definition of liberty, why was it that the government of Great Britain came to be perceived as a government no longer legitimate?

## SECURITY AND THE REVOLUTION

American whigs were not ambiguous about what they believed was the most general threat to their liberty. It was arbitrary power. The king and Parliament, Connecticut's legislators resolved when determining to support independence, were attempting to "subject our property to the most precarious dependence on their arbitrary will and pleasure."[3] Certainly American whigs had no difficulty persuading British radicals that their liberty was menaced by arbitrary power. The radicals were concerned with the same threat—and from the same government of Lord North—to their own liberty in Great Britain. It was on behalf of the colonists that London's lord mayor, alderman, and livery petitioned the king, saying that, "As we would not suffer any man or body of men to establish arbitrary power over us, we cannot acquiesce in any attempt to force it upon any part of our fellow-subjects."[4]

It will no longer do to dismiss petitions of this sort as politically motivated. The people who presented them were in opposition partly because of the way they defined liberty and perceived arbitrary power. Within the traditional meaning of both concepts, the charge made by London's leaders could be documented. From the constitutional perspective of colonial whigs and British radicals, the legislation to which they objected represented an attempt by Parliament to rule Americans by substituting its will and pleasure in place of customary procedural ways that constituted the rule of law. For them the asserted parliamentary power was undeniably arbitrary, as it lacked any criteria on which to base decisions except the subjective caprice of a majority of the members of each house of Parliament.

It was the effect of that power that raised American concerns about a second threat to traditional liberty. For it would have deprived them of security to property. The colonies were part of an empire and should be subject to "some supreme regulating power," the New York General Assembly acknowledged, yet that power "by no means comprehends a right of binding us in all cases whatsoever; because a power of so unbounded an extent, would totally deprive us of security, and reduce us to a state of the most abject servitude." In other words, if Parliament had the power it claimed, Americans had no liberty because they had no security. They were "completely *tenants at will*, and have no permanent property."[5]

The American whig case may seem strongly stated, but in terms of the liberty of the constitution it was not farfetched. A Scots lawyer who had served as admiralty judge in Ireland, for example, went further than did most colonial whigs and claimed that the doctrine of security even protected American charters from parliamentary nullification. He did so on the constitutional premise that "the nature of a free government is such, that all property is inviolable," including charters of incorporation. In 1774 a London newspaper printed a constitutional complaint as extreme as any stated by American whigs. Referring to the British and not to the Americans, it charged that due to recent parliamentary legislation, "[n]o men, or bodies of men in this nation, have now any property which is secure to them, and they can call their own." Interestingly, the writer had in mind much the same threat to security that had aroused the Scots lawyer. For the acts of Parliament that he said "robbed" Britons "of their rights and properties" had altered the charter of the East India Company. From the perspective of both liberty and security, the constitutional criticism of these East India Acts was almost identical to American whig objections to acts altering the government of Massachusetts Bay and closing the port of Boston to private shipping. They were arbitrary in the same consitutional sense, for all were exercises of parliamentary power that was perceived to be unprecedented in its operation and unlimited in its potential. If such power constitutionally belonged to Parliament, the South Carolina convention resolved, the average British subject residing in America would have "not even the shadow of liberty to his person, or security of his property."[6]

The progression of constitutional logic led to revolution. Parliament's claim to legislative supremacy threatened the security of Americans because, in Joseph Hawley's words, it was "absolutely inconsistent with the fundamentals of Government, *British* rights, *English* liberties, or the security of life, liberty, and property." To endanger security was to threaten liberty, because liberty could not survive when property was not secure. People had a right to defend liberty, even to the last extreme of armed rebellion. If Parliament persisted in its claims, the British constitutional imperatives left Americans no alternatives but resistance or the loss of liberty. Their course of action was obvious, Gad Hitchcock warned the last royal governor of Massachusetts Bay. "Our danger is not visionary, but real—Our contention is not about trifles, but about liberty and property; and not ours only, but those of posterity, to the latest generations."[7]

## TAXATION AND THE REVOLUTION

Parliamentary taxation was one of the two major American grievances leading to the Revolution. It was also the one most easily understood and fiercely debated on both sides of the Atlantic. One reason the constitutional premises were so well understood is that the issue of taxation without consent involved two of the best-known doctrines of British constitutional law; for, in addition to the rule of government by consent, there was the principle of security.[8]

The question whether Parliament had authority to tax the colonies was not considered an exclusively constitutional issue. The liberty argument—it might even be called the liberty grievance—was raised relatively frequently, although nowhere near as frequently as the constitutional issue. One reason may be that questions could easily be phrased in liberty terms, that is, in a combination of liberty and constitutional terms,[9] or the liberty grievance could be stated by itself, without discussing the constitutional issue. "[I]nvoluntary Taxes and Impositions are absolutely and necessarily excluded from a State of Liberty," New York representatives told George III. "It is essential to a free state," a Brookfield, Massachusetts, congregation was told, "that no member of it shall have his property taken from him by taxation, or any other way, unless by his own consent, given personally, or by his representative." Americans were not enjoying the British privilege of free government "if they are taxed without being represented," John Wesley was told. "It is an axiom which cannot be too forcibly impressed on the mind— 'Government cannot be free, Where property is TAKEN NOT GIVEN.'"[10]

The case against taxation without consent could also be stated in terms of the principle of security and the doctrine of liberty. In fact, that was how the question was then perceived in the mother country. A writer in the *Political Register*, discussing "liberty" and not the American controversy, explained in 1769: "Great Britain is that happy kingdom, and her people, in preference to the subjects of all other states, can most truly say—we are free, we have a property we can call our own, we can freely dispose of it agreeable to our inclinations without controul, it is not liable to be seized by rude violence."[11]

Even more revealing of the common source of British and American liberty rhetoric are the arguments that had been made in the mother country against the cider excise, just two years before passage of the Stamp Act. In common with the Americans of the next decade, some Britons protested the cider tax on both constitutional and liberty grounds, sometimes in similar if not identical language. The methods of collecting excises, London's Common Council complained, were "in their Nature arbitrary and inconsistent with the Principles of Liberty, and the happy Constitution of your Majesty's government." The council asked the king to veto the excise bill—to do so "to protect their liberty, and to keep them happy, and at Ease, free from the Apprehension of being disturbed in their Property." Of course the relation between a tax and liberty was not easy to resolve. "It would be difficult," a critic of the excise wrote, "to suggest any mode of taxation, which, without the help of much ingenuity, might not be proved in some degree prejudicial to liberty."[12]

### CONSENT AND REVOLUTION

It would be well to resist thinking that there was a dichotomy of arguments, or that a relative importance was accorded to arguments, depending on their perceived significance. The primary aspect of the American whig quarrel with the mother country was constitutional. That fact does not mean that the liberty grievance was secondary, articulated more as a matter of emotional rhetoric, lending color to legal substance, than as a part of the legal substance itself. What must not be forgotten is that liberty and constitutionalism were one in the eighteenth century. Liberty was constitutionalism, and the constitution was liberty. There could be no dichotomy between the constitutional grievance and the liberty grievance.

It was because liberty and constitutionalism were so interwined that the liberty argument could be substituted freely for the

constitutional argument, seemingly wrapping liberty up in the
guise of the constitution, that is, making a claim on behalf of liberty
that had the appearance of a substantive, constitutional argument.[13]

The fact may be surprising, but the concept of constitutional
liberty was used more persuasively as an argument against
legislation without consent than against taxation without consent.
The reason is that the doctrine that taxes could not be imposed
without consent of the persons taxed was a much stronger, more
familiar, and ancient doctrine in English and British constitutional
law. Because it was so strong, American whigs could build a
persuasive case against parliamentary taxation without mentioning such rhetorical arguments as liberty, the rights of man, or
natural law. The case against legislation without consent was less
strong and certainly less familiar to nonlawyers. As a result, the
constitutional argument against legislation without consent lacked
the long history and rich documentation of the constitutional case
against taxation without consent. It is for that reason, because the
constitutional complaint was less familiar against legislation
without consent than against taxation without consent, that the
liberty component of the complaint was either more important or
had the appearance of being more significant. The liberty
grievance, after all, unlike more traditional constitutional
arguments, needed neither contemporary law, legal precedent,
nor historical example to sustain it. Also important, perhaps, was
the fact the liberty grievance was easily stated. Parliamentary
supremacy over the colonies, according to citizens of Accomack
County, Virginia, could not "be admitted without the utter
destruction of American liberty." According to people in Chester
County, Pennsylvania, it would be "subversive to the very idea of
liberty." And according to Joseph Hawley, it was "as repugnant to
every idea of freedom as life and death, blessing and curse, are
opposite to each other."[14]

Unless we keep in mind that these were British arguments, some
may seem too extreme to be serious. "I see not how they can be
called free subjects by others, nor arrogate freedom to themselves,"
an anonymous author observed of the colonists, if "they make not
their own laws, nor have . . . any share in the making of them," for
"these are the characteristics and criterion of freedom."[15] The
argument seems persuasive, but when applied to the eighteenth

century it meant that just about no people had liberty, as hardly anyone but the British enjoyed government by constitutional consent. Yet it is informative that, when the issue was next raised in Great Britain, by the Irish in 1780, the rhetoric of liberty was repeated in almost exactly the same arguments. "IRELAND is not FREE," it was claimed, "whilst England has the power of binding Ireland by British acts of Parliament," and Parliament's exercise of legislative supremacy was called "a Tissue of Oppression on the People" of Ireland. [16]

Governor George Johnstone was one of several members of Parliament who said that Britons were among the very few people who were "yet free" because they were among the very few who retained the privilege of government by consent. It reveals much about the association between the rhetoric of liberty and the principle of security that, when addressing the Commons, Johnstone pleaded for the American right to legislative consent not only on the grounds of liberty but also on the grounds of security. "The most learned writer on government," he said, referring to Locke, "has defined civil and political liberty to consist in a perfect security as to a man's rights: After the acts of parliament of last year, can any man on the great continent of America say that he feels that security?" [17]

# 12

# Slavery and the Revolution

Americans appreciated what loss of their liberty would mean. Loss of liberty meant slavery, and fear of slavery was used in the colonies to motivate people to action. This motivation took two forms. In the early days of the revolutionary controversy, fear of slavery was cited to motivate Americans to be less dependent on British manufactures. "[A]s long as our backs are cloathed from *Great-Britain,* they will lay what burthens upon them they please," the Sons of Liberty were told in 1766; "industry is our best barrier against slavery." Later, fear of slavery became a motivation for taking up arms. "[W]e will, to the utmost of our power," the whig committee of Worcester County, Maryland, resolved after the battle of Lexington, "oppose the detested ministerial plan for enslaving us—a plan calculated to divest us of every privilege which can render life valuable and desirable."[1]

The literature concerning slavery and the motivation for the American Revolution is so enormous it would be impossible even to cite each time the argument was made. There is no need, however, for what was said was not much different from the argument on behalf of liberty. Slavery, after all, was the other side of liberty, and fear of slavery was but fear of liberty lost.

The word appeared at the very beginning of the revolutionary debate. During January 1765, when taxation of the colonies was first being mentioned in the House of Commons, Charles Townshend urged "the supremacy of this country over the colonies," saying that he "would not have them emancipated." That statement, complained William Beckford, future lord mayor of London, implied that Americans were slaves.[2] From then until independence was declared in 1776, "slave" was probably the most frequently used word by both American whigs and their British supporters, and to no issue was it more often applied than that of parliamentary taxation. As demonstrated by the following instructions voted by the town of Boston in May 1772, the word was used not in the sense of chattel slavery.

> An exterior Power claims a Right to govern us, & have for a number of Years been levying an illegal tax on us; whereby we are degraded from the rank of Free Subjects to the despicable Condition of Slaves. For its evident to the meanest Understanding that Great Britain can have no Right to take our Moneys from us without our consents unless we are her Slaves, unless our bodys [and] our Persons are her property she surely cannot have the least claim to dispose of our earnings.[3]

The legal theory why parliamentary taxation meant slavery for America was explained by a Rhode Island governor, when he argued that to hold property at the will and pleasure of Parliament was the same as having no property to call your own. "They who have no property can have no freedom, but are indeed reduced to the most abject slavery," he wrote. A Connecticut clergyman further elaborated the fear when he told a Norwalk congregation that "PROPERTY is a blessing when accompanied with liberty; then it renders life comfortable and pleasant; but to be stript of all we can call our own, and be dependent upon others for our support and subsistence . . . 'tis but the life of a slave, and but half living at best."[4]

As the incredibly voluminous colonial literature on taxation and slavery must be passed over as repetitious, only one point remains to be made. It is that the use of the word "slave" to describe a person taxed without consent was not original with American whigs, but was traditional English legal usage. Even so, the proimperialist Martin Howard, who was a lawyer, mocked its use. When James Otis argued that "If we are taxed, . . . without our own consent; we are in the miserable condition of slaves," Martin Howard criticized him. "In this place," Howard contended, "he hath combined together the idea of slavery, with that of being taxed without our consent, which is very artful, and an effectual way to extinguish all regard to acts of parliament."[5]

Artful the word "slaves" may have been when applied to people taxed without consent, but like the word "slave" describing the subjects of arbitrary government, it had a long history. Lord Clarendon, who had been a royalist lawyer and a chief lieutenant of Charles I's, was remembered during the age of the American Revolution as having said that the fundamental objection against shipmoney had not been the tax itself or the arbitrary imprisonments imposed to collect it. "It is that our BIRTHRIGHT is destroyed, and that there hath been an endeavor to reduce us to *a lower state than villainage.*" The state lower than villenage was slavery, a word that the prosecutor of Charles I used when he said that shipmoney would have made the English "absolute slaves." In 1748, a London author had summarized the legal principle in words no different from those American whigs would be using two generations later. "The Power of *Raising Money,*" he observed, "is justly accounted the *grand Bulwark* of the People's Liberties; for the Moment this is seised [*sic*] by the King, and yielded by the People, He become[s] *absolute,* they *Vassals* and *Slaves.*"[6]

During the age of the American Revolution, the constitutional premise that arbitrary taxation created political slaves was as familiar in Great Britain as it was in the colonies.[7] Certainly members of Parliament were told often enough that they were enslaving the Americans with their taxation statutes to appreciate that in this context the word "slavery" had constitutional connotations sufficient to arouse resistance. Colonial assemblies, William Pitt pointed out during the Stamp Act debates, "have ever been in possession of the Exercise of this, their constitutional Right, of giving and granting their own Money.—They would have been Slaves, if they had not enjoyed it." Eight years later Edmund Burke was still repeating the theme in the same House of Commons:

> Sir, let the gentlemen on the other side call forth all their ability, let the best of them get up and tell me, what one character of liberty the Americans have, and what one brand of slavery they are free from, if they are . . . made pack-horses of every tax you choose to impose, without the least share in granting them. . . . The Englishman in America will feel that this is slavery—that it is *legal* slavery will be no compensation either to his feelings or his understanding.[8]

## Slavery and Parliamentary Supremacy

It is almost repetitious to turn from the issue of consent to taxation to constitutional consent in general. For lawyers the legal issues are different, and the material merits separate treatment. To non-lawyers the arguments may seem the same. Because of the nature of eighteenth-century constitutional law and the legal history of the power to tax, people living in the age of the American Revolution thought the two issues quite distinct. Certainly, they discussed them separately, treating the question of consent to taxation as the more important of the two, yet knowing that it was consent to legislation that led to the final break.

The constitutional principle could become lost in the rhetoric of slavery. Should Parliament make good its claim to legislative supremacy, the Pennsylvania Provincial Congress told the world, "the colonists will *sink* from the rank of freemen into the class of slaves, overwhelmed with all the miseries and vices, proved by the history of mankind to be inseparably annexed to that deplorable condition." Put more simply, the constitutional position was that if Parliament exercised a supreme legislative authority, in which the colonies "have no share, they cannot be considered as a free people. For they are subject to laws and regulations not of their own making, which is the very definition of slavery."[9]

The Declaratory Act was a key factor in the equation about slavery and parliamentary supremacy. It was the statute in which Parliament declared that it had "full power and authority" to make laws binding on the colonies "in all cases whatsoever," and was the prime symbol for American whigs explaining why they thought they were being enslaved by legislation. Today or in the nineteenth century the claim of legislative sovereignty contained in the Declaratory Act would be uncontroversial. During the eighteenth century, however, there were still people—perhaps a majority of Americans and a large part of the British population—who could not abide the thought of any governmental body, not even one consisting wholly of elected representatives, exercising such arbitrary power. The "wit of man," the Pennsylvania Congress lamented, "cannot possibly form a more clear, concise, and comprehensive definition and sentence of slavery, than these expressions contain." "Dreadful power indeed!" Richard Price exclaimed. "I defy any one to express slavery in stronger language."[10]

Scotland's most distinguished jurist, Lord Kames, even thought that the Navigation Acts portended slavery for the colonies. The charge is interesting because American whigs never objected to these laws on the grounds of unconstitutionality. They did not particularly like them and thought them unfair and unequal, but they admitted they were constitutional and therefore not a grievance in the controversy with the mother country. Yet Kames condemned them, saying that "To bar a colony from access to the fountain-head for commodities that cannot be furnished by the mother-country but at second-hand, is oppression; it is so far degrading the colonists from being free subjects to be slaves."[11]

Other acts were occasionally singled out for enslaving the Americans. Lord Camden said that the Quebec Act imposed "slavery," and William Beckford said that the Dockyard Act of Henry VIII, authorizing trial in England of Americans charged with crimes committed in the colonies, made them "absolute slaves." But the statutes that convinced most colonists that they faced the danger of "slavery" were of course the acts of Parliament that made the American Revolution inevitable, the Intolerable or Coercive laws. These acts, altering the government of Massachusetts Bay and closing the harbor of Boston to commerce, the whig committee of New York's Cumberland County resolved, "have a direct tendency to reduce the free and brave *Americans* into a state of the most abject slavery and vassalage."[12]

The American whig constitutional case against the Coercive Acts is so important that it deserves to be restated. The colonists especially objected to those provisions of the statutes that changed the Massachusetts charter and transferred certain types of criminal actions outside the place of venue. What should be noted is that American whigs were not raising the grievance of legislation without consent. It was, rather, unrestrained legislative sovereignty that disturbed them. Although whigs were alarmed by the specific provisions of the statutes, they were even more alarmed by parliamentary assertions of power and the implications for constitutional change contained in the statutes. If the Coercive Acts were legal, they meant that legislative mandates were supreme over custom, "law," vested rights, and even security of property. That possibility shocked eighteenth-century people, especially those of the country or old-whig persuasion. "Upon the principles which the British Legislature have adopted," William Gordon, later to be one of the Revolution's first historians, told a Massachusetts congregation, "I see not how we can be certain of any one privilege—nor what hinders our being in a state of slavery to an aggregate of masters, whose tyranny may be worse than that of a single despot." Remember that in the 1770s law was still thought of as restraint upon government, and liberty was still measured by the absence of coercive power. Parliament's claim, to have the constitutional power to alter the fundamental right of trial by jury and to sweep aside a provincial charter with all its customary and historical rights and privileges, meant "slavery by legislative authority."[13]

If the words seem overblown and the rhetoric melodramatic, the reason may be that we have lost the eighteenth-century meaning of liberty and slavery. Most of all, we have changed our perception of legislative authority and of sovereignty. We no longer think of constitutional or "legitimate" government mainly in terms of restraint or impotency; as a result, our definition of liberty is different from that of people for whom the word "slavery" conjured images of arbitrary rule rather than of bondsmen picking cotton. We are able to understand American loyalists when they tell us that whig committees enforcing nonimportation agreements acted "lawlessly," but we do not understand whigs telling us that the British army was an "unlawful assembly" or that the Boston mob was not illegal. By the same measure of vocabulary, we understand the loyalists' claim that arbitrary and "extralegal" whig committees and congresses made them slaves, but we think the same word misused when whigs complained that they were enslaved by statutes "legally" enacted by the Parliament of Great Britain.[14]

Yet for all these difficulties, it must be apparent that there was something very useful in words that could convey so much meaning about complicated, controversial subjects. We may wonder why the word "slave" was inserted into a sentence, or we may think of African chattel slavery, but the New York Provincial Congress expected contemporaries to know it was speaking of liberty and of the opposite of liberty when it told the inhabitants of Quebec that "[t]he great question between *Britain* and her Colonies is, whether they are subjects, or whether they are slaves." The earl of Buckinghamshire also expected to be understood when he told the House of Lords that "[t]he question now was, not about the liberty of North America, but whether we were to be free, or slaves to our colonies."[15] So too did the author of a pamphlet, who attempted to summarize the entire revolutionary controversy by reducing it to the single concept of slavery. "Our right of legislation over the Americans, unrepresented as they are, is the point in question. This right is asserted by most, doubted of by some, and wholly disclaimed by a few. But to put the matter in a stronger light, the question, I think, should be, Whether we have a general right of making slaves, or not?"[16]

The word "slavery" did outstanding service during the revolutionary controversy, not only because it summarized so many political, legal, and constitutional ideas and was charged with such content. It was also of value because it permitted a writer to say so much about liberty. Consider how Joseph Priestley used the word to make a point about the relationship between liberty and imperialism. "How preposterous is it," he wrote, "that those, who glory in a free constitution for themselves, should wish for a power over *their fellow subjects*, which would make them the most abject slaves, of which there is any account in history." People who now think of chattel slavery might smile at Priestley's exaggeration, but what he said was no exaggeration by the norms of eighteenth-century language. He meant slavery as his fellow Britons understood the term, and as Hugh Baillie, a Scots advocate, used it when justifying the American whig resort to arms. "It is true," Baillie concluded, "they have raised troops, named generals, &c. but not for independency, but to defend their country and *Great Britain* against slavery and arbitrary power."[17]

# 13

# The Rhetoric of Liberty

In the eighteenth century the concept of liberty was more than the sum of all its elements—the other sides of licentiousness and slavery, the rule of law, the security of property, and the principles of the constitution. It was also rhetoric, a way of arguing, or urging action, and of audience expectation. The rhetoric of liberty, so familiar, so anticipated, so persuasive because it was shared by all literate English-speaking people, was a potent force in eighteenth-century politics and constitutional debate.[1] It helped to set not only the tone of forensic exchange but also the political programs that men would initiate.

The coming of the American Revolution was a great theater for the rhetoric of liberty. People on both sides of the controversy employed the words of liberty as a form of shorthand or code of cherished beliefs with which to argue, persuade, and motivate. Opponents could be condemned and allies praised by selecting the correct expression, hoping to provoke predictable reaction with charged meanings, conditioned prejudices, and historical fears. *Brutus* knew the right words to use when telling Virginians that tories were the "degenerate tools of lawless power" and whigs the "upright sons of constitutional liberty."[2] Today, *Brutus's* words appear to be political bombast. In the eighteenth century they said more than that opponents were wicked and friends good. They elicited responses to arbitrariness, prerogativism, rule of law, restraint upon government, and constitutionalism.

The words and expressions employed may not be evidence of what concepts, ideas, or values persuaded people in the eighteenth century to take action on behalf of liberty. They are, however, evidence of what words, ideas, or values eighteenth-century people thought could persuade others to take action. At the very least, they were expected to incite certain reactions.

This discussion of incitement by the rhetoric of liberty can be confined to evidence from the American Revolution. Liberty arguments during that constitutional controversy were typical of eighteenth-century liberty arguments made about other issues and at other times, on both sides of the Atlantic. We may not be surprised that American whigs, thinking they were upholding liberty, described their cause as liberty, irresistable to all open-minded people who were not tools of lawless power. "Born of the bright Inheritance of *English* Freedom," New York City's whig committee told London's Common Council, "the Inhabitants of this extensive Continent, can never submit to the ignominious Yoke, nor move in the galling Fetters of Slavery." More concisely put, in the words of South Carolina's Congress to Governor Lord William Campbell, American whigs preferred "death to slavery" and expected other right-thinking—or perhaps a better description is "liberty-thinking"—people to prefer it, too.[3]

What may surprise us is the fact that the enemies of colonial whigs often predicted the same reaction to the same incitement from the same concept. There were few loyalists more militant than Pennsylvania's Joseph Galloway. He frequently urged London to crush the colonial revolution with armed might. Yet even he believed that his fellow Americans could be incited by liberty. "No people in the world have higher notions of liberty," he warned the British. "It would be impossible to eradicate them." Rather than try, it would be better to accept the fact that the colonists, who could not be enslaved, would unite with the mother country only "upon principles of English liberty."[4]

In Great Britain there were many writers and members of Parliament who said the same as Galloway. The most articulate, Edmund Burke, not only insisted that Americans were incited to liberty and would react to any threat against it, but that the leaders of Britain had to tailor imperial governance to this reality and temper imperial rule with the rhetoric of liberty. "If there be one fact in the world perfectly clear it is this: 'That the disposition of the people of America is wholly averse to any other than a free government;' and this is indication enough to any honest statesman how he ought to adapt whatever power he finds in his hands to their case."[5]

## THE MINISTERIAL VIEW OF LIBERTY

As the revolutionary controversy progressed and the possibility of civil war grew, American whigs came to see the confrontation as one between loyalty and liberty.[6] That the confrontation was with the mother country provided the concept of liberty with a special poignancy.[7] The liberty to defend was the liberty of the constitution, and that very fact helped make civil war inevitable. For, to defend their constitutional rights, Americans had to oppose a rule that their opponents thought to be the true constitution of liberty. It is often forgotten that those opponents honored the same constitutional values and employed the same constitutional rhetoric as colonial whigs. From their perspective, it was Great Britain that was defending liberty. "Our wish," Lord North told General John Burgoyne, "is not to impose on our fellow-subjects in America any terms inconsistent with the most perfect liberty." We may be certain that North was sincere. What would lead to civil war was that American whigs could not credit that sincerity, and the reason was that North's applied liberty was not their applied liberty.

The difference was not of definition but of priority of emphasis. Members of Parliament had to maintain the supremacy of Parliament when confronted with American whig claims that parliamentary supremacy threatened their liberty. They had to do so not due to any constitutional imperative that Parliament be supreme over the colonies, but because in Great Britain the survival of constitutional liberty was understood to depend upon Parliament's supremacy over the Crown. Moreover, there was a distinctive difference of emphasis concerning what constituted threats to liberty. Proadministration members of Parliament and American loyalists tended to worry about anarchy and the breakdown of government as the chief threat to liberty. American whigs and their British supporters tended more to fear that liberty was threatened by government power. To North and his colleagues in the British government, and to colonial loyalists, the definition of liberty was the same as it was to American whigs—a concept embodying the values, principles, and restraints on government discussed in earlier chapters. But where the whigs' emphasis was on restrained legality, theirs was on order through legality. Primarily, liberty was the guaranteed order of constitutional government, securing and enforcing civil behavior above other competing values, even if need be, above security of property. To attack government in the name of liberty was a contradiction, for to attack government was to attack liberty itself. "[L]et me entreat you," Governor James Wright admonished Georgia's legislators, "to take care how you give sanction to trample on Law and Government; and be assured it is an indisputable truth, that where there is no law there can be no liberty. It is the due course of law and support of Government which only can insure to you the enjoyment of your lives, your liberty, and your estates; and do not catch at the shadow and lose the substance."[8]

The lesson is not that American whigs were urged to be cautious about shouting liberty and defying authority in the cause of freedom. It is rather that caution was the defense of liberty because authority was liberty. To justify resistance to authority, the sins of government had to be so serious that they were destroying or threatened to destroy liberty. And the reason why nothing less should justify resistance was that resistance to government was itself destructive of liberty.

For American loyalists the destructiveness of resistance to ordered liberty was indisputably demonstrated by colonial whigs banding together in extralegal associations to compel others to resist parliamentary authority. In the cause of liberty, people were forced by threats, intimidation, and violence to oppose the edicts of the imperial government. Loyalists' protests, phrased in the political vocabulary of the transatlantic British constitutional tradition, warned of "zeal" for liberty and of the risks inherent in any change of government. The warnings, however, were not always on behalf of loyalty to the London government or to the Crown, but quite often on behalf of ordered liberty through the established rule of law.[9]

Tories did not have to dismiss the whig argument on behalf of liberty as farfetched, too extreme, or constitutional error. One could acknowledge its merits and yet say it was too strong a reaction because the threat was too insignificant. In defense of liberty, it jeopardized liberty to an extent that no friend of liberty could support. "I know of no ill consequence that can ever attend a *decent, candid* disquisition of matters which concern the *publick* in general," Jonathan Sewall, attorney general of Massachusetts, explained. "[B]ut when this *liberty* is prostituted to the pernicious purpose of *alienating* the affections of the people from all in *author-*

*ity,* it is unhinging government itself—it is stabbing at the very
vitals of society." Many years later, James Pittman, Sewall's
successor and the last royal attorney general of Massachusetts Bay,
lamented that the warning had not been heeded. The worse had
come to pass, and American liberty had been lost. "My countrymen
have got their independence (as they call it) and with it in my
opinion, have lost the true Substantial Civil liberty."[10]

LIBERTY AND EMPIRE

Most participants in the revolutionary debates, concentrating on
the constitution, thought the dynamics of imperialism irrelevant to
the question of liberty. Remarkably little attention was paid to the
relationship between liberty and imperial government. The extent
of territory might make the preservation of freedom more difficult, but did not diminish the right or alter the constitution. One of
the very few politicians to disagree was Sir William Meredith, who
felt that size might call for sacrifices, especially as one moved farther
from the center of government. The same argument was sometimes
made in response to a different question: whether the colonies were
capable of sustaining all the blessings of British liberty. Thomas
Bernard provided an interesting variation when speaking in favor of
the Quebec Act. Although not wanting despotism in "any part of a
*free* Empire," he argued, "if the constitution of the *dependent* state
cannot exactly tally with that of the *imperial* state, it had better be
*less* free than *more* free."[11]

American whigs would be generally unpersuaded either by
Meredith's notion that the constitution of liberty could serve as a
guide for diminishing liberty, or by Bernard's notion that they could
enjoy the constitution of liberty without enjoying all constitutional
liberty. If some liberty could be taken away, all could. "Of what
importance is it to us, that our fellow-subjects, three thousand miles
off, should be distinguished from the other Nations of the earth, as
free and happy, while we have no share in the distinction?" a
Philadelphian asked. Liberty, after all, was not merely the social
condition of Britons; it was also their property and, like most other
property, was inviolate, with the special provision that the living
generation had a duty to bequeath it undiminished to generations
yet unborn. One argument why liberty could not be diminished,
despite the exigencies of empire, was that as property liberty was

too absolute an inheritance to be diminished. Civil liberty, John Allen explained, is a right "ever inherent in the people, and cannot be given to kings, nor taken away by any parliament whatsoever; the enjoyment may, but the right cannot; its creation is natural and rises with every generation."[12]

American whigs also rejected the argument of Richard Price that as an institution, no matter what its constitution and libertarian traditions, any imperial government was irreconcilable with civil liberty.[13] Price contended "that the authority of one country over another, cannot be distinguished from the servitude of one country to another; and that unless different communities, as well as different parts of the same community, are united by an equal representation, all such authority is inconsistent with the principles of Civil Liberty."[14] Put in terms of slavery rather than of liberty, a critic of Price's summarized his argument as claiming "that the slavery of one state subjected to another is worse, on several accounts, than any slavery of private men to one another."[15]

Not only American whigs but also most British commentators, those favoring suppression of the colonies as well as those supporting colonial arguments, disagreed with Price. They did so for the same reason they disagreed with Meredith: to be ruled by the British constitution meant to be ruled by the liberty of the constitution, no matter the extent of empire. Some British statesmen would accept the empire on no other terms than the constitution of liberty. "I wish this to be an Empire of Freemen," William Pitt boasted in the House of Commons; "it will be the stronger for it and it will be the more easily governed." Edmund Burke would later make the same assertion. "The British Empire must be governed on a plan of freedom for it will be governed by no other," he contended.[16]

Although the administration of imperial liberty was admittedly challenging, few commentators agreed with Richard Price that the task was impossible. It is true that no program for resolving the revolutionary controversy satisfactory to everyone was devised, but difficulty may not be the only reason none was formulated. Because of the concept of liberty, many people seem to have thought a plan not necessary, at least not as we would expect today. If we can credit what some commentators said, there was hope that the dynamics of the concept of liberty alone could solve the imperial constitutional crisis. Surely Governor Thomas Pownall thought the solution was contained within both the liberty of the constitution and the nature of the empire that the constitution had created. Because the British constitution was a constitution of liberty, he explained, it created colonies *"having political liberty,"* a liberty that limited "its own supremacy; which, though in right it goes over the whole empire, cannot, in fact, in the ordinary exercise of it, do any act, within the jurisdictions of the Colonies, which supercedes or destroys that political liberty." If Pownall's conclusion strikes us for what it was, constitutional nonsense, it would be well to consider that to make it he was propelled along by the rhetoric of liberty. Liberty was its own enforcement, just as liberty alone was enough to motivate compliance. "I wish the people of America," he also wrote, "as they love liberty, so to honour true government, which is the only basis on which real liberty can stand *and in that line to see peace."* Put another way, Pownall was saying that if only Americans would be sufficiently motivated by liberty, the governance problems of the empire would be solved.[17]

American whigs felt they were adherents of liberty, and that their notion of liberty was the same as Pownall's, the liberty of the constitution, not abstract or "natural" liberty. For that reason most of them rejected the extreme constitutional theories of men like John Cartwright and Richard Price who, defining liberty as a bundle of natural rights held immediately of God, believed that the constitution should not be a consideration. Liberty was a natural possession that no one could alienate. If Great Britain attempted to "rob" the colonies of it, they could defend themselves no matter what was the law, the customary government, or the constitution.[18]

The solution of Cartwright and Price would have simplified the imperial crisis for those few colonists who wanted independence from the mother country. It did not help the majority whose goal was not separation but constitutional security. That American whigs sought a constitutional solution complicated their case in several ways, primarily because they were seen in London to be challenging British constitutional government. After all, by saying that Parliament was not sovereign in every division of the empire, they appeared to be diminishing the one institution guaranteeing liberty in Great Britain, parliamentary supremacy.

British supporters of the colonial whig cause used the concept of liberty to reverse that perception, pointing out that it was not the

Americans who were seeking to alter the British imperial constitution but the British administration that was seeking to alter the local American constitutions. To do that unilaterally not only threatened American liberty, it threatened British liberty, and did so because British liberty was the liberty of the constitution. Moreover, the liberty of the British constitution was one with the liberty of the American constitution, for they were a unit, the same constitutional liberty. For Great Britain to coerce the colonies, therefore, posed a danger for British liberty. If British constitutionalism was employed to enslave Americans, the total of liberty in the mother country would be diminished, because a constitution capable of imposing slavery on one part of the empire could no longer be the same constitution of liberty in another part, even at home. The premises, the conventions, and the institutions of that constitution might not in any respect be altered, but it would be a different constitution. It would be less free. [19]

## The Empire of Liberty

The rhetoric of liberty served the colonial whig cause well. It permitted Americans to defend local institutions by arguing for traditional British values, using the phraseology of English constitutionalism. It also permitted American whigs to answer what was the most serious charge leveled against them from the tory view of liberty, the usurpation of power by whig committees and congresses. These bodies appeared to be self-appointed, to operate not only outside the norms of British constitutionalism but also to be destructive of the liberty of the constitution. One defense, legitimate in English constitutional law but always debatable, was to employ the doctrine of necessity. Another was to utilize the rhetoric of liberty and to exclaim that whig bodies were the expression of liberty, not its antithesis:

> The *American Congress* derives all its power, wisdom and justice, not from scrolls of parchment signed by Kings, but from the *People*. . . . It is founded upon the principles of the most perfect liberty. A freeman in honouring and obeying the Congress, honours and obeys *himself*. The man who refuses to do both, is a slave. He knows nothing of the dignity of his nature. He cannot govern himself.

> Expose him for sale at publick vendue. Send him to plant
> Sugar with his fellow slaves in *Jamaica*. Let not the air of
> *America* be contaminated with his breath.[20]

One of the strengths of the rhetoric of liberty was that the writer
could always assume that the reader knew what was meant. There
was no need to explain when rhetoric and familiar vocabulary would
do as well.[21] But the question must be asked, what did the American
whigs seek as liberty? An answer was provided by a British author
writing from Bristol. What they sought was the liberty of the
constitution: "[I]t is the liberty of enjoying, in peace and security,
those invaluable rights and privileges which were handed down to
us under the laws and civil institutions of our fathers; it is the
prerogative of being governed by the laws of the land, *'the old, cool-
headed law of England,'* and not by party, or by men." In other
words, American whigs wanted freedom from arbitrary power, and
they wanted it under the rule of constitutional law. They sought to
avoid the kind of arbitrary rule of which radicals in London had
complained four years earlier, when the House of Commons
arrested and imprisoned without jury trial several city officials for
violating the privileges of the House. From the perspective of
people who defined the rule of law narrowly and traditionally, the
"privileges" of the House of Commons seemed to be nothing more
or less than what a majority of those voting said they were. Arrest
and confinement without trial on such grounds was the very essence
of arbitrary government, an act of power rather than an act of right,
a direct attack on liberty. "It is a Power," Alderman Richard Oliver
warned from his imprisonment in the Tower of London, "which
pretends by Law, total[l]y *unknown*, to wrest from the Subject the
clearest and most important Right of personal Liberty, which he
enjoys by the *known* Laws of the Land." Inhabitants of the ward
of Broadstreet, addressing the lord mayor, who also was in the
Tower, explained the threat to liberty in words that could have been
voted by the people of Boston in New England: "We look with the
greatest Horror upon Power assumed over the Laws of the Land,
which we think more to be dreaded under the Name of Privilege
than Prerogative; (as many Tyrants are worse than one;) and that
such Power, invested in any Set of Men, would reduce us to a State
of the most abject Slavery, which God forbid."[22]

The challenge, Charles Carroll of Carrollton believed, was to maintain the old constitution by balancing power against liberty, "the general superintending and controlling power of England" with the customary incidents of American freedom. "[I]f this freedom and that power are *res dissociabiles,* incompatible, I am sorry for it, but let us retain our liberty whatever becomes of the honour."[23]

American whigs believed that they knew where to strike the balance between their liberty and British imperial power. It was where the liberty of the constitution indicated it should be struck. We may wonder, however, if they knew where the reality of constitutional liberty ended and the rhetoric of liberty began. For never were their words far from the mythology of liberty, from speaking of liberty as an entity, a being, an old friend to be welcomed home and cherished, an emigrant from arbitrary Europe, sprung to renewed health and vigor in the American wilderness, where its deep roots had become part of the American soil.

> May the bright example be fairly transcribed on the hearts and reduced into practice by every *Virginian,* by every *American.* May our hearts be open to receive, and our arms strong to defend, that liberty and freedom, the gift of Heaven, now banishing from its last retreat from *Europe.* Here let it be hospitably entertained in every breast; here let it take deep root, flourish in everlasting bloom; that, under its benign influence, the virtuously free may enjoy secure repose, and stand forth the scourge and terrour of tyranny and tyrants of every order and denomination, till time shall be no more.[24]

# 14

# The Definition of Liberty

For English-speaking people of the eighteenth century, the concept of liberty inspired both pride and fear. Pride came from knowing they were the freest people in the world. They boasted of the fact and gloried in it, making exaggerated, even fantastic claims, such as the incredible assertion by Henry Grattan, exclaiming to his fellow Irish Protestants, "We live in a land of liberty," or Charles Lucas, asking the same Irish Protestants, "What has restored and preserved the *British*, and, with it *our Constitution*, in *happy Freedom* and *pure Religion;* was it not *Liberty?*"[1]

Irish Protestants bragging of liberty were defending the political status quo, and it was defense of the status quo that joined the eighteenth century's pride in liberty with the eighteenth century's fear for the vitality of liberty. Because the British loved liberty, an anonymous writer explained in 1776, "we dream of Grievances that never existed, and foresee Dangers that will never approach us." The point was well taken and explains why so much eighteenth-century rhetoric about liberty had a coloring that twentieth-century observers would label conservative. Writers for liberty in the age of the American Revolution were fearful for the status quo. It would not do to misunderstand that fear. It was less the fear of the political reactionary than defense of an existing system in need of defense. Just to know that the British were the freest people in the world was to know that there were people less free. To know that Great Britain was the only nation on earth to enjoy civil and political liberty was to know that liberty did not exist anywhere else. The British system of government may not have been perfect, but it was threatened by forces far worse. Great Britain was an island surrounded by a sea of absolute tyranny. The "liberty enjoyed by the British nation," Arthur Young reminded his countrymen, was always to be contrasted to "the arbitrary power under which so great a part of the world at present groans."[2]

The fear was arbitrary power, because arbitrary power meant loss of liberty. It would be well, however, to realize what arbitrary power was feared. It was not the arbitrary power of privileged individuals, such as Irish landowners evicting tenants from family farms. Nor was it class legislation duly enacted, such as statutes permitting the enclosure of waste held from time immemorial by a community in common, or the game and poaching laws reserving the animals of the wild for the sport of gentry rather than for the providence of peasantry. Undoubtedly eighteenth-century people understood that actions and statutes such as these could be arbitrary to the individuals affected, but for reasons peculiar to the eighteenth-century legal mind they were not the kinds of arbitrary power that concerned students of liberty. Rather, what was feared in the eighteenth century was the power of government acting without restraint. To be subject to arbitrary governmental power was to live without liberty. For the British this meant the rule of the "Grand Turk" or the king of France, and, potentially, a resurgence of Stuart monarchism at home. For Americans the fear became rule by a Parliament in which they were not represented and which they could not restrain. Thomas Hutchinson understood this fear but could not wholly share it, as he feared more the anarchy of the whig mob unrestrained by the rule of law. Lord North never appreciated it. Perhaps he understood it, but he could not accept it, as solution of American fears on colonial whig terms could have imperiled British liberty at home by weakening Parliament in proportion to the increased role of the Crown in the governance of the empire.

## THE EQUALITY OF LIBERTY

Pride in liberty and fear of arbitrariness, licentiousness, and slavery dominated eighteenth-century thoughts about human freedom, and it is those thoughts that have been the focus of this book. We have been concerned with liberty as a generic term: with what the idea and ideal meant to people who commented upon and attempted to influence public affairs during the age of the American Revolution and the germinal years of the federal republic; and with how the concept was employed by them, how it motivated them, and only incidently how they defined it.[3] This is not to deny that eighteenth-century constitutional theorists provided several definitions of liberty; most of the definitions have been considered and discussed indirectly. Here attention should be given to a specific definition selected not because it contains every element mentioned in the previous discussion, but because it is representative: a summary of political and legal theory about liberty in the age of the American Revolution, including the typical eighteenth-century admonishment to members of the lower classes to be satisfied with their lot because it was enough for them to know that they lived in a land of liberty. Published in 1776, this definition has the additional merit of having been formulated by one of the numerous anonymous London pamphleteers offering solutions to the revolutionary controversy.

> Freedom or Civil Liberty does not at all consist in every individual exercising a right in framing the laws, by which such individuals are to be governed; but in the power of doing whatever the laws permit, conformably to rules of equity and justice, which operate indiscriminately on all orders and degrees of men, and by which, the meanest individual is protected from the insults and oppressions of the great. He who is protected in the peaceable enjoyment of his rights is a Freeman, and enjoys Civil Liberty, tho' he has no sort of right in framing the laws, by which he is governed.[4]

There are two aspects of this definition making it especially relevant to the American revolutionary controversy. First, it endorsed an eighteenth-century British notion about representative government that most Americans, loyalists as well as whigs, were reluctant to accept. Second, it was based on the peculiarly English political theory that equality was maintained best by the doctrine of security, an idea that Americans generally supported at the time of the Declaration of Independence, but which they would be abandoning by the 1790s and the federal constitution.

The divergent perspectives may be glimpsed by considering the distinction between the British and American understanding of how representation should intermix with liberty. Although not everyone concurred, the basic eighteenth-century British constitutional philosophy endorsed by people we today would call "conservatives" was that security of property and protection of government were more important to liberty than popular participation in the legislative process through consent by electing representatives. By the time that Americans understood that to retain liberty they would have to separate from Great Britain, their thinking about the relationship between representation and liberty was changing. The altered perception was summarized in the famous *Essex Result,* the statement of constitutional principles issued by a Essex County, Massachusetts, convention that is especially significant as it has always been depicted as a conservative document, drafted for the purpose of continuing in the new republic the British doctrine of security of property. "Political liberty," the *Essex Result* contended, "is by some defined, a liberty of doing whatever is not prohibited by law. The definition is erroneous. A tyrant may govern by laws. . . . Let it be thus defined; political liberty is the right every man in the state has, to do whatever is not prohibited by laws, TO WHICH HE HAS GIVEN HIS CONSENT."[5]

There were, to be sure, British constitutional theorists who associated liberty with representation even before the American revolutionary controversy began.[6] The idea gained currency, however, as the realization grew among people in Great Britain that Parliament possessed or was coming to possess arbitrary power over law. As a result, even though liberty continued to be defined as rule of constitutional law, more and more observers came to associate its reality with direct representation.[7] The notion would be promulgated even more widely in the 1780s and 1790s, largely due to the parliamentary reform movement that drew much inspiration from the American Revolution and its constitutional aftermath.[8] One of the most prolific writers championing equal representation as an element of liberty was John Cartwright. "A state may be free, with or without a King; or with or without nobles; but without *representation* there is no liberty," he wrote in 1797.[9] This new or "radical" constitutional theory was a departure from the British tradition of defining liberty without having its preservation depend on specific institutions, presaging the nineteenth century and the general British acceptance of what in the eighteenth century had been constitutional heresy—that liberty and arbitrary power are not incompatible, if the power that is arbitrary is "representative." A point

that should be made, however, is that the new theorists did not
necessarily abandon the traditional rhetoric of liberty. Even Cartwright explained the association between liberty and representation in terms of security: representation provided security for life,
liberty, and property. "[L]iberty, or freedom," he wrote as the
third article of a proposed *Declaration of Rights*, "consists in having
*an actual share*, either in the legislation itself, or in the appointing
of those who are to frame the laws, and be the guardians of every
man's peace, property, liberty, and life."[10] By the new constitutional theory, representation would become the means by which
the constitution secured the security essential to liberty.

Slavery was a second traditional concept that, for postrevolu-
tionary British reformers, linked liberty to representation. "Those
Englishmen who have *no* votes for electing representatives, are *not*
free men," Cartwright charged, "but are *enslaved* to the representatives of those who have the votes: For, to be enslaved, is to have *no
will of our own* in the choice of law-makers, but to be governed by
legislators whom *other men have set over us.*"[11] This was another
relatively new and narrow definition of slavery, that came to be
widely propagated during the 1780s by parliamentary reform orga-
nizations such as the Society for Constitutional Information. "Are
not these the very definitions of slavery?" the Society asked, repeating Cartwright's words. "And are not Englishmen thus degraded to
a level with the very cattle in the field, and the sheep in the fold,
which are a property to these who rule over them, and have no voice
to say, Why are we bought and sold?"[12]

The concept of equality had a more mixed relationship to the
eighteenth-century definition of liberty than did the right of
representation. There was simply no agreement about what that
relationship should be. In the decades before the American
Revolution, there had been constitutional theorists who thought
equality destructive of liberty. Certainly most commentators did
not associate economic equality with liberty; the fact that one
person was not economically equal to another person did not lessen
either person's liberty.[13] True, there were a few legal theorists who
disagreed, a few who insisted that liberty could never subsist
without equality.[14] Unfortunately they did not say what they meant
by equality in the context of liberty. Aside from the certainty they
were not thinking of economic equality, the historian is confronted
with a term used with even less legal precision than "liberty." The

definitional vagueness of the word "equality" during the age of the American Revolution is perhaps best demonstrated by instances of "liberty" and "equality" being combined into a single concept, as when equality was employed both to support and to limit liberty. "We are contending for freedom," the *Essex Result* pleaded. "Let us all be equally free." "The spirit of our Constitution I define in two words; 'Equal Liberty,'" an English pamphleteer announced in 1768. "*Equal Liberty*," John Cartwright agreed, was "God's eternal law." The equality to which people were entitled, it would seem, was the quantum of liberty.[15]

It would be unwise to puzzle over the meaning of "equal liberty." What seems vague to us had clarity for the eighteenth-century legal and political mind, and we need only recall the premises and the values that that mind associated with liberty to uncover clues as to "equal liberty." Equality of liberty, after all, was probably just a way of restating the familiar argument that liberty was the rule of law—with, of course, the injunction that law be applied equally. "In a word," J. L. De Lolme concluded, "to live in a state where the laws are equal for all, and sure to be executed (whatever may be the means by which these advantages are attained), is to be free."[16]

In the age of the American Revolution the concept of "legal liberty," or liberty under law, did not mean that law should make people "equal." It was not individuals, but the law, or application of law, that was to be equal. The slogan we have inherited from the eighteenth century is "equal justice under law," not "equal men." "Equality," Lord Carysfort explained in the year that Great Britain acknowledged American independence, did not mean that "there can be no legal or accidental distinction between man and man in a government having freedom for its object. . . . A free government is a government by law, and wherever a citizen finds himself in such a situation, that he can fear nothing from any other citizen, as long as he keeps within the bounds of law, there is an equality."[17]

## THE LIMITS OF LIBERTY

We must be careful to avoid anachronistic conclusions. To say that liberty espoused the equal application of law but eschewed abstract economic or social equality is to mention two values that people in the eighteenth century thought of as positive constitutional doctrines. The attitude today would be more negative, as there has come to be a greater attachment to the ideal of equal people. The eighteenth-century emphasis was upon freedom from arbitrary government power, not upon how arbitrary power could be utilized to benefit citizens. Fear of power made security a more appealing abstraction than equality. Eighteenth-century constitutional theory could not contemplate the use of government to work for equality in the form of social or economic justice, because it could not trust government. Government was necessary, there could be no liberty without the state, but government was power, and power had to be restrained or it was not constitutional. That was the role of liberty, to be a barrier against government, but the liberty that could perform that task was the liberty that came from security, the liberty encased in law and manifested by equal treatment before the law. [18]

It was because liberty as a defense against government was encased within the ancient, endurable common law, that the eighteenth-century legal mind thought of it as a dynamic entity and stressed its characteristic of refugee itinerancy and its quality of resilience, and knew that these offset its famed frailty. The barrister James Ibbetson had these capacities in mind when telling readers that due to liberty there was no need to be alarmed by recent historical arguments that Parliament had been created by post-Norman kings and was not secured as part of an immemorial ancient constitution. Liberty, he contended, "cannot be usurped, because it is our right; it cannot arise from innovation, because it is inherent." "The *rights* of *liberty*," another lawyer, Capel Lofft, wrote, "are such as neither the *violence* of times, nor the *power* of magistrates, nor the *authority* of the *whole people*, which in other cases is *sovereign*, can shake or impair." [19] In fact, liberty was almost, but not quite indestructable. There was only one way it could fail the people and that was if the people failed it. [20] They could, of course, but the possibility was unlikely. Even the most pessimistic social critics, writers such as the widely read John Brown, who lamented "the decline of Manners" among the British and complained of "the few remaining Virtues we have left," conceded that the British retained "the Spirit of Liberty." This spirit "happily, still subsists among us: Not indeed in its genuine Vigour; for then, it would work its genuine Effects. Yet, that the Love of Liberty is not extinguished, appears from the *united Voice of a divided People*. . . . But it is remarkable, that in Proportion as this Spirit hath grown weak in *Deeds*, it hath gained strength in *Words;* and of late run out, into unbounded License."[21]

Once again we seem to have encountered the circuity of eighteenth-century legal thought. Liberty was the British citizen's protection against the power of government and yet, as Pennsylvania governor William Keith remarked, liberty was "that Freedom and Power of Action, which men can be supposed to enjoy, under some certain regular Form of Civil Government." The explanation, of course, is a peculiarity of eighteenth-century legal thought in which liberty was characterized as the rule of law and identified as security of person and property. Today we better understand Lord Chancellor Hardwicke's statement that "Law without liberty is tyranny" than we do his contrasting maxim that "Liberty without law is anarchy and confusion;" or, in words more common to the eighteenth century, that liberty without law is licentiousness. The event of twentieth-century totalitarianism has conditioned us to emphasize liberty, and in these more ordered, policed times has caused us to forget the dangers once posed by "confusion" and licentiousness. But the eighteenth century viewed power from a different perspective, and political and legal theorists were then as apt to worry about liberty without law as they were to worry about law without liberty. And the reason why is explained less by the word "anarchy" or the word "licentiousness" than by the word "arbitrary," as the earl of Bolingbroke suggested when distinguishing between threats to private and public liberty. "[A]s *private Liberty* cannot be deem'd secure under a Government, wherein *Law,* the proper and sole Security of it, is dependent on *Will,*" Bolingbroke observed, "so *publick Liberty* must be in Danger, whenever a *free Constitution,* the proper and sole Security of it, is dependent on *Will;* and a *free Constitution* like ours is dependent on *Will,* whenever the *Will of one Estate* can direct the Conduct of *all Three.*"[22] The word "will"—or, as it was more familiarly phrased in eighteenth-century legal parlance, "will and pleasure"—was another way of expressing arbitrary government. Arbitrary government was the danger that threatened liberty then, a fact that we may find difficult to take seriously if we apply theory to fact and realize that what Bolingbroke warned about is nothing less than the twentieth-century British constitution. Great Britain is today governed by one estate, by one house of its tripartite Parliament, and law is the will of the party in power. We may not think of it as an arbitrary government, but eighteenth-century Britons and Americans would have thought so. From the legal premises with which they defined liberty, twentieth-century Great Britain does not know liberty.

## CONCLUSION

The conclusion that twentieth-century Great Britain does not enjoy liberty in the eighteenth-century meaning of liberty should not be resisted but deserves reflection. It may tell us nothing about the governance of twentieth-century Britain. It tells us much about the meaning of the word "liberty" in the eighteenth century. It may not explain why nineteenth-century Great Britain abandoned that eighteenth-century concept of liberty and embraced the constitutionalism of legislative majoritarianism. It does help explain why the eighteenth-century Americans, fearful of majoritarianism, turned to written constitutions to preserve the rule of law.

Our emphasis, therefore, is on words. To dwell on words may appear too narrow a focus, but words merit our attention because unless we are careful they are apt to mislead. We encounter an eighteenth-century word and it seems to be the same as our word, for we believe we understand the meaning; yet when we look closely the usage may be different.

Today we may rediscover a great deal about what people in the eighteenth century meant by "liberty" and "slavery," but we may wonder if we will ever understand how they expected those words to motivate thoughts and actions. We may wonder, we may even doubt, if "liberty" and "slavery" were capable of motivating deeds and events. Only a materialist with a remarkably closed mind, however, could doubt that eighteenth-century Britons and Americans believed that their fellow citizens could be motivated by either concept. Whether they were or not is another matter.[23]

Thoughts must not be carried too far. In seeking to understand eighteenth-century usage we might easily mislead ourselves. To say the word "liberty" motivated implies political action: that the word was employed to direct otherwise free choices, persuading the listener or reader to endorse a party or a program. Adhering to the distinction between "political" and "legal," however, we may think of the usage of "liberty" in the eighteenth century more accurately as finding law than as promoting political programs. For the word liberty was less a descriptive than a normative concept. It was both a right possessed by individuals and a standard for defining other rights—rights that restrained the legitimacy of governmental power. Had the eighteenth-century British judicial system possessed the constitutional jurisdiction of the later American judicial system, the concept of the right to liberty could have furnished norms similar to those furnished nineteenth-century constitutional law by the right of contract or the right to equality, and to twentieth-century constitutional law by the right to privacy or the right to equal representation.

Because the concept of liberty was not subject to judicial redefinition we are forced to understand it on eighteenth-century terms rather than by premises with which we are more familiar. The legal dimensions of the eighteenth-century concept are less precise than they would be if interpreted by twentieth-century American courts. Ambiguity is much more a luxury of British than American constitutional law. Surely it is reasonable to suppose that, given the dynamics of judicial activism, liberty would have become a more absolute concept in American law, in line with the absolutist precedents propagated by the concepts of "freedom of the press" and "freedom of speech." It is because eighteenth-century British law was less judicially oriented that twentieth-century Americans find some of its precepts not only more ambiguous but more troublesome than do twentieth-century Britons. An example is the famous paradox apparent in Blackstone's insistence that, when speech is punished according to law, "the *liberty of the Press*, properly understood, is by no means infringed or violated." Blackstone's formulation of "liberty of the press" became a paradox for constitutional theorists only after the United States Supreme Court threw the protection of constitutional privilege over speech that merely expressed opinion, speech that did not intentionally incite either violence or crime.

The remarkable fact is not how far we have departed from Blackstone's jurisprudence, but rather the certainty that we no longer understand his legal theory because the vocabulary of liberty has been so changed that we read his words—"liberty," "freedom," "licentiousness"—and attach to those words our meanings, not his meanings. Consider the words and phrases that Blackstone used when formulating that constitutional doctrine regarding liberty of the press. What he said became both the rule of liberty for his own day and the most liberal standard for free speech in the nineteenth century. It is only in recent decades that it has been repudiated as inconsistent with the very constitutional freedoms that Blackstone intended to secure.

> The liberty of the press is indeed essential to the nature of a free state: but this consists in laying no *previous* restraints upon publications, and not in freedom from censure for criminal matter when published. Every freeman has an undoubted right to lay what sentiments he pleases before the public: to forbid this, is to destroy the freedom of the press: but if he publishes what is improper, mischievous, or illegal, he must take the consequence of his own temerity. . . . [T]o punish (as the law does at present) any dangerous or offensive writings, which, when published, shall on a fair and impartial trial be adjudged of a pernicious tendency, is necessary for the preservation of peace and good order, of government and religion, the only solid foundations of civil liberty. Thus the will of individuals is still left free; the abuse only of that free will is the object of legal punishment.[24]

It might be argued that we have not so much rejected Blackstone's legal premises as altered our perceptions about "what is improper, mischievous, or illegal." That conclusion may be true if we realize that the difference is less in the argument that some speech may be punished than in the contrasting theories why it is or is not consistent with liberty to punish certain categories of speech. "[T]o censure the licentiousness," Blackstone explained, "is to maintain the liberty, of the press."[25] That is the difference. It is not so much that we now have other ideas concerning what commentary is "improper, mischievous, or illegal," or what "is necessary for the preservation of peace and good order," but that Blackstone's century protected liberty by punishing licentiousness; that is, the preservation of liberty lay in curbing its excesses. As a pragmatic, working constitutional doctrine, the concept of liberty taught not what the individual was free to do, but what the rule of law permitted. All eighteenth-century constitutional theorists demarcated a legal distinction between personal liberty and civil liberty, acknowledging that personal restraint by the rule of law did not diminish the totality of British civil liberty. "A citizen of the freest republic in the world," William Paley, archdeacon of Carlisle, reminded his numerous readers, "may be imprisoned for his crimes; and though his personal freedom be restrained by bolts and fetters, so long as his confinement is the effect of a beneficial public law, his civil liberty is not invaded."[26]

To understand Blackstone's formulation of subsequent restraint as "liberty" *for* the press we must give attention to more than the eighteenth-century meaning of "liberty." It is necessary to heed related words as well, such as "licentiousness" when Blackstone tells us that "to censure the licentiousness, is to maintain the liberty, of the press." For "licentious," too, was more a normative than a descriptive term in the eighteenth century, helping to set the perimeters of governmental coercion by providing phraseology for standards restraining individual social conduct.

A third word whose twentieth-century meaning must not be projected back onto eighteenth-century constitutional values is "property." It is simply wrong to think that the framers of the Declaration of Independence, when they altered the familiar common-law trilogy from "life, liberty, and property" to "life, liberty, and the pursuit of happiness" were turning American law away from the constitutional principle of security of property. That supposition became constitutionally defensible only after definitions changed and the concept of property, ceasing any longer to embrace liberty or rights, was relegated to the material. The basic premise that we may easily overlook, but which eighteenth-century people never forgot, is that liberty in the eighteenth century was personal property. Indeed, it was the concept of property that bestowed on liberty much of its substance as a constitutional entity and provided one of the enigmas of eighteenth-century constitutional thought— a puzzle for us, not for the eighteenth century. For, as everyone then appreciated, liberty existed through security of property and yet, as John Dickinson said, liberty itself was the *only security* of property.

A final word that has misled us is "slavery." When we encounter eighteenth-century political and legal commentators writing of "slavery" we should not think they were drawing analogies to chattel slavery. We should never have thought that in the first place. More importantly, we should take the word "slavery" seriously. It was not a hyperbole to be snickered at, but a term that was charged with normative meaning in the seventeenth and eighteenth centuries. If we think of it in its eighteenth-century

context we will better understand eighteenth-century constitutional thought. There is much to be learned about the eighteenth-
century British constitution by contemplating the astonishing fact
that chattel slavery was said not to be the worst type of slavery. The
question that deserves deep cognition is why people familiar with
chattel slavery, who saw it in daily operation and were witnesses to
its dehumanizing harshness, could believe that it was a lesser evil
than life under arbitrary government?

When we find eighteenth-century constitutional theorists warning against slavery we should keep in mind the danger they warned
about. The fear of slavery was not an apprehension of bondage but of
governmental arbitrariness. It was not enough to say that there was
liberty if people, through security of property, had obtained "independence." For if security of property was to constitute liberty it
had to be absolute, and security of property could only be absolute if
not subject to the will and pleasure of government. It is important to
dwell on the implications of that conclusion, for they tell us why the
concept of liberty in the eighteenth century was so different from
the concept of liberty in today's Great Britain. Security under British constitutionalism could be absolute only if law were still primarily constitutional custom and not the command of the
sovereign. British liberty today is measured by the fairness, consistency, and equality of government's command. Government's
constitutional power to command what it wills was the death knell of
the eighteenth-century concept of liberty.

Liberty in the age of the American Revolution was not the sum of
enumerated rights, the rights to speech, press, security, property,
or isonomy. It was rather government by the rule of law, government by the customary British constitution. If put in terms of freedom, liberty would not be defined as freedom of speech, freedom of
the press, or any other such freedom now familiar in contemporary
constitutional law, but as freedom from arbitrary power, from government by will and pleasure, from government by a sovereign,
unchecked monarch or from government by a sovereign, unchecked Parliament.

The lesson of this book is not that British whig and British tory, or
government and opposition, shared a common rhetoric of liberty.
The lesson is that the rhetoric of liberty uniting government and
opposition at home was the same rhetoric of liberty employed by

American rebels. They, too, were heirs of a common past. Indeed, following independence Americans continued to use it, and leaders of the new republic would despair of the rhetoric of liberty heard from their political opponents just as British ministers had despaired of the rhetoric of liberty employed by colonial whigs. Consider what a future governor of South Carolina wrote in November, 1786, to a future chief justice of the United States. "It is really very curious to observe how the people of this world are made the dupes of a word," Edward Rutledge lamented to John Jay. "'Liberty' is the motto; every attempt to restrain licentiousness or give efficacy to Government is charged audaciously on the real advocates for Freedom as an attack upon Liberty." Eight years earlier in Massachusetts, Theophilus Parsons, principal author of the *Essex Result*, had also worried that liberty misdefined might become liberty misapplied. The 1770s, he thought, was a good epoch in which to be framing the country's first constitutions. His generation had an opportunity both to redefine liberty as freedom under law and to develop government institutions that would restrain the licentiousness worrying Rutledge. "We live also in an age, when the principles of political liberty, and the foundation of governments, have been freely canvassed, and fairly settled," Parsons noted in the *Result*. "Yet some difficulties we have to encounter. Not content with removing our attachment to the old government, perhaps we have contracted a prejudice against some part of it without foundation. The idea of liberty has been held up to dazzling colours, that some of us may not be willing to submit to that subordination necessary in the freest States." The arguments that Parsons and his fellow constitution makers framed resulted in the Massachusetts Constitution of 1780, the great document that contemporaries eventually recognized as joining the American need for government to the British principle of ordered liberty through law. In time, as the arbitrary power of Parliament became more and more apparent, and theorists of liberty recognized that Great Britain was losing its government of restrained authority, the American model came be viewed not as a novelty but with nostalgia. Thirteen years later, a young British radical, Henry Yorke, reached back to the old metaphor of female liberty wandering in exile and thought of her finding a secure haven in the English-speaking republic beyond the seas.

It is not impossible that the nations of the earth would have been at this day sunk in apathy and ignorance, had not the ever memorable revolution of America promoted a spirit of inquiry and discussion, that soon made men long after Freedom. At this period, Reason, with her offspring Liberty, were recalled from their long exile, into the cabinets of Philosophers, and the strangers were welcomed into the homely mansions of Poverty.[27]

# Acknowledgments

The research for this study was supported by a number of sources. Leave from teaching duties at New York University School of Law was provided by the Filomen D'Agostino Greenberg and Max E. Greenberg Faculty Research Fund at the School of Law, and by Norman Redlich, dean of the School of Law. Work at the Huntington Library in San Marino, California, was supported by a Huntington Library–National Endowment for the Humanities Fellowship. The weeks spent at the Cambridge University Library were made easier by the invaluable guidance of Lloyd Bonfield, of Tulane University Law School. The finished manuscript benefited from the attention paid it by a distinguished band of legal historians: Norman Cantor, William E. Nelson, Barbara Kern, and the student members of the New York University School of Law Colloquium in Legal History. A special debt is owed to one member of the Colloquium, Michael Les Benedict, who gave these chapters remarkably close readings, offered many insights from his vast knowledge of the eighteenth-century constitution, and was particularly helpful when he insisted that the title not be changed. Martin Ridge, of the Huntington Library, made two significant contributions to the final version when he insisted that the last should be first and that the University of Chicago Press would be the perfect publisher. Another member of the Colloquium, Seth Agata, verified all citations and text. Any errors are his responsibility. An immeasurable debt is owed to Diana Vincent-Daviss of New York University Law Library and to Virginia Renner of the Huntington Library, and to their staffs, for being the professionals they always are. Finally there is one other member of the New York University School of Law Colloquium in

Legal History, Lawrence Fleischer of Seton Hall University School of Law. It was he who found the 1849 newspaper reporting the speech by Franklin Pierce in which Pierce regretted that licentiousness was no longer what it had once been.

# Notes

## INTRODUCTION

1. For discussion of these rights, unrelated to the concept of liberty, see *Authority of Rights,* at 16–86.

2. For a historian's perception of this lawyer's characteristic (which should not be confused with how lawyers understand courts to function, or whether they "make" or "find" law), see Gough, *Fundamental Law,* at 6–7.

3. Pocock, *Ancient Constitution.*

4. McDonald, *Novus,* at 10.

5. Bailyn, *Origins of Politics,* at 18.

6. Langford, *Excise Crisis.*

7. See petitions and other documents printed in 32 *London Magazine* (1763), at 166, 256, 289; 33 *Gentleman's Magazine* (1763), at 187; 34 *Gentleman's Magazine* (1764), at 226.

8. The opposition cry was "liberty and property and no excise." [Ruffhead], *Considerations,* at 15. For a comparison with the Stamp Act, see *Authority to Tax,* at 277–78.

9. 7 *Political Register* (1770), at 382; Anon., *Considerations on Information.*

10. *Authority of Rights,* at 193–98.

11. See documents in 2 *Town and Country Magazine* (1770), at 127–28, 202; *Public Advertiser,* 8 January 1770, reprinted in *Franklin's Letters to Press,* at 172.

12. See speeches by Sawbridge and Glynn, and "Junius on the Priveleges of the House of Commons," in 1 *Hibernian Magazine* (1771), at 125–28, 182–89.

13. London Resolves, 24 June 1775, 45 *Gentleman's Magazine* (1775), at 348; London's *Public Ledger,* reprinted in *Boston Post-Boy,* 11 September 1769, at 1, col. 1; *Authority of Rights,* at 21–22.

14. See speeches in 42 *Gentleman's Magazine* (1772), at 490–91; "engagement" in 44 *Gentleman's Magazine* (1774), at 444.

15. Anon., *Letter to North on East-India Bill*, at 36; Petition of 24 May 1773, 43 *Gentleman's Magazine* (1773), at 252.

16. Address of London, 44 *Gentleman's Magazine* (1774), at 248; Petition of 18 June 1774, *Addresses and Petitions of Common Council*, at 50.

17. McDonald, *Novus*, at 36–37.

18. Diggins, *Lost Soul*, at 28. See also Pole, *Paths to Past*, at 93; McDonald, *Novus*, at 3; Wood, *Creation*, at 22.

19. Appleby, *Capitalism*, at 17–18.

20. John Adams wrote, "Property must be secured, or liberty cannot exist." Kammen, *Spheres of Liberty*, at 27. See also "To the Electors of Great-Britain," 43 *Gentleman's Magazine* (1773), at 212.

21. "Classical republicism . . . has been variously referred to as civic humanism, republican ideology, classical politics, the commonwealth tradition, dissent and opposition, and radical Whig thought." Diggins, *Lost Soul*, at 9.

22. Pocock, *Machiavellian Moment*, at 362–63. "From the time of the Glorious Revolution, Englishmen in the ruling class could feel themselves in possession of this classical liberty because their mixed, constitutional monarchy had created a new sovereign, that of the King in Parliament." Appleby, *Capitalism*, at 16. Appleby says that Tom Paine "defined a republic as a sovereignty of justice, in contrast to a sovereignty of will," a definition that, if the word "law" was substituted for "justice," was the very essence of common-law constitutionalism. Appleby, "Republicanism," at 20.

23. Appleby, *Capitalism*, at 18.

24. Hexter, "Review Essay," at 331, 334. "The language of liberty that this view of politics generates does not allow much time in its ordinary discourse for talk about civic virtue, participation, patriotism, political animals, citizen militia, or corruption. It tends to go on and on about prerogative, authority, obedience, arbitrary power, and reason of state, about limited government, property, due process, rule of law, and fundamental law." Id., at 335.

25. Bailyn, *Ideological Origins*, at 77.

26. This raises a related point of contention to which this study of eighteenth-century liberty takes serious exception. For both Britons and Americans, Bailyn notes, "[t]he skeleton of their political thought was Lockean—concerned with inalienable rights and the contract theory of government." Bailyn, *Origins of Politics*, at 41.

27. Ibid., at ix–x. See also ibid., at 56, 136. For a summary of Bailyn's theory, see Appleby, "Republicanism," at 22.

28. Admittedly, the Bailyn thesis commands wide support. Wood, *Creation*, at 15–16; Banning, *Jeffersonian Persuasion*, at 54–59; Foner, *Tom Paine*, at 10–11; Pole, *Representation*, at 342; Aptheker, *Revolution*, at 144–45. See also Toohey, *Liberty and Empire*, at 8.

29. This is a story that cannot be developed in this book. It should be noted, however, that it was much better understood by contemporaries than it has been by subsequent scholars of the American Revolution. "The contest with America seems to have produced a strange overturn in the political systems of the two great parties who divide this kingdom. The Tories, by acknowledging the supreme power of the British parliament over the whole British empire, appear to be turned Whigs; and the Whigs, in attempting to extend the power of the King's prerogative beyond the controul of his parliament, shew themselves to be Tories." "A Revolutionary Whig," 37 *Scots Magazine* (1775), at 646. "It is a Matter of Indignation to observe the Persons who at present imprudently call themselves *Whigs*, endeavouring to exalt the Prerogative of the Crown in the most absolute and essential Manner; by petitioning the King to *dissolve the Parliament*, and annihilate the Power of the House of Commons, which is the only true, great, and constitutional Bulwark of our Liberties." Anon., *Address to Junius*, at 18. Similarly, see [Macfarlane], *George the Third*, at 320; Anon., *Candid Thoughts*, at 61n.

30. Greene, "Review," at 20.

31. Ibid., at 20–21.

32. Boucher, *Causes and Consequences*, at 363.

33. This insistence on "law" may help answer the puzzle posed by John Diggins's cynicism about the influence of ideas. "It is difficult to see how either Machiavellianism or Lockeanism could explain why the Founders feared democracy and why they assumed they could succeed in doing what no contemporary American politician would dare to do—tell the people that they are not to be trusted." Diggins, *Lost Soul*, at 76. The explanation is to be found not in fear of democracy but fear of arbitrary power. What was trusted was neither the majority nor the "rulers," but the rule of law.

34. Nelson, "Ideology in Search of Context," at 745–48.

35. For a summary of Blackstone's liberty rhetoric, see Boorstin, *Mysterious Science of Law*, at 154–66, 23n. 15.

36. This last point deserves emphasis. It is implicit in the argument that follows that neither British constitutional law nor English common law in the eighteenth century was perceived as the command of the sovereign. Rather, law was, at least in the dominant theory of the day, a restraint on government and was, therefore, the security of liberty. This thesis—that positive law was the liberty-securing restraint on government—rejects the historical theory, advanced even by lawyers, that during the early nineteenth century the nature of American law was transformed by the law-

as-command theory, supplanting a natural-law theory. In fact, natural law was never the dominant source of law, and perhaps not even a significant one. What happened in nineteenth-century America was not the rise of positive law and the decline of natural law, but the rise of one version of positivism—law as the command of the sovereign—and the decline of an older positivism—law as restraint on the sovereign or the sovereignty of law. Contrast "In the Taught Tradition," to Nelson, "Eighteenth Century" and Horwitz, *Transformation*.

## Chapter One

1. Price, *Two Tracts: Tract Two*, at 5; 6 *Hibernian Magazine* (1776), at 77.

2. Meeting of the Accomack County (Virginia) Committee, 27 June 1775, 2 *American Archives*, at 1113; Address from James Rivington to the Continental Congress, 20 May 1775, id., at 837.

3. Letter from Vice-Admiral Graves to Philip Stephens, 6 September 1775, *Dartmouth American Papers*, at 373; Message from the House of Burgesses to Governor Lord Dunmore, 12 June 1775, 2 *American Archives*, at 1204.

4. Letter from John Wilkes to London Liverymen, 10 March 1768, in Anon., *Battle of the Quills*, at 4. See generally, Rude, *Wilkes and Liberty*.

5. Anon., *Experience Preferable to Theory*, at 17; [Goodricke], *Observations on Price's Theory*, at 79–80; Fish, *Joy and Gladness*, at 10; Cumings, *Thanksgiving Sermon*, at 21. See also Bailyn, *Origins of Politics*, at 19.

6. Hitchcock, *Sermon at Plymouth*, at 17; [Nedham], *Excellencie of Free State*, at xiv; Champion, *Connecticut Election Sermon*, at 14 (see similarly *Boston Gazette*, 10 May 1756, at 1, col. 1; Fish, *Joy and Gladness*, at 17); Hallifax, *Sermon at St. Margaret's*, at 8, 12–13. See also [Robertson], *Liberty, Property, and Religion*, at 5; Price, "Introduction to Two Tracts," at vi note (quoting Edmund Burke); Young, *Constitution Safe*, at 60–61.

7. Stevens, *Election Sermon*, at 12; Hitchcock, *Sermon at Plymouth*, at 19; Clark, *British Opinion*, at 162 (quoting "Will Chatwell," Robinhood Society, 1770); Thornton, "Introduction and Notes," at 190 (quoting Governor Thomas Pownall, speech in Commons on American rights).

8. Anon., *Application of Political Rules*, at 39; Anon., *Fair Trial*, at 234n; Cook, *Codification Movement*, at 38 (quoting 1808 Philadelphia pamphlet). (Darling:) Champion, *Connecticut Election Sermon*, at 5; Baldwin, *New England Clergy*, at 88 (quoting Samuel Bird, 1758). (Enemies:) [Sharp], *Defence of Strictures*, at 9. (Friends:) [Brown], *Civil Liberty*, at 17, 117; Anon., *Political Balance*, at 19. (Learning:) Howard,

*Election Sermon,* at 392; Payson, *Election Sermon,* at 337. (Best Friend:) [Brooke], *Liberty and Common Sense,* at 13.

9. [Brooke], *Liberty and Common Sense: Letter II,* at 4; Fish, *Joy and Gladness,* at 10; Anon., *Rights Asserted,* at 45. See also [Sharp], *Defence of Strictures,* at 14; Barnard, *Election Sermon,* at 20; Anon., *Battle of the Quills,* at 6. For a striking example of this rhetoric by a sometime governor of Pennsylvania see Keith, *Papers and Tracts,* at 141.

10. Foster, *Short Essay,* at 24; Barnard, *Election Sermon,* at 35; Montgomery, *Sermon at Christiana Bridge,* at 24; Letter from James Habersham to William Knox, 29 January 1766, *Habersham Letters,* at 56; Fish, *Joy and Gladness,* at 10. See also Anon., *Liberty in Two Parts,* at 77. For the perilous state of liberty on both sides of the Atlantic in the age of the American Revolution see Anon., *Observations of Consequence,* at 80; Charles, Bishop of St. David's, *Sermon to Lords,* at 18; Langdon, *Government Corrupted,* at 233–34. "LIBERTY and FREEDOM, the great Pillars of the Constitution, are, by Force and Fraud undermined, and tumbling into Ruins." *The Crisis,* 21 February 1775, at 25.

11. 1 *Collection of Letters,* at 222; Letter from Æquus, 16 January 1766, 35 *London Magazine* (1766), at 34; Anon., *Justice and Policy,* at 16; Anon., *Serious and Impartial Observations,* at 6; Anon., *Fair Trial,* at 234; Anon., *What Should be Done,* at 34. See also Anon., *Critical Review of Liberties,* at 3; Anon., *O Liberty,* at 1; Rude, "London Mob," at 13–14.

12. Anon., *Serious Exhortation,* at 32; Anon., *Critical Review of Liberties,* at 11 (quoting Charles Lucas). See also Bailyn, *Origins of Politics,* at 57, 150.

13. Anon., *Dialogues on Rights of Britons,* at 20. See also, "On the Power of England," 2 *Hibernian Magazine* (1772), at 373; *Collection of Political Tracts,* at 30; Hunn, *Welfare of a Government,* at 18; Frank, "Sketch of an Influence," at 214 (quoting Postlethwayt, *Dictionary of Commerce* [1751]); Gordon, Letter of 15 April 1721, 1 *Cato's Letters,* at 191.

14. Anon., *British Liberties,* at vii; [Rous], *Claim of the Commons,* at 4; Anon., *Dialogue on the State,* at 33; Anon., *Examination of the Legality,* at 3; De Lolme, *Constitution: New Edition,* at 490–91; Dickinson, *Liberty and Property,* at 143 (quoting *An Essay on Liberty and Independency* [1747]). See also Instructions of Deputies from Pennsylvania Counties to Representatives, 21 July 1774, 43 *London Magazine* (1774), at 585; Sydney, *Discourses Concerning Government,* at 499; [Young], *Political Essays,* at 21.

15. Barnard, *Election Sermon,* at 37; Anon., *Court of Star Chamber,* at 16; Allen, *American Crisis,* at 48. Similarly, see Wright, *Grand Jury Speech,* at 2; Anon., *Letter on Parliamentary Representation,* at 28.

16.  Baldwin, *New England Clergy*, at 86 (quoting Hunn, 1747); Hunn, *Welfare of a Government*, at 17–18, 24; White, *Connecticut Election Sermon*, at 23; Welsteed, *Dignity and Duty*, at 33; Address of Judge William Henry Drayton to the Camden District (S. C.) Grand Jury, November Session, 1774, 44 *London Magazine* (1775), at 126.

17.  Rossiter, *Political Thought*, at 46–47 (quoting Witherspoon).

18.  Barnard, *Election Sermon*, at 37; Anon., *Licentiousness Unmask'd*, at 2. See also Priestley, *First Principles*, at 189–90. The argument could of course be turned around. Instead of saying the British *could not* oppress because of their spirit of liberty, it was said they *should not*. "I should have thought," a speaker opposing the suppression of the Caribs explained, "that our generosity, as Englishmen, would have taught us to consider the liberty and property of others as sacred." Speech of Lord Folkestone, Commons Debates, 10 February 1773, 35 *Scots Magazine* (1773), at 291. See also Anon., *Honor of Parliament*, at 38–39; Anon., *New Preface to Mollyneux*, at vii. The last writer explained that it was not the British people but the British ministry that oppressed Ireland, a conclusion that would have been denied by many theorists who believed the British people and government so controlled by the spirit of liberty that governmental oppression was impossible. Millar, *Observations Concerning Ranks*, at 248–50; Ellys, *Tracts on Liberty*, at 263.

19.  Brewer, *Party Ideology*, at 260 (quoting *An Essay on the Constitution of England* [1766]); Anon., *Licentiousness Unmask'd*, at 3; Speech of Sir Francis Nethersole, 25 March 1628, 2 *Commons Debates 1628*, at 106.

20.  Anon., *Civil Liberty Asserted*, at 83; 1 *Collection of Letters*, at 223. See also 1 [Oldfield], *History of the Boroughs*, at 2; Olson, "Parliamentary Law," at 310.

CHAPTER TWO

1.  Anon., *Serious Exhortation*, at 12; "Junius on the Privileges of the House of Commons," 1 *Hibernian Magazine* (1771), at 188; Toohey, *Liberty and Empire*, at 94 (quoting Price); Hunn, *Welfare of a Government*, at 14; Gordon, Letter of 27 January 1721, 2 *Cato's Letters*, at 257; Lockwood, *Worth and Excellence*, at 24–25. See also Warrington, *Grand Jury Charge*, at 5.

2.  Anon., *Inquiry into the Causes*, at 2; T. M., "Essay on Liberty and Independency," 5 *Political Register* (1769), at 247; Anon., *Protest of a Private Person*, at 6; Rossiter, *Political Thought*, at 109 (quoting *New York Gazette*); William Markham, "Sermon Preached," reprinted in Peach, *Richard Price*, at 262; Payson, *Election Sermon*, at 330. See also Dolins, *Third Charge to Middlesex Juries*, at 19; [Joseph Hawley], "To Inhabitants," 30 March 1775, 2 *American Archives*, at 248; Duchal, *Sermons*, at

171; Barnard, *Election Sermon*, at 18; Brewer, "Wilkites and the Law," at 132.

3. Anon., *No Liberty*, at 5; Anon., *Whigs and Jacobites*, at 45.

4. Letter of 22 October 1764, *Complete Collection of Wilkes*, at 100; *Letters Between Wilkes*, at 218–19; Molesworth, *Principles of a Real Whig*, at 13–14; [Meredith], *Remarks on Taxation*, at 7; Reply of Sir Benjamin Rudyard to the Lord Keeper, 28 April 1628, 3 *State Trials*, at 173; Baldwin, *New England Clergy*, at 87n. 16 (quoting Cogswell sermon to Putnam's Command, 13 April 1757); Hitchcock, *Sermon at Plymouth*, at 39; [Mulgrave], *Letter from a Member*, at 86; 1 *Select Collection of Letters*, at 191; Arbuthnot, *Freeholder's Catechism*, at 14; Anon., *Court of Star Chamber*, at 31; *York Address of January 1781*, at 9; [Priestley], *Present State of Liberty*, at 22; [Nedham], *Excellencie of Free State*, at xiv; Anon., *Civil Prudence*, at 12; Anon., *Defence of the People*, at 149; [Sharp], *Defence of Strictures*, at 39n; Patten, *Discourse at Hallifax*, at 11, 19–20; Hind, *Sermon at St. Margaret's*, at 16; Anon., *Fatal Consequences*, at 2; Gordon, Letter of 20 October 1722, 3 *Cato's Letters*, at 284; [Marat], *Chains of Slavery*, at 1; 3 Burgh, *Political Disquisitions*, at 415; Anon., *Considerations on Information*, at 18–19; Address from John Wilkes to the Freeholders of Middlesex, 23 March 1768, in Anon., *Battle of the Quills*, at 61; Lowth, *Durham Assize Sermon*, at 11; Anon., *Fair Trial*, at 245; Toohey, *Liberty and Empire*, at 69.

5. *Boston Evening-Post*, 14 October 1765, at 1, col. 1; Letter from Æquus, 16 January 1766, 35 *London Magazine* (1766), at 34; Anon., *O Liberty*, at 1–2. See also Sheridan, *Observations on the Doctrine*, at 5–6.

6. Howard, *Election Sermon*, at 362; Anon., *Fair Trial*, at 241; [Howard], *Defence of the Letter*, at 6 (quoting *Boston Gazette*, 24 September 1764); Book Review, 44 *London Magazine* (1775), at 315. See also Anon., *Application of Political Rules*, at 36; "Preface," 1 *Cato's Letters*, at xxii.

7. Letter from John Wilkes to Aylesbury Electors, 22 October 1764, *Complete Collection of Wilkes*, at 79; Anon., *O Liberty*, at 3. A candidate for Parliament proclaimed: "The spirit of LIBERTY, and not of PARTY, has guided all my actions." Second Address of Sir William Beauchamp Procter to Middlesex, 24 November 1768, Wilkes, *English Liberty*, at 213. See also, Hitchcock, *Sermon at Plymouth*, at 11; Anon., *Observations upon the Authority*, at 1; [Meredith], *Question Stated*, at 67.

8. Lowth, *Durham Assize Sermon*, at 8; Champion, *Connecticut Election Sermon*, at 14; Robertson, *Chatham*, at 99. See also, Speech of Isaac Barre, Commons Debates, 9 December 1772, 42 *London Magazine* (1773), at 114; Hallifax, *Sermon at St. Margaret's*, at 13. For an opposing theory as to why liberty motivated human actions see, [Nedham], *Excellencie of Free State*, at 18.

9. [Bernard], *Appeal to the Public*, at 28; Dickerson, "Writs," at 71 (quoting Opinion of Attorney General Edward Thurston, 31 August 1771); Anon., *Letter to Egremont and Halifax*, at 13, 31, 16.

10. *Boston Post-Boy*, 7 January 1765, at 3, col. 2; Anon., *Political Balance*, at 17; [Drinker], *Observations on the Measures*, at 13; [Goodricke], *Observations on Price's Theory*, at 80. "A Cry of Liberty has gone Abroad in this Country ever since the Revolution, which, tho' it prevents arbitrary Encroachments by the Crown, subjects the People to every Species of Political Imposition." Anon., *Political Conduct of Chatham*, at 1.

11. 1 Valentine, *Lord North*, at 347; [Priestley], *Present State of Liberty*, at 21; Anon., *Considerations on Information*, at 36. "An *Attachment* [was] . . . a Commitment to Prison by a Court of Record, for a Contempt to the Process of that Court from which it issues" *Id.*, at 26. See also, Patten, *Discourse at Hallifax*, at 17–18.

12. Anon., *Civil Prudence*, at 16; Anon., *Political Balance*, at 30. Liberty was also invoked to motivate people to the highest standards of civilized legalism. E.g., Anon., *Whigs and Jacobites*, at 45.

## CHAPTER THREE

1. Admittedly, eighteenth-century political commentators sometimes did discuss liberty in terms of the country-court dichotomy, usually to disparage the assumed argument of the opposition. E.g., [Grange], *Late Excise*, at 79–80.

2. Speeches of Sir Robert Phelips and Sir Dudley Digges, 25 March 1628, in 2 *Commons Debates 1628*, at 106, 105.

3. Kriegel, "Liberty and Whiggery," at 255.

4. *Authority of Rights*, at 65–145; "In Accordance with Usage," at 335–68; "In Our Contracted Sphere," at 21–47; "In an Inherited Way," at 1109–29. A point of law sometimes misunderstood is that the colonial charters were not one of the authorities on which the colonists claimed their rights. *Authority of Rights*, at 159–68; "In the First Line of Defense," at 177–215.

5. For a study of these rights in the American revolutionary controversy, see *Authority of Rights*.

6. Hitchcock, *Sermon at Plymouth*, at 12.

7. For the different contracts, see *Authority of Rights*, at 132–58; *Authority to Tax*, at 53–84; "In Our Contracted Sphere."

8. Patten, *Discourse at Hallifax*, at 12; "Extract of a Letter from Virginia," *Boston Post-Boy*, 12 December 1768, at 1, col. 3; [Young], *Political Essays*, at 19; Petition of several Natives of America to the House of Commons, 2 May 1774, 1 *American Archives*, at 82; Wilkes, *Arms of Liberty and Slavery*, col. 1; Lockwood, *Worth and Excellence*, at 26;

Anon., *No Liberty*, at 5. See also *Boston Gazette*, 10 May 1756, at 1, col. 1; Speech of John Pym, 25 April 1628, 3 *Commons Debates 1628*, at 77.

9. *Authority of Rights*, at 103–13.

10. [Sayre], *Englishman Deceived*, at 11–12. See also Baldwin, *New England Clergy*, at 108 (quoting Adams, 1767).

11. *Gazette & News-Letter*, 6 March 1766, at 2, col. 1. The writer was discussing the British rather than the Massachusetts or the colonial constitution, and by "frame" was not referring to the provincial charter.

12. Trenchard, Letter of 30 December 1721, 2 *Cato's Letters*, at 216; Duchal, *Sermons*, at 170. See also Sydney, *Discourses Concerning Government*, at 449–50; Anon., *Whigs and Jacobites*, at 15–16; Northcote, *Observations on Rights*, at 8–10.

13. Kramnick, "Republican Revisionism," at 648 (quoting Capel Lofft); Bolingbroke, "The Freeholders Political Catechism," 43 *London Magazine* (1774), at 478; Arbuthnot, *Freeholders Catechism*, at 3; Patten, *Discourse at Hallifax*, at 7; [Jones], *Constitutional Criterion*, at 7. See also West, *Election Sermon*, at 273; Duchal, *Sermons*, at 170.

14. Speech of Lord Camden, Lords Debates, February 1766, 16 *Parliamentary History*, at 177; *Boston Gazette*, 10 May 1756, at 1, col. 1; Tuck, *Natural Rights Theories*, at 103 (quoting Dudley Digges, *The Unlawfulnesse of Subjects* [1644]); Anon., *Liberal Strictures*, at 9. A different definition of natural liberty was to act according to physical nature: "Natural Liberty being nothing more than a Creature's power of acting or not acting, in all instances that lie within the Sphere of it's Activity; it follows that all Men . . . have different degrees of Natural power, different Spheres of Activity; but their Liberty of acting or not acting within those limits, will be equally perfect." Hind, *Sermon at St. Margaret's*, at 6.

15. 2 Bracton, *Laws and Customs*, at 29.

16. Hey, *Happiness and Rights*, at 199; [Jones], *Constitutional Criterion*, at 7; Book Review, 55 *Monthly Review* (1776), at 218. See also Price, *Two Tracts: Tract Two*, at 1; Wood, *Creation*, at 21.

17. Book Review, 40 *Critical Review* (1775), at 321; Theophilus, "To the Editor," 43 *London Magazine* (1774), at 483. See also Hobbes, *Leviathan*, at 84, 136–37; Hobbes, *De Cive*, at 109; [Brown], *Civil Liberty*, at 19; [Shebbeare], *Third Letter*, at 11–12.

18. Anon., *Ancient and Modern Liberty*, at 3.

19. 3 Wynne, *Eunomus*, at 32.

20. [Williams], *Essential Rights*, at 6. Williams even proposed a test for determining what part of liberty had been retained and, although it is not certain, may have equated this notion of retained natural liberty with the concept of inalienable rights that some eighteenth-century theorists postulated as rights that could not be surrendered on entering society. The test was "to consider *the Ends* for which Men enter into a State of Govern-

ment. For so much Liberty and no more is departed from, as is necessary to secure those Ends; the rest is certainly our own still." Id., at 5. See also [Johnson], *Some Important Observations*, at 22–23.

21. Arbuthnot, *Freeholder's Cathechism*, at 4. See also Fiske, *Importance of Righteousness*, at 10.

22. Baldwin, *New England Clergy*, at 178 (quoting Rowland, *Thanksgiving Sermon* [Providence, 1766]).

23. [Goodricke], *Observations on Price's Theory*, at iii; 1 Rutherforth, *Natural Law*, at 146; Anon., *Liberal Strictures*, at 9; Anon., *Philosophical Survey of Nature*, at 86. See also Anon., *Ancient and Modern Liberty*, at 2; Adam Ferguson, "Remarks on a Pamphlet," reprinted in Peach, *Richard Price*, at 254. "Liberty, to the individual, is nothing more than freedom from restraint." [Rous], *Claim of the Commons*, at 6.

24. 2 Burke, *Writings & Speeches*, at 229. See also, Forster, *Northampton Assize Sermons*, at 33; Anon., *Licentiousness Unmask'd*, at 8; Anon., *Civil Liberty Asserted*, at 30; R. H., "On the guilt of the present civil war," 38 *Scots Magazine* (1776), at 202 (reprinting *London Chronicle*, 20 April 1776); Burlamaqui, *Politic Law*, at 18; Stevens, *Election Sermon*, at 9; [Boucher], *Letter from a Virginian*, at 8–9; 2 Rutherforth, *Natural Law*, at 386.

25. Dodgson, *Assize Sermon*, at 9; Sydney, *Discourses Concerning Government*, at 162; Stevens, *Election Sermon*, at 9. See also Millar, *Observations Concerning Ranks*, at 248n; Anon., *Whigs and Jacobites*, at 15–16.

26. Hopkins, *Rights*, at 507; [Goodricke], *Observations on Price's Theory*, at iii; Anon., *Ancient and Modern Liberty*, at 2.

27. Anon., *Civil Liberty Asserted*, at 7; Anon., *Critical Review of Liberties*, at 10; Stevens, *Election Sermon*, at 70; Anon., *Application of Political Rules*, at 79.

28. Anon., *Knowledge of the Laws*, at 2; "Thoughts on the late Declaration," 46 *Gentleman's Magazine* (1776), at 404.

29. "Three Letters to Dr. Price," 55 *Monthly Review* (1776), at 152 (quoting John Lind); John Lind, "Three Letters to Price," reprinted in Peach, *Richard Price*, at 243; [Lind], *Letters to Price*, at 24 (and see at 20). See also Anon., *Letter to Robert Morris*, at 32. Burke disagreed that the line could be exact. It was important, therefore, to fix it on the side of liberty: "Liberty, too, must be limited in order to be possessed. The degree of restraint it is impossible in any case to settle precisely. But it ought to be the constant aim of every wise public counsel to find out by cautious experiments, and rational, cool endeavours, with how little, not how much, of this restraint the community can subsist: for liberty is a good to be improved, and not an evil to be lessened." 2 Burke, *Writings & Speeches*, at 229.

30. Anon., *Liberal Strictures,* at 11n (quoting *Martin's Remarks on Human Liberty*). For a contrary perspective see *Boston Gazette,* 10 May 1756, at 1, col 1.

CHAPTER FOUR

1. Price, *Nature of Civil Liberty,* at 3; Price, *Two Tracts: Tract One,* at 3; Priestley, *First Principles,* at 13; *They Preached Liberty,* at 146 (quoting Stevens, *Election Sermon*); Stevens, *Election Sermon,* at 54; Hitchcock, *Sermon at Plymouth,* at 12–13; 1 Blackstone, *Commentaries,* at 244. But see Peckard, *Nature and Extent of Liberty,* at 3n (complaining that some writers define "Civil Liberty" as "nothing Positive. It is an Absence. The Absence of Coercion").

2. Gordon, 20 January 1721, *Cato's Letters,* at 248–49.

3. *In a Defiant Stance,* at 110–14, 133–34, 164; Letter to James Rivington, 2 *American Archives,* at 349; Dolins, *Third Charge to Middlesex Juries,* at 3; Anon., *Letter to Common Council on Pratt,* at 35; Gordon, Letter of 15 April 1721, 1 *Cato's Letters,* at 191; [Brooke], *Liberty and Common Sense: Letter II,* at 5. See also Anon., *Liberal Strictures,* at 24–25; [Goodricke], *Observations on Price's Theory,* at 85.

4. West, *Election Sermon,* at 313; Zubly, *Stamp-Act Repealed,* at 26; Evans, *Constitutional Liberty,* at 30; Anon., *Licentiousness Unmask'd,* at 5; [Shebbeare], *Third Letter,* at 11; Peckard, *Nature and Extent of Liberty,* at 7. See also Lockwood, *Worth and Excellence,* at 16–17.

5. Porteus, *Sermon on Charles I,* at 25–26; Hallifax, *Sermon at St. Margaret's,* at 13. The king hoped Chatham would restore "that subordination to Government which alone can preserve that inestimable Blessing Liberty from degenerating into Licentiousness." Letter from George III to William Pitt, 29 July 1766, 1 *Correspondence of George III,* at 385. See also [Squire], *Historical Essay on Ballance,* at viii.

6. Speech of Lord North, December 1770, 41 *Gentleman's Magazine* (1771), at 291; Book Review, 19 *Critical Review* (1765), at 205. See also Lediard, *Charge to Westminster Jury,* at 28–29; [Egmont], *Faction Detected,* at 6–7; Anon., *Case of Presbyterians,* at 4; Anon., *Court of Star Chamber,* at 13; Alphonso, "To Lord North," 11 *Political Register* (1772), at 334–35; Hallifax, *Sermon at St. Margaret's,* at 9; Wood, *Creation,* at 403.

7. [Brown], *Civil Liberty,* at 14. See also [Brooke], *Liberty and Common Sense: Letter II,* at 6, 13; West, *Election Sermon,* at 291; Dolins, *Third Charge to Middlesex Juries,* at 20; Anon., *Civil Liberty Asserted,* at 22; [Mather], *America's Appeal,* at 65.

8. Anon., *Present Dangerous Crisis,* at 47; Price, *Nature of Civil Liberty,* at 12–13. See also [Stewart], *Letter to Dr. Price,* at 16; Price, *Two Tracts: Tract One,* at 13; Gerard, *Liberty Cloke of Maliciousness,* at 19; Anon., *Considerations on Information,* at 18–19.

9. But see [Brooke], *Liberty and Common Sense: Letter II*, at 13–14; [Meredith], *Question Stated*, at 69.

10. (Equally dangerous:) Anon., *Letter to Common Council on Pratt*, at 36; [Brooke], *Liberty and Common Sense: Letter II*, at 6. (Licentiousness more serious:) [Phelps], *Rights of the Colonies*, at 7; Hunn, *Welfare of a Government*, at 14. (Confused with liberty:) [Squire], *Historical Essay on Ballance*, at viii; Charles, Bishop of Saint David's, *Sermon to Lords*, at 19. See also [Howard], *Defence of the Letter*, at title page (quoting Judge Foster); Anon., *Letter to Common Council on Pratt*, at 35–36.

11. [Blacklock], *Remarks on Liberty*, at 27; West, *Election Sermon*, at 273 (also 320–21); [Brooke], *Liberty and Common Sense: Letter II*, at 13; 4 Blackstone, *Commentaries*, at 153; [Meredith], *Question Stated*, at 69. See also 5 Hume, *History*, at 164 (quoting Sir Thomas Wentworth, 1628); [Brown], *Civil Liberty*, at 42; *They Preached Liberty*, at 99 (reprinting Jonathan Mayhew, 1750).

12. *Boston Evening-Post*, 14 January 1771, at 1, col. 1; Quincy, *Memoir*, at 304. For discussion see Nelson, *American Tory*, at 188–89. Howard wrote that a third Massachusetts lawyer, James Otis, "cannot relish liberty, unless it is stained with the mixture of licentiousness." [Howard], *Defence of the Letter*, at 30 [*sic* 31].

13. "Extract of a Letter from Philadelphia, to Mr. Rivington, New-York, Dated February 16, 1775," 1 *American Archives*, at 1231; Resolutions of Newtown, Connecticut, 6 February 1775, id., at 1215. See similarly, Resolutions of Ridgefield, Connecticut, 30 January 1775, id., at 1202; Protest of 52 persons to the Worcester (Massachusetts) Resolves of 20 June 1774, 36 *Scots Magazine* (1774), at 411.

14. Speech of Isaac Wilkins, New York Assembly Debates, 23 February 1775, 1 *American Archives*, at 1295. See similarly, Letter from Gouverneur Morris to Mr. Penn, 20 May 1774, id., at 343; Letter from Daniel Coxe to Cortland Skinner, Attorney General of New Jersey, 4 July 1775, 11 *Revolution Documents*, at 38; Letter from Joseph Galloway to Samuel Verplanck, 30 December 1774, 1 *Letters of Delegates to Congress*, at 283.

15. Anon., *Appeal to Reason and Justice*, at 138. For other expressions of "the tory fear" of anarchy see Anon., *Essays Commercial and Political*, at 61; Richard, Bishop of Peterborough, *Sermon on King Charles*, at 21.

16. Hitchcock, *Sermon Preached before Gage*, at 55–56; West, *Election Sermon*, at 303; Price, *Two Tracts: Tract One*, at 14. See also Address of the Virginia Council to the People, 15 May 1775, 2 *American Archives*, at 587; Address of the Frederick County Committee to the *Virginia Gazette*, 19 June 1775, and the Richmond County Committee, 25 May 1775, 3 *Revolutionary Virginia*, at 209, 166–67.

17. Cooke, *Election Sermon*, at 21.

### Chapter Five

1. "Moral Liberty enquired into. By the late Dr. Foster," 9 *Town and Country Magazine* (1777), at 488. See also [Young], *Political Essays*, at 48; Peckard, *Nature and Extent of Liberty*, at 8.

2. Gordon, Letter of 21 April 1722, 3 *Cato's Letters*, at 65.

3. Letter from Charles Carroll to Edmund Jennings, 29 May 1766, *Letters of Charles Carroll*, at 117; 44 *Gentleman's Magazine* (1774), at 440 (reprinting a Newport, Rhode Island, circular); [Stephen Hopkins], *A Letter to the Author of the Halifax Letter; Occasioned by his Book, entitled a Defence of that Letter* ([Newport,] 1765), at 6; Zubly, *Stamp-Act Repealed*, at 20; Throop, *Thanksgiving Sermon*, at 10; Langdon, *Government Corrupted*, at 249; Gordon, *Discourse Preached*, at 67.

4. Okoye, "Chattel Slavery," at 3, 16.

5. Kern, *Kingship*, at 88–89; Cook, *King Charls his Case*, at 13; Cook, *King Charles his Case*, at 219–20; [Parker], *Case of Shipmony*, at 44. See also [Saint-John], *Speech or Declaration*, at 2; Cragg, *Freedom and Authority*, at 86.

6. Speech of William Pierrepont to the Lords, 6 July 1647, 1 Rushworth, *Historical Collections: Third Part*, at 327. This statement demonstrates the persistence of the legal notion. A century earlier Thomas More had said that to allow even a good judge to follow his own whim would enslave the people. A century later Chief Justice Thomas Hutchinson told a Massachusetts jury that "the *Judge* should never be the *Legislator:* Because . . . this tends to a State of Slavery." Baker, *English Legal History*, at 91; Hutchinson, Charge to the Grand Jury (1767), Quincy, *Reports*, at 234–35.

7. Speech of Lord Faulkland, 14 January 1640/41, 1 Rushworth, *Historical Collections: Third Part*, at 141. Similarly see, Speech of Lord Digby, in the Commons to the bill of attainder of the earl of Strafford, 21 April 1641, id., at 227.

8. Declaration of the Lords and Commons, 4 August 1642, ibid., at 765 (the word "slavery" was used at least three times in this declaration). See also, Declaration of the Lords and Commons, 14 July 1642, ibid., at 758.

9. *Remonstrance of Many Thousand*, at 7, 3; "Putney Debates," at 96, 89, 90, 71.

10. *Guide to Rights*, at 149 (quoting a 1681 publication); *Boston Gazette*, 7 September 1767, at 3, col. 1. See also 1 [Kames], *History of Man*, at 459; Richard, Bishop of Peterborough, *Sermon on King Charles*, at 16; Anon., *Ancient and Modern Liberty*, at 24; Anon., *Essay on the Constitution*, at 11.

11. Pitkin, "Obligation and Consent," at 994 (quoting Locke); Sydney, *Discourses Concerning Government*, at 10; Locke, *Two Treatises*, at Book 1, Sec. 5, Sec. 1 (see also Book 2, Sec. 17). See similarly Anon., *To the*

*Princess of Wales*, at 18; Mayhew, *Discourse Concerning Unlimited Submission*, at 63; Price, *Two Tracts: Tract Two*, at 86.

12. [Claridge], *Defence of Government*, at 1; Barnes, *Dominion of New England*, at 88; "Declaration of 1689," at 14.

13. Trenchard, Letter of 18 February 1720, 1 *Cato's Letters*, at 113 (see also Letter of 22 September 1722, vol. 3, at 245; Gordon, Letters of 19 November 1720, vol. 1, at 14; 15 April 1721, vol. 1, at 186; 14 October 1721, vol. 2, at 107; 21 October 1721, vol. 2, at 116); Dickinson, *Liberty and Property*, at 140–41 (quoting *London Journal*, 1 September 1733); Langford, *Excise Crisis*, at 163. See also Brisco, *Economic Policy of Walpole*, at 114.

14. Anon., *Court of Star Chamber*, at 24; Anon., *Britannia Libera*, at 42; "Copy of a Letter from Cork," 5 *Political Register* (1769), at 273. See also [Auckland], *Principles of Penal Law*, at 99; Anon., *Honest Grief of a Tory*, at 21; Anon., *Middle Temple Letter to Dublin*, at 10; Anon., *Policy of the Laws*, at 113–19.

15. Petition of the Lord Mayor, Aldermen, and Commons of London to the King, 28 March 1763, 33 *Gentleman's Magazine* (1763), at 187; *Addresses of the Common Council*, at 42; [Heath], *Case of Devon to Excise*, at 31; A Friend to Freedom, "The Cyder Act," 33 *Gentleman's Magazine* (1763), at 447; Baillie, *Letter to Shebear*, at 43.

16. Egerton, *American Revolution;* Headlam, "Constitutional Struggle"; McIlwain, *Revolution;* Mullet, *Fundamental Law;* Schuyler, *Empire.*

17. "In the Taught Tradition," at 931–74.

18. 2 Rutherforth, *Natural Law*, at 671; Anon., *Detector Detected*, at 14.

19. [Douglas], *Seasonable Hints*, at 25; Anon., *Court of Star Chamber*, at 30–31; *Petition of Middlesex to King, 24 May 1769*, at 10; *Cambridge Magazine*, at 221.

20. "A Real Friend to the People," *Declaration of those Rights of the Commonalty of Great-Britain with which they cannot be Free* (broadside printed in London, c. 1775, Huntington Library No. 141710).

21. Lofft, *Observations on Wesley's Address*, at 34; 1 *Select Collection of Letters*, at 92. See also, [Marat], *Chains of Slavery*, at 181n; Evans, *Reply to Fletcher*, at 37–38. "If the members of the house of commons are not obliged to regard the instructions of their constituents, the people of this country chuse a set of despots every seven years, and are as perfect slaves as the Turks, excepting the few months of a general election." 43 *London Magazine* (1774), at 537.

22. Price, *Nature of Civil Liberty*, at 100. See similarly Anon., *Evidence of Common and Statute Laws*, at iii–iv; Bonwick, *English Radicals*, at 64 (quoting Joseph Priestley); [Keld], *Polity of England*, at 485.

23. *The Crisis*, 20 January 1775, at 3, 5; Anon., *North-Country Poll*, at 34.

24. Anon., *Proposition for Peace*, at 13–14.

25. James Duane's Notes of Debates, 22 February 1776, 3 *Letters of Delegates to Congress*, at 295; [Anderson], *Free Thoughts*, at 14, col. 1n; Mayhew, *Snare Broken*, at 4 (quoted by Okoye, "Chattel Slavery," at 26), 13; Price, *Two Tracts: Tract Two*, at 3–4; Fletcher, *Vindication of Wesley*, at 64–66.

26. Resolves of Danbury, 12 December 1774, 1 *American Archives*, at 1038–39; Anon., *Evidence of Common and Statute Laws*, at 23. See also Ebenezer Baldwin, "A Settled Fix'd Plan for Inslaving the Colonies," 31 August 1774, *Commemoration Ceremony*, at 54; Cover, *Justice Accused*, at 20–21 (quoting Patrick Henry); Jensen, *Revolution Within*, at 15 (quoting Hooker, *Carolina Backcountry*); Wills, *Inventing America*, at 73 (quoting John Lind).

27. Mayhew, *Snare Broken*, at 17.

28. 1 Montesquieu, *Spirit of Laws*, at 336; Anon., *Evidence of Common and Statute Laws*, at 13–14. Similarly, Anon., *Candid Reflections upon the Judgement*, at 73–74.

29. Gordon, Letter of 24 February 1721, 2 *Cato's Letters*, at 310; "To the Inhabitants of . . . South Carolina," 4 July 1774, 1 *American Archives*, at 512.

## CHAPTER SIX

1. Price, *Two Tracts: Tract Two*, at 11. See also Hopkins, *Rights*, at 507–08; Gordon, Letter of 20 January 1721, 2 *Cato's Letters*, at 249; [Brooke], *Liberty and Common Sense: Letter II*, at 11; Bonwick, *English Radicals*, at 17.

2. [Joseph Hawley], "To the Inhabitants," 9 March 1775, 2 *American Archives*, at 96. See also Sharp, *Law of Nature*, at 4; Gordon, Letter of 12 May 1722, 3 *Cato's Letters*, at 84; Sydney, *Discourses Concerning Government*, at 10; Speech of E. J., Commons Debates, 5 December 1717, *Three Speeches against Army*, at 25; Price, *Nature of Civil Liberty*, at 5; Hobbes, *De Cive*, at 109; Rogers, *Empire and Liberty*, at 102.

3. Missing, *Letter to Mansfield on Instructions*, at 7; [Brooke], *Liberty and Common Sense: Letter II*, at 6. "[T]he only worse State than that of Civil Slavery" is "Anarchy and wild Misrule." Hind, *Sermon at St. Margaret's*, at 13. See also Welsteed, *Dignity and Duty*, at 8–9.

4. Anon., *Privileges of Jamaica*, at 45; Baldwin, *New England Clergy*, at 86; Trenchard, Letter of 9 February 1722, 4 *Cato's Letters*, at 81; Evans, *Constitutional Liberty*, at 27. See also Anon., *Political Balance*, at 16; [Stevens], *Revolution Vindicated*, at 51; Peckard, *Nature and Extent of Liberty*, at 8.

5. *Boston Gazette*, 10 May 1756, at 1, col. 1. Bernard Bailyn has

explained what this aspect of "slavery" meant to the colonists: "Slavery as a political concept had specific meaning which a later generation would lose. To eighteenth-century Americans it meant, as a newspaper writer put it in 1747, 'a force put upon humane nature, by which a man is obliged to act, or not to act, according to the arbitrary will and pleasure of another'; it meant, a later pamphleteer wrote, 'being wholly under the power and control of another as to our actions and properties.' It meant the inability to maintain one's just property in material things and abstract rights, rights and things which a proper constitution guaranteed a free people." Bailyn, *Ideological Origins*, at 233. It should be added that liberty meant the same to Britons and Irish Protestants.

6. 1 Montesquieu, *Spirit of Laws*, at 37. See also Instructions to Representatives in Parliament, 24 June 1773, *Addresses and Petitions of Common Council*, at 41; Dobbs, *Letter to North*, at 10; J. J. Zubly, "To Lord Dartmouth," 45 *London Magazine* (1776), at 38; Sydney, *Discourses Concerning Government*, at 10; [Johnson], *Some Important Observations*, at 34.

7. Cumings, *Thanksgiving Sermon*, at 18. A few commentators in the eighteenth century employed the concept of slavery to argue for an ideal constitution; that is, for the constitution they wanted, not the one in operation. "Extract of a Letter from a Gentleman in England to one in New-York, Dated June 22, 1774," 1 *American Archives*, at 437; Anon., *Detector Detected*, at 61; Anon., *Critical Review of Liberties*, at 27–28; Anon., *Serious Exhortation*, at 7; Payson, *Election Sermon*, at 337–38.

8. [Meredith], *Remarks on Taxation*, at 61; Evans, *Remembrance of Former Days*, at 27–28.

9. Anon., *Argument in Defence*, at 92. See similarly Hopkins, *Rights*, at 507–08; Letter from Charles Carroll of Carrollton to Edmund Jennings, 23 November 1765, *Letters of Charles Carroll*, at 99.

10. Cartwright, *People's Barrier*, at 20; "To the Author of the *Centinel*," *American Gazette*, at 45. See also 2 *St. Patrick's Anti-Stamp Chronicle* (1774), at 53; Anon., *Sequel to Essay*, at 37–38; Price, *Two Tracts: Tract One*, at 5, 10, 11; Howard, *Election Sermon*, at 364–65; "James Duane's Speech to the Committee on Rights," 8 September 1774, 1 *Letters of Delegates to Congress*, at 54; Benton, *Whig-Loyalism*, at 179 (quoting Benjamin Church). But see denial that legislation without consent creates slavery. Rather, "he who is molested and interrupted in the free use and enjoyment of his rights, is so far a slave tho' he has a right to assist, and actually does assist at every law that passes." Anon., *Civil Liberty Asserted*, at 17.

11. Dobbs, *Letter to North*, at 9; Philadelphia Grand Jury, 24 September 1770, *Boston Evening-Post*, 5 November 1770, at 4, col. 1.

The words of the presentment were lifted from Dickinson, *Letters*, at 372.

12. Gordon, Letter of 14 October 1721, 2 *Cato's Letters*, at 107; *Boston Evening-Post*, 25 March 1765, at 1, col. 1. See similarly [Priestley], *Present State of Liberty*, at 15; [Squire], *Historical Essay on Ballance*, at iv; Price, *Two Tracts: Tract Two*, at 5; Okoye, "Chattel Slavery," at 7 (quoting but misinterpreting Ebenezer Baldwin).

13. Champion, *Connecticut Election Sermon*, at 14; Hitchcock, *Sermon at Plymouth*, at 17. See also [Johnson], *Some Important Observations;* Gordon, Letter of 20 January 1721, 2 *Cato's Letters*, at 249–50, 251; [Andrews], *Reflections on the Spirit*, at 68; [Ruffhead], *Considerations*, at 30.

14. Okoye, "Chattel Slavery," at 7. For early instances of warnings that political "slavery" would make the English "slavish," see *Clarendon's History Compleated*, at 168–69 (reprinting William Allen, *Killing No Murder* [1650]); Sydney, *Discourses Concerning Government*, at 22.

15. Pym, *Declaration of Grievances*, at 403; Gordon, Letter, *supra* note 13, at 250–51; Anon., *Political Catechism*, at 13–14. For an American example of this language see [Fowle], *Appendix to Eclipse*, at 24.

16. Payson, *Election Sermon*, at 334. See also Barnard, *Election Sermon*, at 12, 35–36; Anon., *Ballance of Civil Power*, at iv–xxiii; Gordon, Letter, *supra* note 13, at 251; [Marat], *Chains of Slavery*, at 103.

17. Anon., *Rights Asserted*, at 55–56; Priestley, *First Principles*, at 55–56; "Extract of a Letter Received in Philadelphia, Dated London, March 11, 1775," 2 *American Archives*, at 119. See also West, *Election Sermon*, at 282–83; [Johnson], *Some Important Observations*, at 51; Anon., *British Liberties*, at ix.

18. Arbuthnot, *Freeholder's Catechism*, at 16; [Brooke], *Liberty and Common Sense: Letter II*, at 15–16; Anon., *Critical Review of Liberties*, at 4; Gordon, Letter of 14 October 1721, 2 *Cato's Letters*, at 111. See also Priestley, *First Principles*, at 55–56; Anon., *Dialogue on the State*, at 4–5; [Andrews], *Reflections on the Spirit*, at 54; Hitchcock, *Sermon at Plymouth*, at 18, 19; Price, *Two Tracts: Tract One*, at 5–6; Price, *Two Tracts: Tract Two*, at 17; Anon., *Compleat View*, at 58–59.

19. 1 Preface, *Cato's Letters*, at xxii; Robbins, *Commonwealthman*, at 124 (quoting *Cato's Letters*). See also Trenchard, Letter of 22 September 1722, *Cato's Letters*, at 244–45; Champion, *Connecticut Election Sermon*, at 14. It was accepted that no people voluntarily would submit to arbitrary authority. Arbuthnot, *Freeholder's Catechism*, at 4; Baldwin, *New England Clergy*, at 97n. 41 (quoting Patten, *Discourse at Hallifax*). See also Anon., *Ministerial Catechise*, at 8. But see suggestion of "the natural disposition or inclination of mankind to *slavery*." Chaplin, *Civil State*, at 6.

20. [Marat], *Chains of Slavery*, at 2; Anon., *Serious Exhortation*, at 7. See also 1 Montesquieu, *Spirit of Laws*, at 332.

21. *Cincinnatus,* "To the Inhabitants of Salem," 30 *Scots Magazine* (1768), at 523; [Marat], *Chains of Slavery*, at 67.

22. [Williams], *Letters on Liberty*, at 29; Resolutions of Hanover County, 20 July 1774, 1 *Revolutionary Virginia*, at 139; Pitt's Speech, Morgan, *Prologue*, at 139; "To the People of England," 17 June 1775, 2 *American Archives*, at 1014–15. See also Letter from the Continental Congress to the People of Great Britain, 5 September 1774, 43 *London Magazine* (1774), at 628.

23. *Briefs of American Revolution*, at 25–26; Letter from Massachusetts General Court to Lord Dartmouth, 29 June 1773, 43 *London Magazine* (1774), at 583; 6 *Revolution Documents*, at 168; Speech of Lord North, Commons Debates, 27 October 1775, 45 *Gentleman's Magazine* (1775), at 464.

24. Resolves of York, Maine, 21 January 1774, Banks, *York,* at 384; General Association of the City and County of New York, 29 April 1775, *Addresses and Petitions of Common Council*, at 93. See also "Phil-Americus," 8 March 1776, 6 *Revolutionary Virginia*, at 282; Sampson, *Sermon at Roxbury-Camp*, at 18; Resolves of the Massachusetts Congress, 29 October 1774, 1 *American Archives*, at 852; Letter from George Washington to Bryan Fairfax, 24 August 1774, Knollenberg, *Growth of Revolution*, at 132; *South-Carolina Gazette*, 10 November 1766, at 1, cols. 1–2; Letter from Robert Alexander to the Maryland Council of Safety, 27 February 1776, Benton, *Whig-Loyalism*, at 150; Ekirch, "North Carolinia Regulators," at 233.

CHAPTER SEVEN

1. [Towers], *Letter to Wesley*, at 11; Anon., *With Respect to America*, at 14. See also [Wilkes], *Letter to Johnson*, at 42–43; [Johnson], *Some Important Observations*, at 7; Eliot, *Give Cesar his Due*, at 36n; "To the Worthy Inhabitants of . . . Boston," 21 July 1774, 1 *American Archives*, at 627; James Howell, *The Preheminence and Pedigree of Parliament* (1644), reprinted in 5 *Somers' Tracts*, at 48. See also discussion in Bailyn, *Ideological Origins*, at 234.

2. For the significance of the concept of "arbitrary" during the age of the American Revolution, see "In Legitimate Stirps," at 459–99.

3. Campbell, *Duty of Allegiance*, at 24–25. This book got Campbell in trouble and he thought it advisable to publish a second edition which is more available in research libraries. In it the quoted passage is altered in words but not in meaning. Campbell, *Nature*, at 41–42, 43.

4. *Political Writings of James Otis*, at 35; [Johnson], *Some Important Observations*, at 34; [Joseph Hawley], "To the Inhabitants of Massachu-

setts," 9 March 1775, 2 *American Archives*, at 96. For negative and positive liberty, see Berlin, *Essays*, at 118–72.

5. Kriegel, "Liberty and Whiggery," at 260; Sydney, *Discourses Concerning Government*, at 386; *South-Carolina Gazette*, 18 January 1768, at 1, col. 4; Anon., *Resistance No Rebellion*, at 17; Petition of Middlesex to the King, June 1769, *Cambridge Magazine*, at 219. See also "The Liberty of the Constitution," 8 *Town and Country Magazine* (1776), at 72; Representation of the Lord Mayor, Aldermen, and Commons of London to their Representatives, 22 March 1763, [Almon], *History of the Late Minority*, at 108; [Care], *English Liberties First Edition*, at 4; Anon., *British Liberties*, at iv; Abingdon, *Thoughts on Burke's Letter*, at lii footnote; *Boston Evening-Post*, 6 April 1767, at 2, col. 1; [Johnson], *Some Important Observations*, at 8. The concept of arbitrary also provided a perspective for redefining liberty. Hey, *Observations on Civil Liberty*, at 34; [Shebbeare], *Third Letter*, at 11; 2 Burgh, *Political Disquisitions*, at 64 (quoting speech to Commons by Lord Strange); Trenchard, Letter of 6 January 1721, 2 *Cato's Letters*, at 231.

6. Hunn, *Welfare of a Government*, at 14–15; Gordon, Letter of 27 February 1721, 2 *Cato's Letters*, at 261. See also Locke, *Two Treatises*, Book 2, Sec. 23; Lockwood, *Worth and Excellence*, at 26.

7. One doctrine of influence for the coming of the American Revolution was the principle that arbitrariness lawfully could be resisted. [Johnson], *Some Important Observations*, at 21, 23; Chauncy, *Civil Magistrates*, at 34; Mayhew, *Discourse*, at 213; William Hicks in *South-Carolina Gazette*, 4 April 1768, at 1, col. 4; 1 *Collection of Letters*, at 215.

8. [Johnson], *Some Important Observations*, at 30; Hamilton, *Duty of Obedience to Laws*, at 15. See also *Political Writings of James Otis*, at 25.

9. (Game laws:) 42 *Gentleman's Magazine* (1772), at 120–21; (Riot Act:) 3 Burgh, *Political Disquisitions*, at 242; (excise:) Instructions to the Representatives of the City, 23 March 1763, *Addresses of the Common Council*, at 39; [Ruffhead], *Considerations*, at 14; (informations:) Anon., *Considerations on Information*, at 11–12, 42; 34 *London Magazine* (1765), at 25.

10. [Sheridan], *Observations on the Doctrine*, at 5; Anon., *Four Letters*, at 19. See also Anon., *Fair Trial*, at 233n; Smith, "1758 Pennsylvania Brief," at 701; "In the Taught Tradition," at 931–74.

11. Petition of the Jamaica Assembly to the King, 28 December 1774, *Gazette & Post-Boy*, 6 March 1775, at 4, col. 2; Suffolk Resolves, 9 September 1774, *Massachusetts Provincial Congresses*, at 601. See also "An American," Boston, 20 June 1774, 1 *American Archives*, at 435.

12. Address, Petition, and Remonstrance from the Livery of London to the King, 4 July 1775, *Petition in Favour of Americans*; [Towers], *Letter to Samuel Johnson*, at 37.

13. Langdon, *Government Corrupted*, at 249; Gordon, *Discourse Preached*, at 8–9; Providence Resolves, 19 January 1774, 7 *Records of Rhode Island*, at 273; *Junius Americanus, Boston Evening-Post*, 15 October 1770, at 1, col. 1.

14. Anon., *Letter to Cooper*, at 30–37. See also Resolves of Bristol, Rhode Island, 28 February 1774, Munro, *Bristol*, at 195.

15. By 1774 it was colonial loyalists, alarmed by the political activities of whig committees, who complained of arbitrariness. That they raised the same issues, in the same language, that the whigs raised against British arbitrariness, is striking evidence of the universality, or the "constitutionality," of the "arbitrary" concept. E.g., Letter from the Town of Pelham to Boston Committee of Correspondence, 16 November 1773, Parmenter, *Pelham*, at 124–25; Suffolk County (N.Y.) Letter, 4 February 1775, 2 *American Archives*, at 1212. For instances of the concept of arbitrariness perceived by American whigs as a threat to particular rights and, therefore, as a factor in the coming of the Revolution, see *Authority of Rights*, at 20, 48–50, 181, 233, 237.

## Chapter Eight

1. Thompson, *Whigs and Hunters*, at 265–66. As Joyce Appleby notes, liberty in the eighteenth century "was associated with a republic—the rule of law—and could not exist . . . where the will of the king or queen was supreme." Appleby, *Capitalism*, at 16. See also Bailyn, *Ideological Origins*, at 57.

2. Montrose, *Precedent in English Law*, at 42 (quoting Edmund Burke); Lord Bolingbroke, "The Freeholders Political Catechism," 43 *London Magazine* (1774), at 478; Arbuthnot, *Freeholder's Catechism*, at 5; [Burnet], *Coronation Sermon*, at 7. See also Dulany, *English Laws*, at 81–82. "The Cyder Act," 33 *Gentleman's Magazine* (1763), at 446; Hind, *Sermon at St. Margaret's*, at 13; "Philonomos," *Liberty of the Subject*, at 36; Dolins, *Third Charge to Middlesex Juries*, at 20; 2 Hoadley, *Works*, at 112, 124; [Brown], *Civil Liberty*, at 24; [Fowle], *Appendix to Eclipse*, at 6.

3. For a minority view—that liberty as law is nonsense—see, "Book Review," 19 *Critical Review* (1765), at 204; "To the Editor," 46 *Gentleman's Magazine* (1776), at 547; Hobbes, *De Cive*, at 158; Jordan, *Men of Substance*, at 176n. 107 (quoting Hobbes).

4. Anon., *Liberal Strictures*, at 10n; [Burnet], *Sermon at Salisbury*, at 15. Similarly, the eighteenth century considered law and rights mutually dependent. *Authority of Rights*, at 75–78.

5. Forster, *Northampton Assize Sermons*, at 37; Boucher, *Causes and Consequences*, at 509 (quoting Locke); [Bolingbroke], *Freeholder's Catechism*, at 3; [Meredith], *Question Stated*, at 53–54. See also [Brooke],

*Liberty and Common Sense: Letter II*, at 10; Anon., *Civil Liberty Asserted*, at 138; [Stewart], *Letter to Dr. Price*, at 8; Anon., *British Liberties*, at xviii.

6. [Brooke], *Liberty and Common Sense: Letter II*, at 15; De Pinto, *Letters on Troubles*, at 9; Speech of Edmund Burke at Bristol, 43 *London Magazine* (1774), at 508; Anon., *Civil Liberty Asserted*, at 138. See also Wooddeson, *Jurisprudence*, at 78.

7. Wesley, *Some Observations on Liberty*, at 4–5; Wesley, "Some Observations on Liberty," reprinted in Peach, *Richard Price*, at 246; Hey, *Observations on Civil Liberty*, at 32. See also Gerard, *Liberty Cloke of Maliciousness*, at 9; 3 Wynne, *Eunomus*, at 54; Anon., *Licentiousness Unmask'd*, at 19; Anon., *Civil Liberty Asserted*, at 8; Locke, *Two Treatises*, Book 2, Sec. 22; Hey, *Observations on Civil Liberty*, at 34; [Chalmers], *Plain Truth*, at 1; Peckard, *Nature and Extent of Liberty*, at 8; 1 Montesquieu, *Spirit of Laws*, at 214; Rossiter, *Political Thought*, at 122 (quoting the *Boston Gazette*, 1767); Hamilton, *Duty of Obedience to Laws*, at 15; 2 Montesquieu, *Spirit of Laws*, at 216; Missing, *Letter to Mansfield on Instructions*, at 7–8; Anon., *British Liberties*, at ii.

8. Montrose, *Precedent in English Law*, at 33 (quoting Burke). For another justification of punishment as a defense of liberty see, Dolins, *Third Charge to Middlesex Juries*, at 27.

9. Richard, Bishop of Peterborough, *Sermon on King Charles*, at 15; Maynard, *Speech in reply to Strafford*, at 3; Porteus, *Sermon on Charles I*, at 29; Anon., *No Liberty*, at 9; Forster, *Northampton Assize Sermons*, at 13; Eliot, *Give Cesar his Due*, at 15; 2 Pownall, *Administration Fifth Edition*, at xi; Sharp, *Law of Nature*, at 6; Peckard, *Nature and Extent of Liberty*, at 8–9; Anon., *Civil Liberty Asserted*, at 8; Anon., *Liberal Strictures*, at 38–39. See also Tuck, *Natural Rights Theories*, at 151 (quoting Henry Parker); Harrington, *Commonwealth of Oceana*, at 170; [Cary], *Answer to Molyneux*, at 76–77; [Moir], *Obedience the best Charter*, at 103; Baldwin, *New England Clergy*, at 36.

10. "Book Review," 22 *Critical Review* (1766), at 456. See also 1 Montesquieu, *Spirit of Laws*, at 262.

11. Carysfort, *Thoughts on Constitution*, at 12. See also Anon., *Civil Liberty Asserted*, at 17; Peters, *Massachusetts Constitution*, at 113 (quoting Nathaniel Niles); Anon., *Political Disquisitions*, at 6–7.

12. "Proceedings of the Freeholders in Granville County, 15 August 1774," 9 *North Carolina Colonial Records*, at 1036. See also "The Liberty of the Constitution," 8 *Town and Country Magazine* (1776), at 72; [Rous], *Letter to Jurors*, at 5; Wright, *Grand Jury Speech*, at 3; Burscough, *Abuse of Liberty*, at 9.

13. Letter from Æquus, 16 January 1766, 35 *London Magazine* (1766),

at 35; Baldwin, *New England Clergy,* at 36n. 20 (quoting Jonathan Mayhew); Anon., *Fair Trial,* at 115, 121; Candidus, *Two Letters,* at 7 (quoting William Markham, archbishop of York).

14. "In the Taught Tradition," at 931–74; *In Defiance of the Law,* at 32–49; Anon., *True Merits of Common Sense,* at iii; Trenchard, Letter of 9 February 1722, 4 *Cato's Letters,* at 81.

15. Boucher, *Causes and Consequences,* at 363 (quoted above in "Introduction," text to note 32). See also 1 Montesquieu, *Spirit of Laws,* at 262–63; Locke, *Two Treatises,* Book 2, Sec. 57; Carlyle, *Political Liberty,* at 148.

16. Letter from Arthur Piggott to "the Gentlemen Electors of the Town of St. George, Grenada," 21 January 1772, 10 *Political Register* (1772), at 293. See also Rude, "London Mob," at 14–15.

17. Barker, *Essays,* at 139 (quoting Blackstone); Tully, *Discourse on Property,* at 44 (quoting Locke); Forster, *Northampton Assize Sermons,* at 37 (quoting Locke); Laslett, "Introduction and Notes," at 111; [Goodricke], *Observations on Price's Theory,* at 87–88; West, *Election Sermon,* at 274.

18. Blackstone, *Tracts,* at 19; William Markham, "Sermon Preached," reprinted in Peach, *Richard Price,* at 263; Candidus, *Two Letters,* at 4; 1 Blackstone, *Commentaries,* at 126. See also 2 Campbell, *Political Survey,* at 289–90; Robert, Bishop of Peterborough, *Sermon to Lords,* at 7. There was one rule of evidence that was particular—that in disputes between power and liberty, the *onus probandi* is on power, not liberty. *New York Evening Post,* 7 December 1747, reprinted in *Boston Evening-Post,* 28 December 1747, at 1, col. 2; De Lolme, *Constitution,* at 431–35.

19. Rossiter, *Political Thought,* at 122 (quoting *Boston Gazette,* 1767); [Auckland], *Principles of Penal Law,* at 3.

20. [Leslie], *Right of Monarchy,* at 18; Letter from Edmund Burke to the Sheriffs of Bristol, April 1774, *Burke on American Revolution,* at 194. See also 1 Burgh, *Political Disquisitions,* at 2; Anon., *Liberal Strictures,* at 11n; Anon., *Civil Liberty Asserted,* at 32–33.

21. Anon., *Civil Liberty Asserted,* at 32; [Burnet], *Coronation Sermon,* at 7–8. For excellent American summaries of the balance see Eliot, *Give Cesar his Due,* at 36n; Dickinson, *Connecticut Election Sermon,* at 11.

22. Mayhew, *Discourse Concerning Unlimited Submission,* at 95n. A variation on the theme was to say there are "but two sorts of government, that of law, and that of *force.*" Candidus, *Two Letters,* at 5 (quoting Archbishop Markham); William Markham, "Sermon Preached," reprinted in Peach, *Richard Price,* at 263.

23. Peckard, *Nature and Extent of Liberty,* at 12; Eliot, *Give Cesar his Due,* at 14–15; Anon., *British Liberties,* at ii; Anon., *Application of*

*Political Rules*, at 39–40. See also 1 Montesquieu, *Spirit of Laws*, at 213; Boucher, *Causes and Conquences*, at 363; Price, *Two Tracts: Tract Two*, at 28.

24. Anon., *Political Mirror of Summary Review*, at 39; Instructions to Jasper Mauduit, 1762, *Mauduit Letters*, at 40.

CHAPTER NINE

1. Moss, *Connecticut Election Sermon*, at 19; Mulford, *Speech to New York Assembly*, at 6. For the positiveness of rights as law in the age of the American Revolution, see *Authority of Rights*, at 75–78.

2. Anon., *Letter Concerning Home and Abroad*, at 6; Anon., *Civil Liberty Asserted*, at 30–31.

3. Williams, *Election Sermon*, at 14; Baillie, *Letter to Shebear*, at 25; Earl of Abingdon, "Great Outlines of the English Constitution," 9 *Town and Country Magazine* (1777), at 454. See also *Petition of Middlesex to King, 24 May 1769*, at 4. For another aspect of the American Revolution and security of property, see *Authority of Rights*, at 34–46.

4. Locke, *Two Treatises*, Book 2, Secs. 221–22; Anon., *British Liberties*, at lvi (quoting Locke). See also Jones, *Fear of God*, at 30; Larkin, *Property in Eighteenth Century*, at 1.

5. Speech of Sir Thomas Wentworth, 1 May 1628, and Speech of the Archbishop, 25 April 1628, 3 *Commons Debates 1628*, at 203, 85, 74, 90; Message from the King delivered by Secretary Cook, Commons Debates, 2 May 1628, 3 *State Trials*, at 180. See also Speech of Mr. Cresswell, Commons Debates, 24 March 1627/28, 3 *State Trials*, at 74 (quoting Sir John Davis, "Case of Tanistry Customs").

6. Articles of the Commons against Archbishop William Laud, 26 February 1640/41, 1 Rushworth, *Historical Collections: Third Part*, at 196; House of Commons Remonstrance to the King, 1 December 1641, id., at 445; Speech of Harbottle Gremston, Commons Debates, 9 November 1640, id., at 34–36; Resolves of the Lords and Commons, 18 June 1642, id., at 658; "His Majesties Message for a Treaty, March 3, 1643," Charles I, *Several Speeches*, at 73; Cook, *King Charles His Case*, at 10; *True Copy*, at 48. See also Speech of Charles, 22 January 1648/49, and Charles's Speech Upon the Scaffold, *Clarendon's History Compleated*, at 99, 123; [Claridge], *Defence of Government*, at 7; Articles of Impeachment against John Finch, 14 January 1640/41, and Speech by "a certain Member" of Commons, 22 December 1640, 1 Rushworth, *Historical Collections: Third Part*, at 138, 131; Jones, *Country and Court*, at 133.

7. Robert, Bishop of Peterborough, *Sermon to Lords*, at 13; [Johnson], *Some Important Observations*, at 33; [Stevens], *Discourse on Constitution*, at 39–40.

8. Thomas Gordon, Letter of 27 January 1721, 2 *Cato's Letters*, at 258–59; Price, *Two Tracts: Tract Two*, at 15; Charge of Chief Justice Hutchinson to the Suffolk Grand Jury, March Term 1769, Quincy, *Reports*, at 306–07.

9. Anon., *British Liberties*, at xvii, iii; 1 Montesquieu, *Spirit of Laws*, at 261–62; [Joseph Hawley], "To the Inhabitants," 30 March 1775, 2 *American Archives*, at 247; Anon., *Civil Liberty Asserted*, at 17; "The Liberty of the Constitution," 8 *Town and Country Magazine* (1776), at 72; Speech of Lord Falkland, Commons Debates, 7 December 1640, 3 *State Trials*, at 1260.

10. Protests of 22 January 1723 and 18 March 1727, *Protests of the Lords of Ireland*, at 63, 71. Similarly, see Wright, *Grand Jury Speech*, at 2–3; Anon., *Serious Address*, at 12–13; [Johnson], *Some Important Observations*, at 8–9; Candidus, *Two Letters*, at 4–5; Baldwin, *New England Clergy*, at 87 (quoting Jonathan Mayhew). No matter what procedural safeguards guaranteed security, the primary object of the law's security was property. Stevens, *Election Sermon*, at 17–18; 3 Blackstone, *Commentaries*, at 119; [Williams], *Essential Rights*, at 5; Dolins, *Third Charge to Middlesex Juries*, at 31.

11. Welles, *Patriotism Described*, at 17; John Dickinson, "Address," 25 April 1768, 30 *Scots Magazine* (1768), at 526.

12. Anon., *Serious Exhortation*, at 6. See also Adam Ferguson, "Remarks on a Pamphlet," reprinted in Peach, *Richard Price*, at 257.

13. Gordon, Letter of 3 March 1721, 2 *Cato's Letters*, at 321; Jensen, *Revolution Within*, at 74 (quoting *Boston Gazette*, 22 February 1768). See also Kriegel, "Liberty and Whiggery," at 257; Hudson, "Penn's *English Liberties*," at 581.

14. Dickinson, *Essay*, at 41; Evans, *Reply to Fletcher*, at 35. See also Speech of Henry Ireton, 1 November 1647, "Putney Debates," at 121; Dolins, *Third Charge to Middlesex Juries*, at 4. But see Filmer, *Observations upon Aristotle*, at 225.

15. Rossiter, *Political Thought*, at 112 (quoting *Boston Gazette*); Arbuthnot, *Freeholder's Catechism*, at 3; Gordon, Letter of 3 March 1721, 2 *Cato's Letters*, at 321–22. See also Hill, *Upside Down*, at 272 (quoting Charles Cooke in 1656). For a related discussion of the association of liberty with property in the eighteenth century, see *Authority of Rights*, at 31–33, 44–46.

16. Hill, *Century of Revolution*, at 188 (quoting Sir Thomas Aston), and at 45; Speech of Lord Falkland, Commons Debates, 7 December 1640, 3 *State Trials*, at 1260; Anon., *Serious Address*, at 13; Dolins, *Third Charge to Middlesex Juries*, at 31; Lediard, *Charge to Westminster Jury*, at 19; Trenchard, Letter of 6 October 1722, 3 *Cato's Letters*, at 272; "Putney Debates," at 71; Dickinson, *Liberty and Property*, at 310 (quoting Smith,

*Wealth of Nations*); Young, *Political Arithmetic*, at 122; Thompson, *Whigs and Hunters*, at 241–44.

17. *Authority of Rights*, at 98–113.

18. Fiske, *Importance of Righteousness*, at 10; De Lolme, *Constitution*, at 237–38; "The Cyder Act," 33 *Gentleman's Magazine* (1763), at 446. See also De Lolme, *Constitution: New Edition*, at 99–100; Charles I, Speech upon the Scaffold, *Clarendon's History Compleated*, at 123.

19. Sydney, *Discourses Concerning Government*, at 348; Morgan, *Challenge*, at 55. See also Anon., *Treatise on Government*, at 21; Throop, *Thanksgiving Sermon*, at 11.

20. Price, *Two Tracts: Tract One*, at 17. See also Chauncy, *Civil Magistrates*, at 8–9.

21. Young, *Political Arithmetic*, at 5–6; Hunn, *Welfare of a Government*, at 14–15; Welles, *Patriotism Described*, at 16; Gordon, Letter of 20 January 1721, and Trenchard, Letter of 24 February 1721, 2 *Cato's Letters*, at 248–52, 310.

22. Peckard, *Nature and Extent of Liberty*, at 8; Gordon, Letter of 20 January 1721, 2 *Cato's Letters*, at 245.

## Chapter Ten

1. Resolutions of Monmouth County, New Jersey, 19 July 1774, 1 *American Archives*, at 610.

2. Cumings, *Thanksgiving Sermon*, at 18; [Joseph Hawley], "To the Inhabitants," 9 March 1775, 2 *American Archives*, at 97; Duchal, *Sermons*, at 170–71; [Ferguson], *Remarks on a Pamphlet*, at 13; Evans, *Constitutional Liberty*, at 20. See also Anon., *Critical Review of Liberties*, at 17; Anon., *No Liberty*, at 22.

3. Evans, *Remembrance of Former Days*, at 25. See also Lowth, *Durham Assize Sermon*, at 7–8; Anon., *Political Disquisitions*, at 7. "They, who talk of *Liberty* in *Britain* on any other Principles than Those of the *British Constitution*, talk impertinently at best, and much Charity is requisite to believe no worse of Them." [Bolingbroke], *Dissertation*, at 148.

4. 1 Montesquieu, *Spirit of Laws*, at 215; Missing, *Letter to Mansfield on Instructions*, at 9 (quoting Blackstone); Petition from the New York General Assembly to the House of Commons, 25 March 1775, 1 *American Archives*, at 1321. See also Lofft, *Observations on Wesley's Address*, at 32; Anon., *Fatal Consequences*, at 2; Hallifax, *Sermon at St. Margaret's*, at 12; Resolves of North Carolina Provincial Congress, 27 August 1774, 9 *North Carolina Colonial Records*, at 1047; Evans, *Constitutional Liberty*, at 10; Speech of Edmund Burke at Bristol, 16 October 1774, 1 *American Archives*, at 877; Mayhew, *Snare Broken*, at 24; Peckard, *Nature and Extent of Liberty*, at 26; Anon., *Britannia Libera*, at 42. For other aspects of

the eighteenth-century emphasis on the "end" of government or the constitution, see *Authority of Rights*, at 78–81.

5. "Debates in a Newly established Society," 41 *Gentleman's Magazine* (1771), at 291.

6. 1 Montesquieu, *Spirit of Laws*, at 260; "The Liberty of the Constitution," 8 *Town and Country Magazine* (1776), at 72; Peckard, *Nature and Extent of Liberty*, at 6; Anon., *Letter to Common Council on Pratt*, at 36–37; Price, *Two Tracts: Tract Two*, at 8.

7. De Lolme, *Constitution: New Edition*, at 375; Memorial from New York General Assembly to House of Lords, 25 March 1775, 1 *American Archives*, at 1317. See also Anon., *Civil Liberty Asserted*, at 32; Maier, *Resistance*, at 29–30. For the best revolutionary era statement of how the British constitution was the guarantor and definition of liberty, see Evans, *Constitutional Liberty*, at 9.

8. Hamilton, *Duty of Obedience to Laws*, at 15; Anon., *Ancient and Modern Constitution*, at 13–14; Protest of 7 March 1732, 1 *Protests of the Lords*, at 420–21; Speech of Lord Chancellor Northington, Lords Debates, 10 February 1766, 16 *Parliamentary History*, at 171.

9. For exceptions by lawyers, see Canning, *Letter to Hillsborough*, at 36; Baillie, *Letter to Shebear*, at 43.

10. Courtney, *Montesquieu and Burke*, at 94–95 (quoting Burke); [Williams], *Essential Rights*, at 6; Anon., *Letter Concerning Home and Abroad*, at 2; [Mortimer], *National Debt*, at 53. A special procedure upon which liberty depended (still being mentioned in the revolutionary era) was parliamentary control of the standing army. Price, *Two Tracts: Tract Two*, at 47; Anon., *Considerations on Militias*, at 1; Trenchard, Letter of 9 November 1723, 4 *Cato's Letters*, at 321; Pocock, *Machiavellian Moment*, at 410 (quoting 1675 pamphlet). See also Anon., *Letter to People of Ireland*, at 15; *In Defiance of the Law*, at 6–110.

11. Dolins, *Third Charge to Middlesex Juries*, at 22–23; *Guide to Rights*, at v; Letter from the Continental Congress to the People of Great Britain, 5 September 1774, 43 *London Magazine* (1774), at 628.

12. Anon., *Fair Trial*, at 1. Bernard Bailyn has provided important evidence of the role that the concept "power" played in eighteenth-century political thought. Bailyn, *Ideological Origins*, at 57–59. He is correct to emphasize the extent to which "power" and "right" were conceived to be independent entities. What must be added, however, is that both "power" and "right" were normative jurisprudential measures. Not only was an act of "power" outside constitutional norms, and an act of "right" within constitutional norms, but the concepts "power" and "right" were long standing tests for common law and for the validity of custom and of customary law restraints. "In the Taught Tradition," at 947–61.

13. Anon., *Vox Populi*, at 31–32; Botein, "Religion and Politics," at 21 (quoting Eliot). See also [Sheridan], *Review of Three Questions*, at 42, 39.

14. Hallifax, *Sermon at St. Margaret's*, at 9; 1 Montesquieu, *Spirit of Laws*, at 214. For theories of how the balance could be maintained in constitutional government, see 1 Blackstone, *Commentaries*, at 142; [Williams], *Letters on Liberty*, at 8; To the Inhabitants of Quebec, 26 October 1774, *Journal of the First Congress*, at 110–11; Stevens, *Election Sermon*, at 9.

15. Anon., *Considerations on Information*, at 4–5.

16. It must be understood that this discussion pertains to prerogative law or prerogative constitutionalism, not to political prerogativism manifested by such matters as "corruption," patronage, "placemen," or the "king's party." Prerogative *constitutional* power was controversial in only three significant areas during the two decades before 1776: (1) general search warrants, which were invalidated by the courts on the grounds that they were not sanctioned by Parliament; (2) prerogative colonial taxation, invalidated by King's Bench in *Campbell* v. *Hall;* (3) suspension of the corn law, requiring parliamentary action to render constitutional. For *Campbell* v. *Hall*, see *Authority of Rights*, at 155–58. For the corn embargo, see Speeches of Lords, 13 May 1778, 19 *Parliamentary History*, at 1244–51; 29 *Scots Magazine* (1767), at 409, 457, 478; 5 Campbell, *Lives of Chancellors*, at 265–66; Ritcheson, *British Politics*, at 75.

17. For some of the debate during the reign of Charles I, see Davis, *Reports*, "Preface" at 5; Jordan, *Men of Substance*, at 153 (quoting Henry Parker); [Parker], *Observations upon some Answers*, at 17–18; Speech of Sir Thomas Wentworth, 14 May 1628, 3 *Commons Debates 1628*, at 406; [Strafford], *Brief and Perfect Relation*, at 10, 63; Cragg, *Freedom and Authority*, at 84; 4 *Somers' Tracts*, at 120; Anon., *Advice to a Member*, at 18–20; Speech of the Lord Keeper, 2 June 1628, and Speech of Charles I, 7 June 1628, 4 *Commons Debates 1628*, at 52, 193; Speech of John Pym, Commons Debates, 25 November 1640, 4 *Somers' Tracts*, at 217; Charge of High Treason, *Clarendon's History Compleated*, at 97.

18. 1 Montesquieu, *Spirit of Laws*, at 23; Anon., *Court of Star Chamber*, at 3; *Boston Evening-Post*, 1 March 1773, at 2, col. 3.

19. Carroll, "First Citizen," at 126; Smith, "John Adams," at 81; Wilson, "Speech in the Pennsylvania Convention," at 179; Wilson, "Speech of 1775," at 753.

20. Samuel, Bishop of St. David's, *Sermon on Charles I*, at 13–14. But see Anon., *Secret Springs*, at 39.

21. Anon., *Perspective View of Complexion*, at 1–2.

22. [Bolingbroke], *Freeholder's Catechism*, at 3; Arbuthnot, *Free-*

_holder's Catechism_, at 5. See also Dobbs, _Letter to North_, at 8–9; [Allen], _Watchman's Alarm_, at 5; Gray, _Doctor Price's Notions_, at 101n (quoting Mollineux, _Case of Ireland_); Pole, _Representation_, at 82 (quoting William Penn); Rossiter, _Political Thought_, at 159 (quoting the _Essex Result_); Greene, "Paine and Modernization," at 85 (quoting Thomas Paine).

23. Sydney, _Discourses Concerning Government_, at 3; Carlyle, _Political Liberty_, at 122 (quoting Sydney); _Political Writings of James Otis_, at 22 (quoting Locke); Anon., _British Liberties_, at xvii–xviii (quoting Locke); Boucher, _Causes and Consequences_, at 533n (quoting "Libertye and the Weale Publick reconciled in a Declaration to the late Court of Elections in Newtown, the 17th of the 3d Month, 1637").

24. Anon., _North-Country Poll_, at 20–21; Priestley, _First Principles_, at 12–13. See also Blackstone, _Tracts_, at 203–4. Joyce Appleby suggests that indirect participation by voting may not have been sufficient participation. "To have liberty was to share in the power of the state, to be actively involved in making and executing decisions." Appleby, _Capitalism_, at 16.

25. Price, _Two Tracts: Tract One_, at 7. For the significance of Price's writings, see Bailyn, "Year of Challenge," at 439.

26. Anon., _Civil Liberty Asserted_, at 16–17; Gerard, _Liberty Cloke of Maliciousness_, at 9; 38 _Scots Magazine_ (1776), at 230 (reprinting _London Chronicle_). See also Anon., _Experience preferable to Theory_, at 18–19; Shebbeare, _Essay on National Society_, at 70; John Wesley, "Some Observations on Liberty," reprinted in Peach, _Richard Price_, at 247; "His Majesties Reasons . . . (22 January 1648/49)," 5 _Somers' Tracts_, at 213; _Speech upon the Scaffold_, at 9–10; Willcox, _Age of Aristocracy_, at 4.

27. Price, "Introduction to Two Tracts," at viii–ix; Anon., _Case of Great Britain_, at 6.

28. Anon., _Prospect of the Consequences_, at 15–16; Dolins, _Third Charge to Middlesex Juries_, at 28–29. See also Trumbull, _Discourse at New Haven_, at 27. For a discussion of consent as a restraint on government, see Pulteney, _Thoughts on Present State_, at 7–8.

29. Virginia Memorial to House of Lords, _Massachusetts Gazette & News-Letter_, 21 March 1756, at 2, col. 1. See also Fiske, _Importance of Righteousness_, at 32; Price, _Two Tracts: Tract One_, at 6–7; [Mulgrave], _Letter from a Member_, at 12–13.

30. Instructions of Newburyport, 21 October 1765, _Boston Post-Boy_, 4 November 1765, at 1, col. 1; Missing, _Letter to Mansfield on Instructions_, at 7.

31. Anon., _Considerations on Information_, at 1–2.

32. (Annual elections:) [Ramsay], _English Constitution_, at 11; Price, _Nature of Civil Liberty_, at 10; (Independent Commons:) Arbuthnot, _Freeholder's Catechism_, at 18; Anon., _O Liberty_, at 2; (Judiciary:) Anon., _Letter to Robert Morris_, at 66.

33. [Brooke], *Liberty and Common Sense: Letter II*, at 16–17; Anon., *Critical Review of Liberties*, at 19; Champion, *Reflections on Parties*, at 60–61. For a contrary appraisal, see Thompson, *Whigs and Hunters*, at 189.

34. Champion, *Reflections on Parties*, at 61; Clark, *British Opinion*, at 269 (quoting *London Magazine*, February 1766, at 80); Courtney, *Montesquieu and Burke*, at 94 (quoting Burke).

35. "Book Review," 46 *Gentleman's Magazine* (1776), at 126; [Shipley], *Intended Speech*, at 4. "Conceiving of liberty, then, as the exercise, within the boundaries of the law, of natural rights whose essences were minimally stated in English law and custom, the colonists saw in the balance of powers of the British constitution 'a system of consummate wisdom' that provided an effective 'check upon the power to oppress.'" Bailyn, *Pamphlets*, at 51.

## CHAPTER ELEVEN

1. Petition of the Continental Congress to the King, 26 October 1774, 44 *London Magazine* (1775), at 68. See also Instructions to Jasper Mauduit, 1762, *Mauduit Letters*, at 40–41; Representation from New York General Assembly to the House of Commons, 45 *Gentleman's Magazine* (1775), at 249; Patten, *Discourse at Hallifax*, at 13.

2. 1 Pownall, *Administration Fifth Edition*, at 86; Anon., *Honor of Parliament*, at 63; Canning, *Letter to Hillsborough*, at 26–27; Anon., *Civil Liberty Asserted*, at 49. See also [Phelps], *Rights of the Colonies*, at 4–5.

3. Resolution to Instruct Connecticut Delegates to Vote for Independence, June 1776, 15 *Colonial Records of Connecticut*, at 414. Compare that statement to one made a century and a half before, during the English constitutional crisis: Larkin, *Property in Eighteenth Century*, at 52 (quoting *England's Monarch* [1644]).

4. Petition of Lord Mayor, Aldermen, and Livery of London to King, 24 June 1775, 2 *American Archives*, at 1073.

5. Memorial from New York General Assembly to House of Lords, 25 March 1775, 1 *American Archives*, at 1316; Stearns, *View of the Controversy*, at 19. See also John Dickinson's Draft Address to the Inhabitants of America (January 1776), 3 *Letters of Delegates to Congress*, at 139; Address of the Grand Jury to the Quarter Session Justices, New York, 10 February 1775, 1 *American Archives*, at 1227.

6. [Baillie], *Appendix to a Letter*, at 34; 2 *St. Patrick's Anti-Stamp Chronicle* (1774), at 53 (reprinting a London newspaper); Petition of the East-India Company to Commons, 3 May 1773, 43 *London Magazine* (1774), at 315; 43 *Gentleman's Magazine* (1773), at 247–48; Resolves of the South Carolina Convention, 8 July 1774, 1 *American Archives*, at 526. See also Gordon, *Discourse Preached*, at 7; 1 Aikin, *Annals of George III*, at 58;

Price, *Two Tracts: Tract One*, at 35; Northcote, *Observations on Rights*, at 19; Address of the Massachusetts Congress, 9 February 1775, 1 *American Archives*, at 1332–33.

7. [Joseph Hawley], "To the Inhabitants," 6 April 1775, 2 *American Archives*, at 290; Hitchcock, *Sermon Preached before Gage*, at 46–47.

8. Letter from Daniel Dulany to Arthur Lee, May 1774, 1 *American Archives*, at 355; Resolutions of 5 November 1773, 18 *Boston Town Records*, at 143; Anon., *Inquiry into the Causes*, at 28–29. See also John Dickinson, "Address," 25 April 1768, 30 *Scots Magazine* (1768), at 526; Speech of Lord Camden, Lords Debates, February 1766, 16 *Parliamentary History*, at 180–81.

9. Petition of several Natives of America, 2 May 1774, 1 *American Archives*, at 82. See also Address of the Massachusetts Congress, 9 February 1775, id., at 1333; Toohey, *Liberty and Empire*, at 73 (quoting James Burgh); Jedrey, *World of Cleaveland*, at 131–32 (quoting *Essex Gazette*, 25 October 1768).

10. Petition of New York Representatives to King, 18 October 1764, *New York Journal of Votes*, at 771; Fiske, *Importance of Righteousness*, at 32; Anon., *Constitutional Answer to Wesley*, at 12. See also Report of 18 October 1769, 16 *Boston Town Records*, at 304; 35 *Gentleman's Magazine* (1765), at 562.

11. T. M., "An Essay on Liberty and Independency," 5 *Political Register* (1769), at 248–49.

12. Petition to the King, 28 March 1763, *Addresses of the Common Council*, at 42; Anon., *Present Dangerous Crisis*, at 21n. The liberty argument against taxation without consent, of course, had roots far earlier than the second half of the eighteenth century. E.g., Judson, "Henry Parker," at 139 (quoting *The Case of Shipmoney* [1640]).

13. For important examples of the liberty argument dressed up as a constitutional argument, see Declaration of 14 October 1774, *Commemoration Ceremony*, at 97; Memorial to Inhabitants of Colonies, 21 October 1774, id., at 115.

14. Resolutions of Accomack County, 27 July 1774, 1 *American Archives*, at 639; Resolves of Chester County, 18 June 1774, id., at 428; [Hawley], "To the Inhabitants," 6 April 1775, 2 *American Archives*, at 290. See also Price, *Nature of Civil Liberty*, at 19.

15. Anon., *Prospect of the Consequences*, at 14–15. See also 2 Pownall, *Administration Fifth Edition*, at 49; Anon., *Inquiry into the Causes*, at 37; Anon., *Observations of Consequence*, at 30.

16. Dobbs, *Letter to North*, at 10; Anon., *Moderation Unmasked*, at 10 note. See also Letter from Thomas Northcote to the Irish Reform Committee, 15 October 1783, *Collection of Irish Letters*, at 95.

17. Speech of George Johnstone, Commons Debates, 18 May 1775, 37 *Scots Magazine* (1775), at 249; Johnstone, *Speech on American Affairs*, at 17.

## CHAPTER TWELVE

1. Anon., *Discourse to Sons of Liberty*, at 7; Resolves of Worcester County Committee, 7 June 1775, 2 *American Archives*, at 924.

2. Thomas, quoting Townshend and Beckford, *British Politics*, at 88. Earlier Bostonians had voted that taxation without representation reduced them "from the character of free Subjects to the miserable state of tributary slaves." Instructions of 24 May 1764, *Boston News-Letter*, 31 May 1764, at 2, col. 2. Similarly see Letter to Agent Mauduit, 13 June 1764, *Massachusetts Representatives Journal*, at 74.

3. Instruction of 20 May 1772, 18 *Boston Town Records*, at 83. For a similar explanation that implies thoughts of chattel slavery, see [John Cleaveland], "To the Inhabitants," 18 April 1775, 2 *American Archives*, at 340.

4. Hopkins, *Rights*, at 516; Throop, *Thanksgiving Sermon*, at 11. Samuel Adams wrote the most interesting analysis, indicating that slavery by taxation was a condition below that of indentured servitude, and leaving the impression he thought it a status above chattel slavery. 1 Adams, *Writings*, at 270–71 (reprinting *Boston Gazette*, 19 December 1768).

5. [Howard], *Defence of the Letter*, at 16.

6. Evans, *Reply to Fletcher*, at 36n.; Cook, *King Charles his Case*, at 219–20; Cook, *King Charls his Case*, at 13; Anon., *Character of Charles I*, at 21.

7. For British discussion of unrepresented taxation as "slavery," see Speech of Isaac Barre, Commons Debates 1766, "Stamp Act Debates," at 571; Evans, *Political Sophistry detected*, at 25; Anon., *Prospect of the Consequences*, at 17; [Evans], *Letter to John Wesley*, at 13.

8. *Massachusetts Gazette & News-Letter*, 8 May 1766, at 2, col. 3 (quoting Pitt); *Prior Documents*, at 59 (quoting Pitt); Speech of Edmund Burke, Commons Debates, 19 April 1774, *Burke on American Revolution*, at 65. See also Speech of Mr. Aubrey, Commons Debates, 15 May 1775, 44 *London Magazine* (1776), at 676.

9. Instructions of the Pennsylvania Provincial Congress to the Deputies to Continental Congress, 15 July 1774, 43 *London Magazine* (1774), at 585; Anon., *Inquiry into the Causes*, at 21. See also Dickinson, "Address," 25 April 1768, 30 *Scots Magazine* (1768), at 525; [Bancroft], *Remarks*, at 10; Okoye, "Chattel Slavery," at 4 (quoting Alexander Hamilton); Higginbotham, "Iredell and Origins," at 107; Stout, *Perfect Crisis*, at 32.

10. 6 George III, cap. 12; Instructions . . . , *supra* note 9, at 585; Price, *Two Tracts: Trace One*, at 34; [Joseph Hawley], "To the Inhabitants," 9 March 1775, 2 *American Archives*, at 100.

11. 1 [Kames], *History of Man*, at 504n; 43 *London Magazine* (1774), at 543.

12. Speech of Lord Camden, Lords Debates, 17 May 1775, 37 *Scots Magazine* (1775), at 242; 5 *Political Register* (1769), at 277; Message from the Cumberland Committee to New York Congress, 8 June 1775, 2 *American Archives*, at 935.

13. Gordon, *Discourse Preached*, at 7. See also Letter from Continental Congress to the People of Great Britain, 5 September 1774, 43 *London Magazine* (1774), at 630; Message from Massachusetts Congress to Governor Thomas Gage, 13 October 1774, 1 *American Archives*, at 835; "Brutus," *Virginia Gazette*, 14 July 1775, 3 *Revolutionary Virginia*, at 131; Letter from Charles Chauncy to Richard Price, 30 May 1774, reprinted in Peach, *Richard Price*, at 286.

14. A freeholder of Essex to Stephen Crane, et al., January 1775, 1 *American Archives*, at 1095; Stout, *Perfect Crisis*, at 146–47 (quoting Samuel Seabury and an anonymous pamphlet); Kurland, "Colonies, Parliament, and Crown," at 66 (quoting Lord Wedderburn).

15. Address of the New York Congress to Inhabitants of Quebec, 2 June 1775, 2 *American Archives*, at 893; Stout, *Perfect Crisis*, at 42 (quoting earl of Buckinghamshire, 1 February 1774). See also Anon., *Short and Friendly Caution*, at 7–8; Clark, *British Opinion*, at 228 (quoting John Shebbeare).

16. Anon., *Inquiry into the Causes*, at 39.

17. [Priestley], *Present State of Liberty*, at v; [Baillie], *Some Observations on a Pamphlet*, at 14.

## Chapter Thirteen

1. The topic of the rhetoric of liberty has been either overlooked or ignored. For a brief recognition of its importance in the colonies, see Baldwin, *New England Clergy*, at 88–89.

2. *Brutus*, "To the Inhabitants of Virginia," 19 May 1775, 2 *American Archives*, at 641.

3. Letter from New York General Committee to Mayor, Aldermen, and Common Council of London, 5 May 1775, *Addresses and Petitions of Common Council*, at 86; Address from South Carolina Congress to Governor Lord William Campbell, 20 June 1775, 2 *American Archives*, at 1043. See also Address of Judge William Henry Drayton to Camden District (South Carolina) Grand Jury, November Session, 1774, 44 *London Magazine* (1775), at 126.

4. Savelle, "Nationalism in the Revolution," at 109 (quoting Galloway).

5. Burke, "On Reconcilation," 22 March 1775, reprinted in Peach,

*Richard Price*, at 232; Burke, "Letter to the Sheriffs," reprinted in id., at 272. See also *Americus*, "To the Printer of the Public Ledger, London, Nov. 22, 1765," reprinted in *Massachusetts Gazette & News-Letter*, 6 February 1766, at 1, col. 2.

6. Brown, *Middle-Class Democracy*, at 327 (quoting 3 Adams, *Writings*, at 101–02). See also Instructions of the Freemen of Philadelphia to their Representatives, 30 *Scots Magazine* (1768), at 690; "John Jay's Draft Petition to the King," June 1775, 1 *Letters of Delegates to Congress*, at 441; John Dickinson's Notes for a Speech in Congress, June 1776, 4 *Letters of Delegates to Congress*, at 168. In 1780 an Irish barrister wrote to Britain's prime minister: "We are attached to England, and seek a connexion with her, in preference to the rest of mankind. But, my Lord, our first attachment is to FREEDOM, and every other is a secondary consideration." Dobbs, *Letter to North*, at 11.

7. *They Preached Liberty*, at 121 (quoting John Lathrop, *Thanksgiving Sermon*, 1774).

8. Letter from Lord North to John Burgoyne, 31 July 1775, 1 Valentine, *Lord North*, at 377; Nelson, *American Tory*, at 188–89; Address of Governor James Wright to Georgia Commons House of Assembly, 18 January 1775, 1 *American Archives*, at 1153. See also Browning, *Court Whigs*.

9. [Drinker], *Observations on the Measures*, at 23; "Letter to People of New-Jersey," 19 November 1774, reprinted in *Commemoration Ceremony*, at 134. For loyalists' defense of liberty applied against specific whig activities and institutions, see Allen, *American Crisis*, at 24; Loyalist Association of Massachusetts, December 1774, 1 *American Archives*, at 1057; Resolutions of Marshfield, Massachusetts, 31 January 1774, 36 *Scots Magazine* (1774), at 120; *Maryland Gazette*, 19 January 1775, reprinted in 1 *American Archives*, at 1141.

10. *Boston Evening-Post*, article by Sewall, 14 January 1771, at 1, col. 3; Stark, *Loyalists*, at 380 (quoting Pittman). See also Letter from Peter Van Schaack to the New York Provincial Convention, 1777, *American Tory*, at 44.

11. [Meredith], *Question Stated*, at 54; [Bernard], *Appeal to the Public*, at 24.

12. Camillus, "To the Printers of the Pennsylvania Gazette," 1 March 1775, 2 *American Archives*, at 11; [Allen], *Watchman's Alarm*, at 6.

13. Toohey, *Liberty and Empire*, at 102, 95–96.

14. Price, *Two Tracts: Tract One*, at 90. See also Price, *Two Tracts: Tract Two*, at 5, 29, 76. For a similar argument regarding taxation and empire, see 43 *London Magazine* (1774), at 582; [Priestley], *Address to Dissenters*, at 17–18.

15. [Blacklock], *Remarks on Liberty*, at 29.

16. Speech of William Pitt, Commons Debates, 1766, "Stamp Act Debates," at 573; Koebner, *Empire*, at 155 (quoting Burke); Anon., *Some Seasonable Observations*, at 11; Speech of Edmund Burke at Bristol, 43 *London Magazine* (1774), at 508. See also Speech of Edmund Burke, Commons Debates, 3 February 1766, Ryder, "Parliamentary Diaries," at 273. Contrary see Speech of Lord Irnham, Commons Debates, 6 February 1775, 44 *London Magazine* (1775), at 396. There was also an argument that the British constitution was too much the instrument of liberty to govern any empire successfully. Anon., *Inquiry into the Causes*, at 23–24.

17. 2 Pownall, *Administration Fifth Edition*, at 49; Pownall, *Pownall*, at 268.

18. [Cartwright], *American Independence*, at 54; Price, *Nature of Civil Liberty*, at 1.

19. Anon., *Reflections on the Contest*, at 41; Petition to the House of Lords, 14 March 1775, and Remonstrance to the King, 24 June 1775, *Addresses and Petitions of Common Council*, at 77–78, 104.

20. "Political Observations, Without Order," 14 November 1774, reprinted in *Commemoration Ceremony*, at 136.

21. For an excellent example see Message from the House of Burgesses to Governor Lord Dunmore, 19 June 1775, 13 *Journal of Burgesses*, at 261.

22. [Chalmers], *Answer from Bristol to Burke*, at 84; Answer from Alderman Richard Oliver to the Sheriff and Grand Jury of Pembroke, 27 April 1771, and Address of the Inhabitants of Broad-Street to Lord Mayor Brass Crosby, 2 May 1771, printed in Anon., *Magna Charta Opposed to Privilege*, at 161, 213. The point is worth repeating that when the actions of government were attacked on grounds of liberty, the word "natural" was used occasionally. It must not be allowed to mislead us. Even when the concept of natural liberty was specifically mentioned, it was the liberty of the constitution that Americans sought. Thus a Massachusetts congregation was told: "[W]e have a right to all the natural liberty which is indulged by the constitution we are under. That is to say, we have a right to every branch of liberty, which we have not surrendered. If neither we, nor our fathers have yielded our lives or properties into the hands of others, they are still our own." Patten, *Discourse at Hallifax*, at 12.

23. Letter from Charles Carroll of Carrollton to Mr. Graves, 27 August 1767, *Letters of Charles Carroll*, at 147.

24. Address of the Freeholders of Augusta County to Virginia's Continental Congress Delegates, February 1775, 1 *American Archives*, at 1255.

## CHAPTER FOURTEEN

1. [Grattan], *Mutiny Bill*, at 36; Lucas, *Divelina Libera*, at 6. See also Hamilton, *Duty of Obedience to Laws*, at 15.

2. Anon., *American Resistance Indefensible*, at 7; 46 *Monthly Review* (1772), at 580 (quoting Arthur Young). See also Anon., *Serious Address*, at 17–18; [Bolingbroke], *Dissertation*, at 141. For the eighteenth-century duty to defend "rights" and "law" and, therefore, to defend liberty, see *Authority of Rights*, at 187–89.

3. Had definitions been the topic of concern, greater attention would have been given to the categories into which contemporaries divided liberty, such as "civil liberty," "political liberty," "physical liberty," "religious liberty," "moral liberty." Some small amount of ink was spilled debating these differences, primarily by Richard Price and his critics. The debaters may have thought the distinctions important, but generally their significance belonged to semantics; they had *no* impact on either politics or law. Distinctions were, in truth, drawn much as in the twentieth century they are drawn by debaters about civil rights in American law reviews. One side makes a point by claiming a protection or an extension for a civil right. The other side responds by saying that the privilege extended is not a civil right but an entitlement or a civil liberty. The counterpoint scored is not of substance but semantics.

4. Anon., *Civil Liberty Asserted*, at 17.

5. [Shebbeare], *Third Letter*, at 6–7; *Essex Result*, at 14. The "erroneous" definition was the majority British view, favored by Blackstone, among others. For criticism see Cartwright, *Appeal on Constitution*, at 34n.

6. Dolins, *Third Charge to Middlesex Juries*, at 28–29; [Bolingbroke], *Dissertation*, at 164, 203; Arbuthnot, *Freeholder's Catechism*, at 5; 9 *London Magazine* (1740), at 3–4; Anon., *Second Letter to Member*, at 19; Pole, *Representation*, at 82 (quoting William Penn).

7. [Anderson], *Free Thoughts*, at 21, col. 2; [Jones], *Constitutional Criterion*, at 8; Anon., *To Committee of London Merchants*, at 22–25; [Cartwright], *American Independence*, at 36; Price, *Two Tracts: Tract One*, at 6–7; Anon., *North-Country Poll*, at 20–21; [Ramsay], *Historical Essay*, at 115–16; 5 *Political Register* (1769), at 249; "A Real Friend to the People," *Declaration of those Rights of the Commonalty of Great-Britain with which they cannot be Free* (broadside printed in London, c. 1775, Huntington Library Rare Book No. 141710). For American arguments, see Shute, *Election Sermon*, at 54–55; Tucker, *Election Sermon*, at 49–50; Benjamin Church's Oration (1773), *Massacre Orations*, at 36; Anon., *To Electors of Philadelphia*; Schutz, "Galloway," at 85; Wood, *Creation*, at 24–25, 56–57 (Wood contends [at 62] that colonists believed that "power held by the people was liberty," but quotes none who say that liberty was better preserved by the people than by law).

8. Tucker, *Treatise*, at 140; Letter from the earl of Effingham, *Collection of Irish Letters*, at 61; Lofft, *Observations on Publication*, at 13,

16; Anon., *Duty of Freeman*, at 5–6. Contrary see [Pulteney], *Plan of Reunion*, at 35; Speech of T. Pitt, [Almon], *Free Parliaments*, at 34–35. The right to representation was also postulated on nonliberty grounds. Kramnick, "Republican Revisionism," at 637–38.

9. Cartwright, *Appeal on Constitution*, at 11, 19–20. See also Cartwright, *Appeal Civil and Military*, at 9; Cartwright, *Legislative Rights*, at 36–46; Cartwright, *Postscript*, at 8, 18; Hall, *Apology for Freedom*, at 29; Anon., *Constitutional Answer to Wesley*, at 16; Lofft, *Summary of Treatise*, at 2; [Keld], *Polity of England*, at 278–79, 284, 297, 484–85.

10. Cartwright, *People's Barrier*, at 20. See also [Gray], *Right of the Legislature*, at 6; Anon., *Vindication of the Livery*, at 13.

11. Cartwright, *Postscript*, at 19–20. See also Cartwright, *Constitution Produced*, at 140 (quoting Earl Stanhope); Rokeby, *Further Examination*, at 189; Lofft, *Summary of Treatise*, at 2.

12. Declaration of rights (1782), *Society for Constitutional Information*, at 38–39. Josiah Tucker lit upon this definition, attributed it to Locke and Price, and in ridiculing it, attempted to reduce to absurdities many of the eighteenth-century concepts of liberty that have been discussed in this book. Tucker, *Treatise*, at 85, 140.

13. 2 Hoadly, *Works*, at 112–13; Anon., *Whigs and Jacobites*, at 31–32; Anon., *Compleat View*, at 59–60.

14. Gordon, Letter of 1 July 1721, 2 *Cato's Letters*, at 16. See also Priestley, *First Principles*, at 15–16; [Bollan], *Continued Corruption*, at 69 (quoting Addison). For a 1780 writer who questioned the existence of liberty "where inequalities of property are very great," see Anon., *Essay on Constitutional Liberty*, at 5–10.

15. *Essex Result*, at 11, also 12–13; [Jones], *Constitutional Criterion*, at 6; Cartwright, *Constitution Produced*, at 125. See also Cartwright, *Legislative Rights*, at 2, 50–51.

16. Anon., *Civil Liberty Asserted*, at 17; [Shebbeare], *Third Letter*, at 5; De Lolme, *Constitution*, at 238.

17. Carysfort, *Thoughts on Constitution*, at 11–12.

18. The barrier was against "bad" government which, interestingly, could be seen as a threat to liberty. Some theorists thought that "good" government was not necessarily "destructive of any such Liberty as is good for the whole, but abundantly supports, secures & defends it." Eliot, *Give Cesar his Due*, at 15.

19. [Ibbetson], *National Assemblies*, at 1; Lofft, *Observations on Wesley's Address*, at 32. For more extended wording see Lofft, *Summary of Treatise*, at 2.

20. Anon., *Court of Star Chamber*, at 1–2; *Craftsman* (No. 366), 7 July 1733, at 86–87; [Fowle], *Appendix to Eclipse*, at 7; Warrington, *Grand*

*Jury Charge*, at 7; [Bolingbroke], *Dissertation*, at 214; [Adair], *Dismission of Officers*, at 32–33; [Cooper], *Crisis*, at 4.

21. Brown, *Estimate of Manners*, at 12–13. See also Rokeby, *Further Examination*, at 97.

22. Keith, *Papers and Tracts*, at 123; Browning, *Court Whigs*, at 155, 156 (quoting Hardwicke); [Bolingbroke], *Dissertation*, at 216. See also Rusticus, *Good of Community*, at 42; Evans, *Remembrance of Former Days*, at 27–28; Frink, *Election Sermon*, at 80–81.

23. *Authority of Rights*, at 211–17.

24. 4 Blackstone, *Commentaries*, at 151–52.

25. Ibid., at 153.

26. Paley, *Principles of Philosophy*, at 443.

27. Letter from Edward Rutledge to John Jay, 2 November 1786, 3 *Correspondence and Public Papers of John Jay* 217 (H. P. Johnston, editor, New York, 1891); *Essex Result*, at 11; Yorke, *Reason against Precedent*, at 39–40.

# Short Titles

Abingdon, *Thoughts on Burke's Letter*
Willoughby Bertie, earl of Abingdon. *Thoughts on the Letter of Edmund Burke, Esq; to the Sheriffs of Bristol, on the Affairs of America.* 6th ed. Oxford, England, 1777.

[Adair], *Dismission of Officers*
[James Adair.] *Thoughts on the Dismission of Officers, Civil or Military for their Conduct in Parliament.* London, 1765.

Adams, *Writings*
*The Writings of Samuel Adams.* Edited by Harry Alonzo Cushing. 4 vols. New York, 1904–8.

*Addresses and Petitions of Common Council*
*Addresses, Remonstrances, and Petitions; Commencing the 24th of June, 1769, Presented to the King and Parliament, from the Court of Common Council, and the Livery in Common Hall assembled, with his Majesty's Answers: Likewise the Speech to the King, made by the late Mr. Alderman Beckford, When Lord Mayor of the City of London.* London, [1778].

*Addresses of the Common Council*
*Addresses Presented from the Court of Common Council to the King, On his Majesty's Accession to the Throne, and on various other Occasions, and his Answers. Resolutions of the Court, . . . . Instructions at different Times to the Representatives in Parliament. Petitions to Parliament for different Purposes. . . . Agreed to between the 23d October, 1760, and the 12th October, 1770.* London, [1770].

Aikin, *Annals of George III*
John Aikin. *Annals of the Reign of King George the Third; From its Commencement in the Year 1760, to the General Peace in the Year 1815.* Vol. 1. London, 1816.

Allen, *American Crisis*

William Allen. *The American Crisis: A Letter, Addressed by Permission to the Earl Gower, Lord President of the Council, &c. &c. &c. On the present alarming Disturbances in the Colonies.* London, 1774.

[Allen], *Watchman's Alarm*

[John Allen.] *The Watchman's Alarm to Lord N[ort]h, or, The British Parliamentary Boston Port-Bill Unwrapped. Being an Oration on the Meridian of Liberty; Not to inflame but to cheer the Mind: Or as an Appeal of Gold in the Pictures of Silver for the mourning Captives in America. With some Observations on the Liberties of the Africans. By the British Bostonian.* Salem, Mass., 1774.

[Almon], *Free Parliaments*

[John Almon.] *Free Parliaments: or, a Vindication of the Parliamentary Constitution of England; in Answer to Certain visionary Plans of Modern Reformers.* London, 1783.

[Almon], *History of the Late Minority*

[John Almon.] *The History of the Late Minority. Exhibiting the Conduct, Principles, and Views of that Party, during the Years 1762, 1763, 1764, and 1765.* London, 1766.

*American Archives*

*American Archives, Fourth Series. Containing a Documentary History of the English Colonies in North America From the King's Message to Parliament, of March 7, 1774, to the Declaration of Independence by the United States.* Vols. 1 and 2. Washington, 1837.

*American Gazette*

*The American Gazette. Being a Collection of all the Authentic Addresses, Memorials, Letters, &c. Which relate to the Present Disputes Between Great Britain and her Colonies. Containing also Many Original Papers Never Before Published.* London, 1768.

*American Tory*

*The American Tory.* Edited by Morton Borden and Penn Borden. Englewood Cliffs, N.J., 1972.

[Anderson], *Free Thoughts*

[James Anderson.] *Free Thoughts on the American Contest.* Edinburgh, 1776.

[Andrews], *Reflections on the Spirit*

[John Andrews.] *Reflections on the too prevailing Spirit of Dissipation and Gallantry; Shewing its dreadful Consequences to Publick Freedom.* London, 1771.

Anon., *Address to Junius*

Anonymous. *An Address to Junius, Upon the Subject of his Letter in the Public Advertiser, December 19, 1769.* London, [1770?].

Anon., *Advice to a Member*
Anonymous. *Advice to a Newly Elected Member of Parliament: Inscribed to the Right Honble William Fitzgerald, Commonly called Marquess Kildare.* Dublin, 1764.

Anon., *American Resistance Indefensible*
Anonymous. *American Resistance Indefensible. A Sermon, Preached on Friday, December 13, 1776, Being the Day appointed for a General Fast.* London, [1776].

Anon., *Ancient and Modern Constitution*
Anonymous. *The Ancient and Modern Constitution of Government Stated and compared. And also Some Remarks on the Controversy Concerning the Dependence of Members of Parliament on the Crown.* London, 1734.

Anon., *Ancient and Modern Liberty*
Anonymous. *Ancient and Modern Liberty Stated and Compar'd.* London, 1734.

Anon., *Appeal to Reason and Justice*
Anonymous. *An Appeal to Reason and Justice in Behalf of the British Constitution, and the Subjects of the British Empire. In which the present Important Contest with the Revolted Colonies is impartially considered, the Inconsistency of Modern Patriotism is demonstrated, the Supremacy of Parliament is asserted on Revolution Principles, and American Independence is proved to be a manifest Violation of the Rights of British Subjects.* London, 1778.

Anon., *Application of Political Rules*
Anonymous. *An Application of some General Political Rules, to the Present State of Great-Britain, Ireland and America. In a Letter to the Right Honourable Earl Temple.* London, 1766.

Anon., *Argument in Defence*
Anonymous. *An Argument in Defence of the Exclusive Right Claimed by the Colonies to Tax Themselves, with a Review of the Laws of England, Relative to Representation and Taxation. To Which is Added, An Account of the Rise of the Colonies, and the Manner in which the rights of the subjects within the realm were communicated to those that went to America, with the exercise of those rights from their first settlement to the present time.* London, 1774.

Anon., *Ballance of Civil Power*
Anonymous. *An Historical Essay Upon the Ballance of Civil Power in England, From its first Conqeust by the Anglo-Saxons, to the Time of the Revoluion; in which is introduced a new Dissertation Upon Parties.* London, 1748.

Anon., *Battle of the Quills*

Anonymous. *The Battle of the Quills: or, Wilkes Attacked and Defended.* London, 1768.

Anon., *Britannia Libera*

Anonymous. *Britannia Libera, or a Defence of the Free State of Man in England, Against the Claim of any Man there as a Slave. Inscribed and Submitted to the Jurisconsulti, and the Free People of England.* London, 1772.

Anon., *British Liberties*

Anonymous. *British Liberties, or the Free-born Subject's Inheritance; Containing the Laws that form the Basis of those Liberties, with Observations thereon; also an Introductory Essay on Political Liberty and a Comprehensive View of the Constitution of Great Britain.* London, 1766.

Anon., *Candid Reflections upon the Judgement*

Anonymous. *Candid Reflections Upon the Judgement lately awarded by the Court of King's Bench in Westminster-Hall, On What is commonly called the Negroe-Cause, by a Planter.* London, 1772.

Anon., *Candid Thoughts*

Anonymous. *Candid Thoughts; or, and Enquiry into the Causes of National Discontents and Misfortunes Since the Commencement of the Present Reign.* London, 1781.

Anon., *Case of Great Britain*

[Gervase Parker Bushe or George B. Butler.] *The Case of Great Britain and America, Addressed to the King, and Both Houses of Parliament.* 3d ed. Boston, [1769].

Anon., *Case of Presbyterians*

Anonymous. *The Case of the Scotch Presbyterians of the City of New-York.* New York, 1773.

Anon., *Chains of Slavery*

Anonymous. *The Chains of Slavery. A Work Wherein the Clandestine and Villainous Attempts of Princes to Ruin Liberty are Pointed Out, and the Dreadful Scenes of Despotism Disclosed.* London, 1774.

Anon., *Character of Charles I*

Anonymous. *An Essay Towards Attaining a True Idea of the Character and Reign of K. Charles the First, And the Causes of the Civil War.* London, 1748.

Anon., *Civil Liberty Asserted*

Anonymous. *Civil Liberty Asserted, and the Rights of the Subject Defended, Against the Anarchial Principles of the Reverend Dr. Price.* London, 1776.

Anon., *Civil Prudence*

Anonymous. *Civil Prudence Recommended to the Thirteen United Colonies of North America.* Norwich, Conn., 1776.

Anon., *Compleat View*
Anonymous. *A Compleat View of the Present Politicks of Great-Britain. In a Letter from a German Nobleman, to his Friend at Vienna.* London, 1743.

Anon., *Considerations on Information*
Anonymous. *Considerations on Proceedings by Information and Attachment. Addressed to the Members of the House of Commons. By a Barrister at Law.* 2d ed. London, 1768.

Anon., *Considerations on Militias*
Anonymous. *Considerations on Militias and Standing Armies.* London, 1782.

Anon., *Constitutional Answer to Wesley*
Anonymous. *A Constitutional Answer to the Rev. Mr. John Wesley's Calm Address to the American Colonies.* London, 1775.

Anon., *Court of Star Chamber*
Anonymous. *The Court of Star Chamber, or Seat of Oppression.* London, 1768.

Anon., *Critical Review of Liberties*
Anonymous. *A Critical Review of the Liberties of British Subjects. With a Comparative View of the Proceedings of the H[ous]e of C[ommon]s of I[relan]d, against an unfortunate Exile of that Country; who, in contending for the Rights and Liberties of the Publick, lost his own.* 2d ed. London, 1750.

Anon., *Defence of the People*
Anonymous. *A Defence of the People: or, Full Confutation of the Pretended Facts, Advanc'd in a late, Huge, Angry Pamphlet; call'd Faction Detected. In a Letter to the Author of that Weighty Performance.* London, 1744.

Anon., *Detector Detected*
Anonymous. *The Detector Detected: or, the Danger to which our Constitution now lies exposed, Set in a True and manifest Light.* 2d ed. London, 1743.

Anon., *Dialogue on the State*
Anonymous. *A Dialogue on the Actual State of Parliament.* London, 1783.

Anon., *Dialogues on Rights of Britons*
Anonymous. *Dialogues on the Rights of Britons, between a Farmer, a Sailor, and a Manufacturer. Dialogue the Second.* 2d ed. London, 1792.

Anon., *Discourse to Sons of Liberty*
Anonymous. *A Discourse, Addressed to the Sons of Liberty, at a Solemn Assembly, near Liberty-Tree, in Boston, February 14, 1766.* Providence, [1766].

Anon., *Duty of Freeman*
    Anonymous. *The Duty of a Freeman, Addressed to the Electors of Great Britain.* n.i., n.d. (Distributed by the Society for Constitutional Information.)

Anon., *Essay on Constitutional Liberty*
    Anonymous. *An Essay on Constitutional Liberty: Wherein the Necessity of Frequent Elections of Parliament is shewn to be superseded by the Unity of the Executive Power.* London, 1780.

Anon., *Essay on the Constitution*
    Anonymous. *An Essay on the Constitution of England.* London, 1765.

Anon., *Essays Commercial and Political*
    Anonymous. *Essays Commercial and Political, on the Real and Relative Interests of Imperial and Dependent States, Particularly those of Great Britain and Her Dependencies: Displaying the Probable Causes of, and a Mode of Compromising the present Disputes Between this Country and her American Colonies.* Newcastle, 1777.

Anon., *Evidence of Common and Statute Laws*
    Anonymous. *The Evidence of the Common and Statute Laws of the Realm; Usage, Records, History, with the Greatest and Best Authorities Down to the 3d of George the IIId, in Proof of the Rights of Britons Throughout the British Empire. Addressed to the People.* London. 1775.

Anon., *Examination of the Legality*
    Anonymous. *A Candid Examination of the Legality of the Warrant Issued by the Secretaries of State For Apprehending the Printers, Publishers, &c. of a late Interesting Paper.* London, 1764.

Anon., *Experience Preferable to Theory*
    Anonymous. *Experience Preferable to Theory. An Answer to Dr. Price's Observations on the Nature of Civil Liberty, and the Justice and Policy of the War with America.* London, 1776.

Anon., *Fair Trial*
    Anonymous. *A Fair Trial of the Important Question, or the Rights of Election Asserted; Against the Doctrine of Incapacity by Expulsion, or by Resolution: Upon True Constitutional Principles, the Real Law of Parliament, the Common Right of the Subject, and the Determinations of the House of Commons.* London, 1769.

Anon., *Fatal Consequences*
    Anonymous. *The Fatal Consequences of the Want of System In the Conduct of Public Affairs.* London, 1757.

Anon., *Four Letters*
    Anonymous. *Four Letters on Interesting Subjects.* Philadelphia, 1776.

Anon., *Honest Grief of a Tory*

Anonymous. *The Honest Grief of a Tory, Expressed in a Genuine Letter from a Burgess of* _____, *in Wiltshire, to the Author of the Monitor, Feb. 17, 1759.* London, 1759.

Anon., *Honor of Parliament*

Anonymous. *The Honor of Parliament and the Justice of the Nation Vindicated. In a Reply to Dr. Price's Observations on the Nature of Civil Liberty.* London, 1776.

Anon., *Inquiry into the Causes*

Anonymous. *An Inquiry into the Nature and Causes of the Present Disputes Between the British Colonies in America and the Mother-Country; And their reciprocal Claims and just Rights impartially examined, and fairly stated.* London, 1769 [*sic* 1768].

Anon., *Justice and Policy*

Anonymous. *Justice and Policy. An Essay on the Increasing Growth and Enormities of our Great Cities.* Dublin, 1772.

Anon., *Knowledge of the Laws*

Anonymous. *An Introduction to the Knowledge of the Laws and Constitution of England.* Dublin, 1764.

Anon., *Letter Concerning Home and Abroad*

Anonymous. *A Letter to a Member of Parliament Concerning the present State of Affairs at Home and Abroad. By a True Lover of the People.* London, 1740.

Anon., *Letter on Parliamentary Representation*

Anonymous. *A Letter on Parliamentary Representation, in which the Propriety of Trienial and Septennial Parliaments is Considered. Inscribed to John Sinclair, Esq. M.P.* London, 1783.

Anon., *Letter to Common Council on Pratt*

Anonymous. *A Letter to the Common Council of the City of London. With Remarks on Lord Chief Justice Pratt's Letter to the City of Exeter.* London, 1764.

Anon., *Letter to Cooper*

Anonymous. *A Letter to the Rev. Dr. Cooper, on the Origin of Civil Government; in Answer to his Sermon, Preached before the University of Oxford, on the Day appointed by Proclamation for a General Fast.* London, 1777.

Anon., *Letter to Egremont and Halifax*

Anonymous. *A Letter to the Right Honourable the Earls of Egremont and Halifax, His Majesty's Principal Secretaries of State on the Seizure of Papers.* London, 1763.

Anon., *Letter to North on East-India Bill*

Anonymous. *A Letter to the Right Honourable Lord North on the East-India Bill now depending in Parliament.* London, 1772.

Anon., *Letter to People of Ireland*
Anonymous. *A Letter to the People of Ireland. The Second Edition.* London, 1770.

Anon., *Letter to Robert Morris*
Anonymous. *Letter to Robert Morris, Esq. Wherein the Rise and Progress of our Political Disputes are Considered. Together with some Observations on the Power of Judges and Juries as relating to the Cases of Woodfall and Almon.* London, 1771.

Anon., *Liberal Strictures*
Anonymous. *Liberal Strictures on Freedom and Slavery: Occasioned by the Numerous Petitions to Parliament, for the Abolition of the Slave-Trade.* London, 1789.

Anon., *Liberty in Two Parts*
Anonymous. *Liberty in Two Parts.* London, 1754.

Anon., *Licentiousness Unmask'd*
Anonymous. *Licentiousness Unmask'd; or Liberty Explained.* London, n.d.

Anon., *Magna Charta Opposed to Privilege*
Anonymous. *Magna Charta, Opposed to Assumed Privilege: Being a complete View of the Late Interesting Disputes between the House of Commons and the Magistrates of London.* London, 1771.

Anon., *Middle Temple Letter to Dublin*
Anonymous. *A Letter from a Gentleman of the Middle Temple, to his Friend in Dublin, Relative to the Present Crisis of Affairs in the Kingdom.* Dublin, 1780.

Anon., *Ministerial Catechise*
Anonymous. *A Ministerial Catechise, Suitable to be Learned by all Modern Provincial Governors, Pensioners, Placemen, &c. Dedicated to T[homas] H[utchinson], Esq.* Boston, 1771.

Anon., *Moderation Unmasked*
Anonymous. *Moderation Unmasked; or, the Conduct of the Majority Impartially Considered. By the Author of a Scheme for a Constitutional Association.* Dublin, 1780.

Anon., *New Preface to Mollyneux*
Anonymous. Preface to William Mollyneux, *The Case of Ireland being bound by Acts of Parliament in England, Stated. With a New Preface.* London, 1770.

Anon., *No Liberty*
Anonymous. *No Liberty! No Life! Proper Wages, and Down with Oppression. In a Letter to the Brave People of England. By John Englishman.* 3d ed. London, 1768.

Anon., *North-Country Poll*

Anonymous. *The North-Country Poll; or, an Essay on the New Method of Appointing Members to serve in Parliament*. London, 1768.

Anon., *O Liberty*

Anonymous. *O Liberty, thou Goddess Heavenly Bright*. [New York, 1732].

Anon., *Observations of Consequence*

Anonymous. *Some Observations of Consequence, In Three Parts. Occasioned by the Stamp-Tax, Lately imposed on the British Colonies*. [Philadelphia], 1768.

Anon., *Observations Upon the Authority*

Anonymous. *Observations Upon the Authority, Manner and Circumstances of the Apprehension and Confinement of Mr. Wilkes. Addressed to Free-Born Englishmen*. London, 1763.

Anon., *Perspective View of Complexion*

Anonymous. *A Perspective View of the Complexion of some Late Elections, and of the Candidates. With a Conclusion Deduced from Thence. In a Letter addressed to a Member of Parliament*. London, 1768.

Anon., *Philosophical Survey of Nature*

Anonymous. *A Philosophical Survey of Nature: in which the Long Agitated Question Concerning Human Liberty and Necessity, is Endeavoured to be fully Determined*. London, 1763.

Anon., *Policy of the Laws*

Anonymous. *An Inquiry into the Policy of the Penal Laws Affecting the Popish Inhabitants of Ireland. In which the History and Constitution of that Country, and the Rights of Colonies and Planters are briefly Considered . . . with some Hints respecting America*. London, 1775.

Anon., *Political Balance*

Anonymous. *The Political Balance in which the Principles and Conduct of the Two Parties are weighed*. London, 1765.

Anon., *Political Catechism*

Anonymous. *A Political Catechism, for the Instructions of those who have made the late Protestations concerning the Power and Privileges of Parliament*. [London, 1740?]. (Huntington Library Rare Book #406290, title page missing, but identified as a reprint of a seventeenth-century political catechism by Henry Parker.)

Anon., *Political Conduct of Chatham*

Anonymous. *The Political Conduct of the Earl of Chatham*. London, 1769.

Anon., *Political Disquisitions*

Anonymous. *Political Disquisitions Proper for Public Consideration in the Present State of Affairs in a Letter to a Noble Duke*. London, 1763.

Anon., *Political Mirror or Summary Review*
Anonymous. *A Political Mirror; or, a Summary Review of the Present Reign. With Notes, Explanatory and Historical, and an Authentic List of the Ships and Vessels of War, Taken and Destroyed, Since the Commencement of Hostilities.* London, 1779.

Anon., *Present Dangerous Crisis*
Anonymous. *Considerations on the Present Dangerous Crisis.* Second Edition. London, 1763. (See also [Ruffhead], *Considerations.*)

Anon., *Privileges of Jamaica*
Anonymous. *The Privileges of the Island of Jamaica Vindicated; with an Impartial Narrative of the Late Dispute Between the Governor and House of Representatives, Upon the Case of Mr. Olyphant, A Member of that House.* London, 1766.

Anon., *Proposition for Peace*
Anonymous. *A Proposition for the Present Peace and Future Government of the British Colonies in North America.* London, [1775].

Anon., *Prospect of the Consequences*
Anonymous. *A Prospect of the Consequences of the Present Conduct of Great Britain Towards America.* London, 1776.

Anon., *Protest of a Private Person*
Anonymous. *An Address to the People of England: Being the Protest of a Private Person Against every Suspension of Law that is liable to injure or endanger Personal Security.* London, 1778.

Anon., *Reflections on the Contest*
Anonymous. *Reflections on the American Contest: In which the Consequence of a Formal Submission, and the Means of a Lasting Reconciliation are pointed out, Communicated by Letter to a Member of Parliament, Some Time Since, and now Addressed to Edmund Burke, Esq.* London, 1776.

Anon., *Resistance No Rebellion*
Anonymous. *Resistance No Rebellion: In Answer to Doctor Johnson's Taxation no Tyranny.* London, 1775.

Anon., *Rights Asserted*
Anonymous. *The Rights of the People Asserted, and the Necessity of a More Equal Representation in Parliament Stated and Proved.* Dublin, 1783.

Anon., *Second Letter to Member*
Anonymous. *A Second Letter to a Member of Parliament Concerning the Present State of Affairs.* London, 1741.

Anon., *Secret Springs*
Anonymous. *The Secret Springs of the Late Changes in the Ministry Fairly Explained, by an Honest Man.* London, 1766.

Anon., *Sequel to Essay*
Anonymous. *Sequel to an Essay on the Origin and Progress of Government.* London, 1783.

Anon., *Serious Address*
Anon.. *Serious Address to the People of Great Britain. In which the Certain Consequences of the Present Rebellion, are fully demonstrated.* London, 1745.

Anon., *Serious and Impartial Observations*
Anonymous. *Serious and Impartial Observations on the Blessings of Liberty and Peace. Addressed to Persons of all Parties. Inviting them also to enter into that Grand ASSOCIATION, which is able to secure the Safety and Happiness of the BRITISH EMPIRE.* London, 1776.

Anon., *Serious Exhortation*
Anonymous. *A Serious Exhortation to the Electors of Great Britain: Wherein the Importance of the approaching Elections is particularly proved from our present Situation both at Home and Abroad.* London, 1740.

Anon., *Short and Friendly Caution*
Anonymous. *A Short and Friendly Caution to the Good People of England.* London, 1766.

Anon., *Some Seasonable Observations*
Anonymous. *Some Seasonable Observations and Remarks upon the State of our Controversy with Great Britain; And on the Proceedings of the Continental Congress: Whereby many interesting Facts are related, and Methods proposed for our Safety and an Accommodation.* [Boston,] 1775.

Anon., *To Committee of London Merchants*
Anonymous. *A Letter to the Gentlemen of the Committee of London Merchants Trading to North America: Shewing in what Manner, it is apprehended, that the Trade and Manufactures of Britain may be effected by some late Restrictions on the American Commerce. . . .* London, 1766.

Anon., *To Electors of Philadelphia*
Anonymous. *To the Electors and Freeholders of the City of Philadelphia.* Broadside [Philadelphia, 1774].

Anon., *To the Princess of Wales*
Anonymous. *A Letter to Her R[oya]l H[ighness]s the P[rinces]s D[o]w[a]g[e]r of W[ales] on the Approaching Peace. With a few Words Concerning the Right Honourable the Earl of B[ute], and the General Talk of the World.* 3d ed. London, 1762.

Anon., *Treatise on Government*
Anonymous. *A Treatise on Government: Being a Review of the Doctrine*

*of an Original Contract. More particularly as it respects the Rights of Government, and the Duty of Allegiance.* London, 1750.

Anon., *True Merits of Common Sense*
Anonymous. *The True Merits of a Late Treatise, printed in America, Intitled, Common Sense, Clearly Pointed Out. Addressed to the Inhabitants of America. By a late Member of the Continental Congress, a Native of a Republican State.* London, 1776.

Anon., *Vindication of the Livery*
Anonymous. *A Vindication of the Petition of the Livery of the City of London, to His Majesty, as to the Charge upon the Ministry of raising a Revenue in our Colonies by Prerogative.* n.i., 1769.

Anon., *Vox Populi*
Anonymous. *Vox Populi, Or Old England's Glory or Destruction, in One Thousand, Seven Hundred, and Seventy-Four; Being a Choice Collection of Hints, Found in the Cabinet of a late worthy and noble Lord, To the Free-Holders of Great Britain in their Choice of Members to serve in Parliament at the ensuing General Election.* London, 1774.

Anon., *What Should be Done*
Anonymous. *What Should be Done: or, Remarks on the Political State of Things. Addressed to the Present Administration, the Members of the House of Commons, and the Good People of England.* London, 1766.

Anon., *Whigs and Jacobites*
Anonymous. *The Spirit and Principles of the Whigs and Jacobites Compared. Being the Substance of a Discourse delivered to an Audience of Gentlemen at Edinburgh, December 22, 1745.* London, 1746.

Anon., *With Respect to America*
Anonymous. *Reflections on Government, With Respect to America. To which is Added, Carmen Latinum.* London, 1766.

Appleby, *Capitalism*
Joyce Appleby. *Capitalism and a New Social Order: The Republican Vision of the 1790s.* New York, 1984.

Appleby, "Republicanism"
Joyce Appleby. "Republicanism in Old and New Contexts." 43 *William and Mary Quarterly* (1986):20–34.

Aptheker, *Revolution*
Herbert Aptheker. *The American Revolution 1763–1783.* New York, 1960.

Arbuthnot, *Freeholder's Catechism*
[John] Arbuthnot. *The Freeholder's Political Catechism. Written by Dr. Arbuthnot.* [London,] 1769.

[Auckland], *Principles of Penal Law*
[William E. Auckland.] *Principles of Penal Law.* 2d ed. London, 1771.

*Authority of Rights*
> John Phillip Reid. *Constitutional History of the American Revolution: The Authority of Rights.* Madison, Wis., 1986.

*Authority to Tax*
> John Phillip Reid. *Constitutional History of the American Revolution: The Authority to Tax.* Madison, Wis., 1987.

[Baillie], *Appendix to a Letter*
> [Hugh Baillie.] *An Appendix to a Letter to Dr. Shebbeare. To which are added, Some Observations on a Pamphlet, Entitled, Taxation no Tyranny; In which the Sophistry of the Author's Reasoning is Detected.* London, 1775.

Baillie, *Letter to Shebear*
> Hugh Baillie. *A Letter to Dr. Shebear: Containing a Refutation of his Arguments Concerning the Boston and Quebec Acts of Parliament: and his Aspersions upon the Memory of King William, and the Protestant Dissenters.* London, 1775.

[Baillie], *Some Observations on a Pamphlet*
> [Hugh Baillie.] *Some Observations on a Pamphlet Lately Published, Entitled the Rights of Great-Britain Asserted against the Claims of America, Being an Answer to the Declaration of the General Congress.* London, 1776.

Bailyn, *Ideological Origins*
> Bernard Bailyn. *The Ideological Origins of the American Revolution.* Cambridge, Mass., 1967.

Bailyn, *Origins of Politics*
> Bernard Bailyn. *The Origins of American Politics.* New York, 1968.

Bailyn, *Pamphlets*
> *Pamphlets of the American Revolution, 1750–1776.* Edited by Bernard Bailyn. Vol. 1. Cambridge, Mass., 1965.

Bailyn, "Year of Challenge"
> Bernard Bailyn. "1776: A Year of Challenge—A World Transformed." 19 *Journal of Law and Economics* (1976):437–66.

Baker, *English Legal History*
> John H. Baker. *An Introduction to English Legal History.* 2d ed. London, 1979.

Baldwin, *New England Clergy*
> Alice M. Baldwin. *The New England Clergy and the American Revolution.* Durham, N.C., 1928.

[Bancroft], *Remarks*
> [Edward Bancroft.] *Remarks on the Review of the Controversy Between Great Britain and her Colonies. In which the Errors of its Author are exposed, and the Claims of the Colonies vindicated, Upon the Evidence of Historical Facts and authentic records.* London, 1769.

Banks, *York*
  Charles Edward Banks. *History of York Maine.* 1967 ed. Vol. 1.
Banning, *Jeffersonian Persuasion*
  Lance Banning. *The Jeffersonian Persuasion: Evolution of a Party
  Ideology.* Ithaca, N.Y., 1978.
Barker, *Essays*
  Ernest Barker. *Essays on Government.* Oxford, England, 2d ed. 1951.
Barnard, *Election Sermon*
  Thomas Barnard. *A Sermon Preached before his Excellency Francis
  Bernard, Esq.; Governor and Commander in Chief, the Honourable
  His Majesty's Council, and the Honourable House of Representatives,
  of the Province of the Massachusetts-Bay in New-England, May 25th.
  1763. Being the Anniversary for the Election of His Majesty's Council
  for said Province.* Boston, 1763.
Barnes, *Dominion of New England*
  Viola Florence Barnes. *The Dominion of New England: A Study in
  British Colonial Policy.* New Haven, Conn., 1923.
Benton, *Whig-Loyalism*
  William Allen Benton. *Whig-Loyalism: An Aspect of Political Ideology
  in the American Revolutionary Era.* Rutherford, N.J., 1969.
Berlin, *Essays*
  Isaiah Berlin. *Four Essays on Liberty.* Oxford, England, 1969.
[Bernard], *Appeal to the Public*
  [Thomas Bernard.] *An Appeal to the Public; Stating and Considering
  the Objections to the Quebec Bill.* London, 1774.
[Blacklock], *Remarks on Liberty*
  [Thomas Blacklock.] *Remarks on the Nature and Extent of Liberty, as
  compatible with the Genius of Civil Societies; On the Principles of
  Government and the proper Limits of its Powers in Free States; And, on
  the Justice and Policy of the American War. Occasioned by Perusing the
  Observations of Dr. Price on these Subjects. In a Letter to a Friend.*
  Edinburgh, 1776.
Blackstone, *Commentaries*
  William Blackstone. *Commentaries on the Laws of England.* 4 vols.
  Oxford, England, 1765–69.
Blackstone, *Tracts*
  William Blackstone. *Tracts, Chiefly Relating to the Antiquities and
  Laws of England.* 3d ed. Oxford, England, 1771.
[Bolingbroke], *Dissertation*
  [Henry Saint John, 1st Viscount Bolingbroke.] *A Dissertation Upon
  Parties; In Several Letters to Caleb D'Anvers, Esq.* 3d ed. London,
  1735.
[Bolingbroke], *Freeholder's Catechism*

[Henry Saint John, 1st Viscount Bolingbroke.] *The Freeholder's Political Catechism. Very Necessary to be Studied by every Freeman in America.* New London, Conn., 1769.

[Bollan], *Continued Corruption*

[William Bollan.] *Continued Corruption, Standing Armies, and Popular Discontents Considered; And the Establishment of the English Colonies in America, with Various subsequent Proceedings, and the Present Contests, examined, with Intent to promote their cordial and perpetual Union with their Mother-Country, for their Mutual Honour, Comfort, Strength, and Safety.* London, 1768.

Bonwick, *English Radicals*

Colin Bonwick. *English Radicals and the American Revolution.* Chapel Hill, N.C., 1977.

Boorstin, *Mysterious Science of Law*

Daniel J. Boorstin. *The Mysterious Science of the Law: An Essay on Blackstone's COMMENTARIES Showing how Blackstone, Employing Eighteenth-Century Ideas of Science, Religion, History, Aesthetics, and Philosophy, Made of the Law at Once a Conservative and a Mysterious Science.* Cambridge, Mass., 1941.

*Boston Evening-Post*

*The Boston Evening-Post.* [weekly newspaper.]

*Boston Gazette*

*The Boston Gazette and Country Journal.* [weekly newspaper.]

*Boston News-Letter*

*The Massachusetts Gazette and Boston News-Letter,* also sometimes *The Massachusetts Gazette and the Boston News-Letter,* or *The Boston News-Letter.* [weekly newspaper.]

*Boston Post-Boy*

*The Boston Post-Boy & Advertiser.* [weekly newspaper.]

*Boston Town Records*

*A Report of the Record Commissioners of the City of Boston, Containing the Boston Town Records, 1758 to 1769.* 16th Report. Boston, 1886. *A Report of the Record Commissioners of the City of Boston, Containing the Boston Town Records, 1770 Through 1777.* 18th Report. Boston, 1887.

Botein, "Religion and Politics"

Stephen Botein. "Religion and Politics in Revolutionary New England: Natural Rights Reconsidered." In *Party and Political Opposition in Revolutionary America.* Edited by Patricia U. Bonomi. Tarrytown, New York, 1980, at 13–34.

Boucher, *Causes and Consequences*

Jonathan Boucher. *A View of the Causes and Consequences of the American Revolution; in Thirteen Discourses, Preached in North*

*America between the Years 1763 and 1775: With an Historical Preface.* London, 1797.

[Boucher], *Letter from a Virginian*
[Jonathan Boucher.] *A Letter From A Virginian to the Members of the Congress to be held at Philadelphia on the first of September, 1774.* [Boston,] 1774.

Bracton, *Laws and Customs*
Henry de Bracton. *On the Laws and Customs of England.* Translated and Edited by Samuel E. Thorne. 5 vols. Cambridge, Mass., 1968–.

Brewer, *Party Ideology*
John Brewer. *Party Ideology and Popular Politics at the Accession of George III.* Cambridge, England, 1976.

Brewer, *English Radicalism*
John Brewer. "English Radicalism in the Age of George III." In *Three British Revolutions: 1641, 1688, 1776,* edited by J. G. A. Pocock, at 323–67. Princeton, N.J., 1980.

Brewer, "Wilkites and the law"
John Brewer. "The Wilkites and the law, 1763–74: a study of radical notions of governance." In *An Ungovernable People: The English and their Law in the Seventeenth and Eighteenth Centuries.* Edited by John Brewer and John Styles, at 128–71. New Brunswick, N.J., 1980.

*Briefs of American Revolution*
*The Briefs of the American Revolution: Constitutional Arguments Between Thomas Hutchinson, Governor of Massachusetts Bay, and James Bowdoin for the Council and John Adams for the House of Representatives.* Edited by John Phillip Reid. New York, 1981.

Brisco, *Economic Policy of Walpole*
Norris A. Brisco. *The Economic Policy of Robert Walpole.* New York, 1907.

[Brooke], *Liberty and Common Sense*
[Henry Brooke.] *Liberty and Common Sense to the People of Ireland, Greeting.* London, 1760.

[Brooke], *Liberty and Common Sense: Letter II*
[Henry Brooke.] *Liberty and Common-Sense to the People of Ireland, Greeting: Letter II.* Dublin, 1760.

[Brown], *Civil Liberty*
[John Brown.] *Thoughts on Civil Liberty, on Licentiousness, and Faction.* 2d ed. London, 1765.

Brown, *Estimate of Manners*
John Brown. *An Estimate of the Manners and Principles of the Times.* 7th ed. Boston, 1758.

Brown, *Middle-Class Democracy*

Robert E. Brown. *Middle-Class Democracy and the Revolution in Massachusetts, 1691–1780.* Ithaca, N.Y., 1955.

Browning, *Court Whigs*
Reed Browning. *Political and Constitutional Ideas of the Court Whigs.* Baton Rouge, La., 1982.

Burgh, *Political Disquisitions*
J. Burgh. *Political Disquisitions; or, An Enquiry into public Errors, Defects, and Abuses. Illustrated by, and established upon Facts and Remarks, extracted from a Variety of Authors, Ancient and Modern.* 3 vols. Philadelphia, 1775.

*Burke on American Revolution*
*Edmund Burke on the American Revolution: Selected Speeches and Letters.* Edited by Elliot Robert Barkan. New York, 1966.

Burke, *Writings & Speeches*
*The Writings & Speeches of Edmund Burke in Twelve Volumes.* Beaconsfield edition. New York, 1901.

Burlamaqui, *Politic Law*
J. J. Burlamaqui. *The Principles of Politic Law: Being a Sequel to the Principles of Natural Law.* London, 1752.

[Burnet], *Coronation Sermon*
[Gilbert Burnet.] *A Sermon Preached at the Coronation of William III. and Mary II. King and Queen of England, --- France, and Ireland, Defenders of the Faith; in the Abby-Church of Westminster, April 11, 1689.* London, 1689.

[Burnet], *Sermon at Salisbury*
Gilbert [Burnet.] *A Sermon Preach'd in the Cathedral-Church of Salisbury, on the 29th Day of May, in the Year 1710.* London, 1710.

Burscough, *Abuse of Liberty*
William Burscough. *The Abuse of Liberty. A Sermon Preach'd before the Honourable House of Commons, on the 5th of November, 1722.* London, 1722.

*Cambridge Magazine*
*The Cambridge Magazine: or Universal Repository of Arts, Sciences, and the Belle Letters. For the Year MDCCLXIX.* London, 1769.

Campbell, *Duty of Allegiance*
George Campbell. *The Nature, Extent, and Importance, of the Duty of Allegiance: A Sermon Preached at Aberdeen, December 12, 1776, Being the Fast Day Appointed by the King, on Account of the Rebellion in America.* Aberdeen, 1777.

Campbell, *Lives of Chancellors*
John Lord Campbell. *The Lives of the Lord Chancellors and Keepers of*

*the Great Seal of England, From the Earliest Times till Reign of George IV.* Vol. 5. London, 1846.

Campbell, *Nature*

George Campbell. *The Nature, Extent, and Importance, of the Duty of Allegiance: A Sermon, Preached at Aberdeen, December 12, 1776, Being the Fast Day Appointed by the King, on Account of the Rebellion in America.* 2d ed. Aberdeen, 1778.

Campbell, *Political Survey*

John Campbell. *A Political Survey of Britain: Being a Series of Reflections on the Situation, Lands, Inhabitants, Revenues, Colonies, and Commerce of this Island. Intended to Shew that we have not yet approached near the Summit of Improvement, but that it will afford Employment to many Generations before they push to their utmost Extent the natural Advantages of Great Britain. In Two Volumes.* London, 1774.

Candidus, *Two Letters*

Mystagogus Candidus. *Two Letters: viz. I. A Letter to the Earl of Abingdon, in which his Grace of York's Notions of Civil Liberty are Examined by Liberalis; published in the London Evening Post, November 6th, 1777. II. Vera Icon; or a Vindication of his Grace of York's Sermon, preached on February 21st, 1777.* London, [1777].

Canning, *Letter to Hillsborough*

George Canning. *A Letter to the Right Honourable Wills Earl of Hillsborough, on the Connection Between Great Britain and her American Colonies.* Dublin, 1768.

[Care], *English Liberties First Edition*

[Henry Care.] *English Liberties: Or, the Free-Born Subject's Inheritance, Containing I. MAGNA CHARTA, The Petition of Right, The Habeas Corpus Act; and divers other most Useful Statutes: With Large Comments upon each of them.* London, 1774.

Carlyle, *Political Liberty*

A. J. Carlyle. *Political Liberty: A History of the Conception in the Middle Ages and Modern Times.* Oxford, 1941.

Carroll, "First Citizen"

Charles Carroll. "First Citizen." Reprinted in *Maryland and the Empire, 1773: The Antilon-First Citizen Letters,* edited by Peter S. Onuf. Baltimore, 1974.

[Cartwright], *American Independence*

[John Cartwright.] *American Independence the Interest and Glory of Great Britain; Containing Arguments which prove that not only in Taxation, but in Trade, Manufactures, and Government, the Colonies are entitled to an entire Independency on the British Legislature; and* that it can only by a formal Declaration of these Rights. and forming thereupon a friendly League with them, that the true and lasting Welfare of both Countries can be promoted. In a Series of Letters to the Legislature. Philadelphia, 1776.

Cartwright, *Appeal Civil and Military*

John Cartwright. *An Appeal Civil and Military on the Subject of the English Constitution.* London, 1799.

Cartwright, *Appeal on Constitution*

John Cartwright. *An Appeal on the Subject of the English Constitution.* Boston, England, [1797].

Cartwright, *Constitution Produced*

John Cartwright. *The English Constitution Produced and Illustrated.* London, 1823.

Cartwright, *Legislative Rights*

John Cartwright. *The Legislative Rights of the Commonalty Vindicated; or, Take Your Choice! Representation and Respect: Imposition and Contempt: Annual Parliaments and Liberty: Long Parliaments and Slavery.* 2d ed. London, 1776.

Cartwright, *People's Barrier*

John Cartwright. *The People's Barrier Against Undue Influence and Corruption: Or the Commons' House of Parliament According to the Constitution.* London, 1780.

Cartwright, *Postscript*

John Cartwright. *The Postscript to Major Cartwright's Reply to Soame Jenyns, Esq; Humbly Recommended to the Perusal of Lord North's Admirers, Previous to His Lordship's Next Speech Against a Parliamentary Reform.* London, 1785.

[Cary], *Answer to Molyneux*

[John Cary.] *An Answer to Mr. Molyneux His Case of Ireland's being bound by Acts of Parliament in England, Stated: and His Dangerous Notion of Ireland's being under no Subordination to the Parliamentary Authority of England Refuted; By Reasoning from his own Arguments and Authorities.* London, 1698.

Carysfort, *Thoughts on Constitution*

Lord Carysfort [John Joshua Proby, first earl of Carysfort]. *Thoughts on the Constitution with a View to the Proposed Reform in the Representation of the People, and Duration of Parliaments.* London, 1783.

*Cato's Letters*

*Cato's Letters: or, Essays on Liberty, Civil and Religious, And other Important Subjects. In Four Volumes.* 6th ed. London, 1755.

[Chalmers], *Answer from Bristol to Burke*

[George Chalmers.] *An Answer from the Electors of Bristol to the*

*Letter of Edmund Burke, Esq. on teh [sic] Affairs of America.* London, 1777.

[Chalmers], *Plain Truth*

[James Chalmers.] *Plain Truth; Addressed to the Inhabitants of America, Containing, Remarks on a late Pamphlet, entitled Common Sense. Wherein are shewn, that the Scheme of Independence is Ruinous, Delusive, and Impracticable: That were the Author's Asseverations, Respecting the Power of America, as Real as Nugatory; Reconciliation on liberal Principles with Great Britain, would be exalted Policy: And that circumstanced as we are, Permanent Liberty, and True Happiness, can only be obtained by Reconciliation with that Kingdom.* Philadelphia, 1776.

Champion, *Connecticut Election Sermon*

Judah Champion. *Christian and Civil Liberty and Freedom Considered and Recommended: A Sermon Delivered before the General Assembly of the Colony of Connecticut, at Hartford, on the Day of their Anniversary Election, May 9th, 1776.* Hartford, Conn., 1776.

Champion, *Reflections on Parties*

J. Champion. *Reflections on the State of Parties; on the National Debt, and the Necessity and Expediency of Suppressing the American Rebellion.* 2d ed. London, 1776.

Chaplin, *Civil State*

Ebenezer Chaplin. *Civil State compared to Rivers, all under GOD's controul, and what People have to do when Administration is grievous. In a Discourse Delivered in Sutton, 2d Parish, January 17, 1773. Being the Day preceeding the Town Meeting, Which then stood Adjourned to consider and act upon the LETTER, &c. from Boston.* Boston, 1773.

Charles, Bishop of St. David's, *Sermon to Lords*

Charles, Lord Bishop of St. David's. *A Sermon Preached before the House of Lords, in the Abbey Church of St. Peter, Westminster, on Monday, January 30, 1769, Being the Day Appointed to be Observed as the Day of the Martyrdom of King Charles I.* London, 1769.

Charles I, *Several Speeches*

Charles I. *Several Speeches Delivered by His Majesty to the two Houses of Westminster, And at other Places, since the beginning of this Parliament.* [c. 1647].

Chauncy, *Civil Magistrates*

Charles Chauncy. *Civil Magistrates must be just, ruling in the Fear of God. A Sermon Preached before His Excellency William Shirley, Esq; the Honourable His Majesty's Council, and House of Representatives, of the Province of the Massachusetts-Bay in N. England; May 27, 1747. Being the Anniversary for the Election of His Majesty's Council for the said Province.* Boston, 1747.

*Clarendon's History Compleated*
> The Lord Clarendon's History of the Grand Rebellion Compleated. 3d
> ed. corrected. Dublin, 1720.

[Claridge], *Defence of Government*
> [Richard Claridge.] *A Defence of the Present Government under King*
> *William & Queen Mary. Shewing the Miseries of England under the*
> *Arbitrary Reign of the Late King James, II.* London, 1689.

Clark, *British Opinion*
> Dora Mae Clark. *British Opinion and the American Revolution.* New
> Haven, Conn., 1930.

*Collection of Irish Letters*
> *A Collection of the Letters which have been addressed to the Volunteers*
> *of Ireland, on the subject of a Parliamentary Reform.* London, 1783.

*Collection of Letters*
> *A New and Impartial Collection of Interesting Letters, from the Public*
> *Papers; Many of them Written by Persons of Eminence, On a great*
> *Variety of Important Subjects, which Have occasionally engaged the*
> *Public Attention: From the Accession of his present Majesty, in*
> *September 1765, [sic] to May 1767. In Two Volumes.* London, 1772.

*Collection of Political Tracts*
> *A Collection of Political Tracts.* Edinburgh, 1747.

*Colonial Records of Connecticut*
> *The Public Records of the Colony of Connecticut.* . . . Edited by
> Charles J. Hoadly. Vols. 12, 13, 14, 15. Hartford, Conn., 1881–90.

*Commemoration Ceremony*
> *Commemoration Ceremony in Honor of the Two Hundredth*
> *Anniversary of the First Continental Congress in the United States*
> *House of Representatives.* House Document No. 93-413. 93d
> Congress, 2d Session. Washington, 1975.

*Commons Debates 1628*
> *Commons Debates 1628.* Edited by Robert C. Johnson, Mary Frear
> Keeler, Maija Cole, and William B. Bidwell. 6 vols. New Haven,
> Conn., 1977–1983.

*Complete Collection of Wilkes*
> *A Complete Collection of the Genuine Papers, Letters, &c. in the Case*
> *of John Wilkes, Esq. Elected Knight of Shire of the County of Middlesex.*
> Berlin, [1768].

Cook, *Codification Movement*
> Charles Malcolm Cook. *The American Codification Movement: A*
> *Study of Antebellum Legal Reform.* Westport, Conn., 1981.

Cook, *King Charles his Case*
> John Cook. *King Charles his Case; or, an Appeal to all rational Men,*
> *concerning his Tryal at the High Court of Justice: Being, for the most*

part, that which was intended to have been delivered at the Bar, if the King had pleaded to the Charge, and put himself upon a fair Tryal. 1649. Reprinted in 5 *Somers' Tracts*, at 214–37.

Cook, *King Charls his Case*
John Cook. *King Charl[e]s his Case, an Appeal to all Rational Men, Concerning his Tryal at the High Court of Justice. Being for the most part that which was intended to have been delivered at the Bar, if the King had Pleaded to the Charge, and put himself upon a fair Tryal.* London, 1649.

Cooke, *Election Sermon*
Samuel Cooke. *A Sermon Preached at Cambridge in the Audience of his Honor Thomas Hutchinson, Esq; Lieutenant-Governor and Commander in Chief; The Honorable His Majesty's Council, and the Honorable House of Representatives, of the Province of the Massachusetts-Bay in New-England, May 30th, 1770. Being the Anniversay of the Election of His Majesty's Council for the Said Province.* Boston, 1770.

[Cooper], *Crisis*
[Samuel Cooper.] *The Crisis.* [Boston], 1754.

*Correspondence of George III*
*The Correspondence of King George the Third From 1760 to December 1783.* Vol. *1 1760–1767.* Vol. *2 1768–June 1773.* Vol. *3 July 1773–December 1777.* Vol. *4 1778–1779.* Edited by Sir John Fortescue. London, 1927–28.

Courtney, *Montesquieu and Burke*
C. P. Courtney. *Montesquieu and Burke.* Westport, Conn., 1975.

Cover, *Justice Accused*
Robert M. Cover. *Justice Accused: Antislavery and the Judicial Process.* New Haven, Conn., 1975.

*Craftsman*
*The Craftsman.* Vols. 8–14. London, 1737.

Cragg, *Freedom and Authority*
Gerald R. Cragg. *Freedom and Authority: A Study of English Thought in the Seventeenth Century.* Philadelphia, 1975.

*Critical Review*
*The Critical Review: Or Annals of Literature. By a Society of Gentlemen.* London [Monthly magazine].

Cumings, *Thanksgiving Sermon*
Henry Cumings. *A Thanksgiving Sermon Preached at Billerica, November 27, 1766.* Boston, 1767.

*Dartmouth American Papers*
*Historical Manuscripts Commission. Fourteenth Report, Appendix,*

Part X. *The Manuscripts of the Earl of Dartmouth. Vol. II. American Papers.* London, 1895.

Davis, *Reports*
Sir John Davis [Davies]. *Les Reports Des Cases & Matters en Ley, Resolves & Adjudges en les Courts del Roy en Ireland.* London, 1674.

"Declaration of 1689"
"The Declaration of the Gentlemen, Merchants, and Inhabitants of Boston, and the Country Adjacent. April 18, 1689." Reprinted in 1 *The Andros Tracts,* at 11–20. Prince Society Publication, Vol. 5. Boston, 1868.

De Lolme, *Constitution*
J. L. De Lolme. *The Constitution of England: or, an Account of the English Government: in which it is Compared Both with the Republican Form of Government, and the Other Monarchies in Europe.* A New Edition. London, 1821.

De Lolme, *Constitution: New Edition*
J. L. De Lolme. *The Constitution of England; or, an Account of the English Government; in which it is Compared Both with the Republican Form of Government, and the Other Monarchies in Europe.* New ed. London, 1807.

De Pinto, *Letters on Troubles*
M. De Pinto. *Letters on the American Troubles; Translated From the French.* London, 1776.

Dickerson, "Writs"
O. M. Dickerson. "Writs of Assistance as a Cause of the Revolution." In *The Era of the American Revolution,* edited by Richard B. Morris, at 40–75. New York, 1939.

Dickinson, *Connecticut Election Sermon*
Moses Dickinson. *A Sermon Preached before the General Assembly of the Colony of Connecticut, at Hartford on the Day of the Anniversary Election, May 8th, 1755.* New London, 1755.

Dickinson, *Letters*
John Dickinson. *Letters from a Farmer in Pennsylvania to the Inhabitants of the British Colonies* (1768), reprinted in *The Writings of John Dickinson: Political Writings 1764–1774.* Edited by Paul Leicester Ford, at 305–406. Philadelphia, 1895.

Dickinson, *Liberty and Property*
H. T. Dickinson. *Liberty and Property: Political Ideology in Eighteenth-Century Britain.* London, 1977.

Dickinson, *Essay*
John Dickinson. *An Essay on the Constitutional Power of Great-Britain over the Colonies in America; with the Resolves of the Committee*

*For the Province of Pennsylvania, and their Instructions to their Representatives in Assembly.* Philadelphia, 1774.

Diggins, *Lost Soul*

John Patrick Diggins. *The Lost Soul of American Politics: Virtue, Self-Interest, and the Foundations of Liberalism.* Chicago, 1986.

Dobbs, *Letter to North*

Francis Dobbs. *A Letter to the Right Honourable Lord North on his Propositions in Favour of Ireland.* Dublin, 1780.

Dodgson, *Assize Sermon*

Charles [Dodgson], Lord Bishop of Ossory. *A Sermon Preached the 3d of August, 1766. In the Catheral Church of St. Canice. By the Right Reverend Charles, Lord Bishop of Ossory. And Published at the Request of the Judges of Assize, for the Leinster Circuit.* Dublin, 1766.

Dolins, *Third Charge to Middlesex Juries*

Sir Daniel Dolins. *The Third Charge of Sir Daniel Dolins, Kt. to the Grand-Jury, and other Juries of the County of Middlesex; At the General Quarter-Sessions of the Peace Held the Sixth Day of October, 1726. at Westminster-Hall.* London, 1726.

[Douglas], *Seasonable Hints*

[John Douglas.] *Seasonable Hints From an Honest Man On the Present Crisis of a New Reign and a New Parliament.* London, 1761.

[Drinker], *Observations on the Measures*

[John Drinker.] *Observations on the Late Popular Measures, Offered to the Serious Consideration of the Sober Inhabitants of Pennsylvania, By a Tradesman.* Philadelphia, 1774.

Duchal, *Sermons*

James Duchal. *Sermons Upon the Following Subject . . . .* 2d ed. Vol. 1. London, 1765.

Dulany, *English Laws*

Daniel Dulany, Senior. *The Right of the Inhabitants of Maryland to the Benefit of the English Laws.* 1728. Reprinted in 21 *Johns Hopkins University Studies in Historical and Political Science*, edited by J. M. Vincent, J. H. Hollander, and W. W. Willoughby. Baltimore, 1903.

Dummer, *Defence*

Jer[emiah] Dummer. *A Defence of the New-England Charters.* London, 1765.

Egerton, *American Revolution*

Hugh Edward Egerton. *The Causes and Character of the American Revolution.* Oxford, England, 1923.

[Egmont], *Faction Detected*

[John Perceval, 2d earl of Egmont.] *Faction Detected, By the Evidence of Facts. Containing an Impartial View of Parties at Home and Affairs Abroad.* 5th ed. London, 1743.

Ekirch, "North Carolina Regulators"
A. Roger Ekirch. "The North Carolina Regulators on Liberty and Corruption, 1766–1771." 11 *Perspectives in American History* (1977–1978):199–256.

Eliot, *Give Cesar His Due*
Jared Eliot. *Give Cesar his Due. Or, the Obligation that Subjects are under to their Civil Rulers, As was shewed in a Sermon Preach'd before the General Assembly of the Colony of Connecticut at Hartford, May the 11th, 1738. The Day for the Election of the Honourable the Governour, the Deputy-Governour, and the Worshipful Assistants.* New London, Conn., 1738.

Ellys, *Tracts on Liberty*
Anthony Ellys. *Tracts on the Liberty, Spiritual and Temporal, of the Subjects in England. Addressed to J. N. Esq; at Aix-la-Chapelle. Part II. [Of the Temporal Liberty of Subjects in England.]* London, 1765.

*Essex Result*
*Result of the Convention of Delegates Holden at Ipswich in the County of Essex, who were Deputed to take into Consideration the Constitution and form of Government Proposed by the Convention of the State of Massachusetts-Bay.* Newburyport, 1778.

Evans, *Constitutional Liberty*
Caleb Evans. *British Constitutional Liberty. A Sermon Preached in Broad-mead, Bristol, November 5, 1775.* Bristol, England, [1775].

[Evans], *Letter to John Wesley*
[Caleb Evans.] *A Letter to the Rev. Mr. John Wesley, Occasioned by his Calm Address to the American Colonies.* London, 1775.

Evans, *Political Sophistry detected*
Caleb Evans. *Political Sophistry detected, or, Brief Remarks on the Rev. Mr. Fletcher's late Tract, entitled "American Patriotism." In a Letter to a Friend.* London, 1776.

Evans, *Remembrance of Former Days*
Caleb Evans. *The Remembrance of Former Days. A Sermon Preached at Broad-Mead, Bristol, November 5, 1778.* 2d ed. Bristol, England, [1778].

Evans, *Reply to Fletcher*
Caleb Evans. *A Reply to the Rev. Mr. Fletcher's Vindication of Mr. Wesley's Calm Address to Our American Colonies.* Bristol, England, [1776].

[Ferguson], *Remarks on a Pamphlet*
[Adam Ferguson.] *Remarks on a Pamphlet lately Published by Dr. Price, Intitled, Observations on the Nature of Civil Liberty, the Principles of Government, and the Justice and Policy of the War with America, &c. In a Letter from a Gentleman in the Country to a Member of Parliament.* London, 1776.

Filmer, *Observations upon Aristotle*
> Robert Filmer. *Observations Upon Aristotles Politiques Touching Forms of Government Together with Directions for Obedience to Governours in dangerous and doubtfull Times.* 1652. Reprinted in *Patriarcha and other Political Works of Sir Robert Filmer*, edited by Peter Laslett, at 185–229. Oxford, England, 1949.

Fish, *Joy and Gladness*
> Elisha Fish. *Joy and Gladness: A Thanksgiving Discourse, Preached in Upton, Wednesday, May 28, 1766; Occasioned by the Repeal of the Stamp-Act.* Providence, R.I., 1767.

Fiske, *Importance of Righteousness*
> Nathan Fiske. *The Importance of Righteousness to the Happiness, and the Tendency of Oppression to the Misery of a People; illustrated in two Discourses Delivered at Brookfield, July 4. 1774.* Boston, 1774.

Fletcher, *Vindication of Wesley*
> John Fletcher. *A Vindication of the Rev. Mr. Wesley's "Calm Address to our American Colonies:" In Some Letters to Mr. Caleb Evans.* London, [1776].

Foner, *Tom Paine*
> Eric Foner. *Tom Paine and Revolutionary America.* New York, 1976.

Forster, *Northampton Assize Sermons*
> John Forster. *Two Sermons Preached at Northampton Assizes, April 7, and July 20, 1757.* Cambridge, 1757.

Foster, *Short Essay*
> Dan Foster. *A Short Essay on Civil Government, the Substance of Six Sermons, Preached in Windsor, Second Society, October 1774.* Hartford, Conn., 1775.

[Fowle], *Appendix to Eclipse*
> [Daniel Fowle.] *An Appendix to the late Total Eclipse of Liberty.* Boston, 1756.

Frank, "Sketch of an Influence"
> Jerome Frank. "A Sketch of an Influence." In *Interpretations of Modern Legal Philosophies: Essays in Honor of Roscoe Pound*, edited by Paul Sayre, at 189–261. New York, 1947.

*Franklin's Letters to Press*
> *Benjamin Franklin's Letters to the Press 1758–1775.* Edited by Verner W. Crane. Chapel Hill, N.C., 1950.

Frink, *Election Sermon*
> Thomas Frink. *A King reigning in Righteous, and Princes ruling in Judgment. A Sermon Preached before His Excellency Thomas Pownall, Esq.; Governour, the Honourable His Majesty's Council, and House of Representatives, of the Province of the Massachusetts-Bay, in New-England, May 31. 1758. Being the Anniversary for the Election of His Majesty's Council, for said Province.* Boston, 1758.

*Gazette & News-Letter*
    The Massachusetts Gazette and Boston News-Letter.
*Gazette & Post-Boy*
    The Massachusetts Gazette and Boston Post-Boy and the Advertiser.
*Gentleman's Magazine*
    The Gentleman's Magazine and Historical Chronicle. London
    [monthly magazine].
Gerard, *Liberty Cloke of Maliciousness*
    Alexander Gerard. *Liberty the Cloke of Maliciousness, both in the
    American Rebellion, and in the Manners of the Times. A Sermon
    Preached at Old Aberdeen, February 26, 1778, Being the Fast-Day
    appointed by Proclamation, on account of the Rebellion in America.*
    Aberdeen, Scotland, 1778.
[Goodricke], *Observations on Price's Theory*
    [Henry Goodricke.] *Observations on Dr. Price's Theory and Principles
    of Civil Liberty and Government, Preceded by a Letter to a Friend on
    the Pretensions of the American Colonies, in respect to Right and
    Equity.* York, England, 1776.
Gordon, *Discourse Preached*
    William Gordon. *A Discourse Preached December 15th 1774. Being the
    Day Recommended by the Provincial Congress; And Afterwards at the
    Boston Lecture.* Boston, 1775.
Gough, *Fundamental Law*
    J. W. Gough. *Fundamental Law in English Constitutional History.*
    Oxford, England, 1955.
[Grange], *Late Excise*
    [James Erskine, Lord Grange.] *The Late Excise Scheme Dissected: Or,
    an Exact Copy of the Late Bill, for Repealing several Subsidies, and an
    Impost, Now Payable on Tobacco, &c.* London, 1734.
[Grattan], *Mutiny Bill*
    [Henry Grattan.] *Observations on the Mutiny Bill: With Some
    Strictures on Lord Buckingham's Administration in Ireland* (London,
    1781), reprinted in *Miscellaneous Works of the Right Honourable
    Henry Grattan.* London, 1822.
Gray, *Doctor Price's Notions*
    John Gray. *Doctor Price's Notions of the Nature of Civil Liberty, Shewn
    to be Contradictory to Reason and Scripture.* London, 1777.
[Gray], *Right of the Legislature*
    [John Gray.] *The Right of the British Legislature to Tax the American
    Colonies Vindicated; and the Means of Asserting that Right Proposed.*
    London, 1774.
Greene, "Paine and Modernization"
    Jack P. Greene. "Paine, America, and the 'Modernization' of Political
    Consciousness." 93 *Political Science Quarterly* (1978):73–92.

Greene, "Review"
  Jack P. Greene. "Review." In *Revolution, Confederation, and Constitution*, edited by Stuart Gerry Brown, at 20–22. New York, 1971.
*Guide to Rights*
  *A Guide to the Knowledge of the Rights and Privileges of Englishmen.* London, 1757.
*Habersham Letters*
  *The Letters of Hon. James Habersham.* Collections of the Georgia Historical Society. Vol. 6. Savannah, Ga., 1904.
Hall, *Apology for Freedom*
  Robert Hall. *An Apology for the Freedom of the Press, and for General Liberty.* London, 1793.
Hallifax, *Sermon at St. Margaret's*
  Samuel Hallifax. *A Sermon Preached Before the Honourable House of Commons, at St. Margaret's, Westminster, on Monday, January 30, 1769; Appointed to be Observed as the Martyrdom of King Charles I.* Cambridge, England, 1769.
Hamilton, *Duty of Obedience to Laws*
  Hugh Hamilton. *The Duty of Obedience to the Laws and of Submission to Magistrates. A Sermon Occasioned by the Late Disturbances in the North of Ireland, Preached before the Judges of Assize in the Cathedral Church of Armagh, on Sunday, April 12, 1772.* London, 1772.
Harrington, *Commonwealth of Oceana*
  James Harrington. *The Commonwealth of Oceana.* 1656. Reprinted in *Political Works of James Harrington*, edited by J. G. A. Pocock, at 155–359. Cambridge, England, 1977.
Headlam, "Constitutional Struggle"
  Cecil Headlam. "The Constitutional Struggle With the American Colonies, 1765–1775." In *The Cambridge History of the British Empire. Vol. 1, The Old Empire From the Beginnings to 1783*, edited by J. Holland Rose, A. P. Newton, and E. A. Benians, at 646–84. Cambridge, England, 1929.
[Heath], *Case of Devon to Excise*
  [Benjamin Heath.] *The Case of the County of Devon, With Respect to the Consequences of the New Excise Duty on Cyder and Perry. Published by the Direction of the Committee appointed at the General Meeting of that County to superintend the Application for the Repeal of that Duty.* London, 1763.
Hexter, "Review Essay"
  J. H. Hexter. "Review Essay." 16 *History and Theory* (1977):306–37 [reviewing Pocock, *Machiavellian Moment*].
Hey, *Happiness and Rights*
  Richard Hey. *Happiness and Rights. A Dissertation Upon Several*

*Subjects Relative to the Rights of Man and his Happiness. Rights are Means: Happiness the End.* London, 1792.

Hey, *Observations on Civil Liberty*

Richard Hey. *Observations on the Nature of Civil Liberty, and the Principles of Government.* London, 1776.

*Hibernian Magazine*

*The Hibernian Magazine or Compendium of Entertaining Knowledge Containing The greatest Variety of the most Curious & useful Subjects in every Branch of Polite Literature.* Dublin [Monthly magazine].

Higginbotham, "Iredell and Origins"

Don Higginbotham. "James Iredell and the Origins of American Federalism." In *Perspectives on the American Revolution: A Bicentennial Contribution,* edited by George G. Suggs, Jr., at 99–115. Carbondale, Ill., 1977.

Hill, *Century of Revolution*

Christopher Hill. *The Century of Revolution 1603–1714.* New York, 1961.

Hill, *Upside Down*

Christopher Hill. *The World Turned Upside Down: Radical Ideas During the English Revolution.* Penguin ed. Harmondsworth, England, 1976.

Hind, *Sermon at St. Margaret's*

Richard Hind. *A Sermon Preached before the Honourable House of Commons; at St. Margaret's, Westminster: on Wednesday, January xxx. MDCCLXV.* London, 1765.

Hitchcock, *Sermon at Plymouth*

Gad Hitchcock. *A Sermon Preached at Plymouth December 22d, 1774. Being the Anniversary Thanksgiving, in Commemoration of the first Landing of our New-England Ancestors in that Place, Anno Dom 1620.* Boston, 1775.

Hitchcock, *Sermon Preached before Gage*

Gad Hitchcock. *A Sermon Preached Before his Excellency Thomas Gage, Esq; Governor: The Honorable His Majesty's Council, and the Honorable House of Representatives, of the Province of the Massachusetts-Bay in New-England, May 25th, 1774. Being the Anniversary of the Election of his Majesty's Council for said Province.* Boston, 1774.

Hoadly, *Works*

*The Works of Benjamin Hoadly, D.D. Successively Bishop of Bangor, Hereford, Salisbury, and Winchester.* 3 vols. London, 1773.

Hobbes, *De Cive*

Thomas Hobbes. *De Cive or the Citizen.* Edited by P. Lamprecht. New York, 1949.

Hobbes, *Leviathan*
Thomas Hobbes. *Leviathan or the Matter, Forme and Power of a Commonwealth Ecclesiasticall and Civil.* Edited by Michael Oakeshott. Oxford, England, n.d.

Hopkins, *Rights*
Stephen Hopkins. *The Rights of Colonies Examined.* 1765. Reprinted in Bailyn, *Pamphlets*, at 506–22.

Horwitz, *Transformation*
Morton J. Horwitz. *The Transformation of American Law, 1780–1860.* Cambridge, Mass., 1977.

[Howard], *Defence of the Letter*
[Martin Howard.] *A Defence of the Letter from a Gentleman at Halifax, to His Friend in Rhode-Island.* Newport, R.I., 1765.

Howard, *Election Sermon*
Simeon Howard. *A Sermon Preached before the Honorable Council and the Honorable House of Representatives of the State of Massachusetts-Bay, in New-England, May 31, 1780. Being the Anniversary for the Election of the Honorable Council.* 1780. Reprinted in *Pulpit of American Revolution*, at 355–96.

Hudson, "Penn's *English Liberties*"
Winthrop S. Hudson. "William Penn's *English Liberties: Tract for Several Times.*" 26 *William and Mary Quarterly* (1969):579–85.

Hume, *History*
David Hume. *The History of England From the Invasion of Julius Caesar to the Revolution in 1688.* New ed. Vols. 5 and 6. London, 1763.

Hunn, *Welfare of a Government*
Nathaniel Hunn. *The Welfare of a Government Considered. A Sermon Preach'd before the General Assembly of the Colony of Connecticut, at Hartford, on the Day of their Anniversary Election, May 14th, 1747.* New London, Conn., 1747.

[Ibbetson], *National Assemblies*
[James Ibbetson.] *A Dissertation on the National Assemblies Under the Saxon and Norman Governments.* London, 1781.

"In Accordance with Usage"
John Phillip Reid. "In Accordance with Usage: The Authority of Custom, the Stamp Act Debate, and the Coming of the American Revolution." 45 *Fordham Law Review* (1976):335–68.

*In a Defiant Stance*
John Phillip Reid. *In a Defiant Stance: The Conditions of the Law in Massachusetts Bay, the Irish Comparison, and the Coming of the American Revolution.* University Park, Pa., 1977.

"In an Inherited Way"
John Phillip Reid. "In an Inherited Way: English Constitutional Rights,

the Stamp Act Debates, and the Coming of the American Revolution." 49 *Southern California Law Review* (1976):1109–29.

*In Defiance of the Law*
John Phillip Reid. *In Defiance of the Law: The Standing-Army Controversy, the Two Constitutions, and the Coming of the American Revolution.* Chapel Hill, N.C., 1981.

"In Legitimate Stirps"
John Phillip Reid. "In Legitimate Stirps: The Concept of 'Arbitrary,' the Supremacy of Parliament, and the Coming of the American Revolution." 5 *Hofstra Law Review* (1977):459–99.

"In Our Contracted Sphere"
John Phillip Reid. "'In Our Contracted Sphere': The Constitutional Contract, the Stamp Act Crisis, and the Coming of the American Revolution." 76 *Columbia Law Review* (1976):21–47.

"In the First Line of Defense"
John Phillip Reid. "In the First Line of Defense: The Colonial Charters, the Stamp Act Debate, and the Coming of the American Revolution." 51 *New York University Law Review* (1976):177–215.

"In the Taught Tradition"
John Phillip Reid. "In the Taught Tradition: The Meaning of Law in Massachusetts-Bay Two Hundred Years Ago." 14 *Suffolk University Law Review* (1980):931–74.

Jacob, *New Law Dictionary*
Giles Jacob. *A New Law-Dictionary: Containing the Interpretation and Definition of Words and Terms used in the Law.* 8th ed. London, 1762.

Jedrey, *World of Cleaveland*
Christopher M. Jedrey. *The World of John Cleaveland: Family and Community in Eighteenth-Century New England.* New York, 1979.

Jensen, *Revolution Within*
Merrill Jensen. *The American Revolution, Within America.* New York, 1974.

[Johnson], *Some Important Observations*
[Stephen Johnson.] *Some Important Observations, Occasioned by, and adapted to, the Publick Fast, Ordered by Authority, December 18th, A.D. 1765.* Newport, R. I., 1766.

Johnstone, *Speech on American Affairs*
*Biblotheca Curiosa. Governor Johnston[e]'s Speech on American Affairs on the Address in answer to the King's Speech. 1776.* Edinburgh, 1885.

[Jones], *Constitutional Criterion*
[William Jones.] *The Constitutional Criterion: By a Member of the University of Cambridge.* London, 1768.

Jones, *Country and Court*

J. R. Jones. *Country and Court: England, 1658–1714.* Cambridge, Mass., 1978.

Jones, *Fear of God*
William Jones. *The Fear of God, and the Benefits of Civil Obedience. Two Sermons Preached in the Parish Church of Harwich in the County of Essex, on Sunday, June 21, 1778. And Published at the Request of the Audience.* London, 1778.

Jordan, *Men of Substance*
W. K. Jordan. *Men of Substance: A Study of the Thought of Two English Revolutionaries Henry Parker and Henry Robinson.* Chicago, 1942.

*Journal of Burgesses*
*Journals of the House of Burgesses of Virginia* Vol. 10, *1761–1765.* Vol. 11, *1766–1769.* Vol. 12, *1770–1772.* Vol. 13, *1773–1776. Including the records of the Committee of Correspondence.* Edited by John Pendleton Kennedy. Richmond, Va., 1905–7.

*Journal of the First Congress*
*Journals of the Continental Congress 1774–1789.* Vol. 1. Edited by Worthington Chauncey Ford. Washington, 1904.

Judson, "Henry Parker"
Margaret Atwood Judson. "Henry Parker and the Theory of Parliamentary Sovereignty." In *Essays in History and Political Theory in Honor of Charles Howard McIlwain,* at 138–67. Cambridge, Mass., 1936.

[Kames], *History of Man*
[Henry Home, Lord Kames.] *Sketches of the History of Man. In Two Volumes.* Edinburgh, 1774.

Kammen, *Spheres of Liberty*
Michael Kammen. *Spheres of Liberty: Changing Perceptions of Liberty in American Culture.* Madison, Wis., 1986.

Keith, *Papers and Tracts*
Sir William Keith. *A Collection of Papers and other Tracts, Written occasionally on Various Subjects.* 2d ed. London, 1749.

[Keld], *Polity of England*
[Christopher Keld.] *An Essay on the Polity of England.* London, 1785.

Kern, *Kingship*
Fritz Kern. *Kingship and Law in the Middle Ages.* Translated by S. B. Chrimes. Oxford, 1939.

Knollenberg, *Growth of Revolution*
Bernhard Knollenberg. *Growth of the American Revolution 1766–1775.* New York, 1975.

Koebner, *Empire*
Richard Koebner. *Empire.* London, 1961.

Kramnick, "Republican Revisionism"
> Isaac Kramnick. "Republican Revisionism Revisited." 87 *American Historical Review* (1982):629–64.

Kriegel, "Liberty and Whiggery"
> Abraham D. Kriegel. "Liberty and Whiggery in Early Nineteenth-Century England." 52 *Journal of Modern History* (1980):253–78.

Kurland, "Colonies, Parliament, and Crown"
> Philip B. Kurland. "The Colonies, the Parliament, and the Crown: The Constitutional Issues—Some Reflections of a Twentieth Century Lawyer." In *Political Separation and Legal Continuity: Papers prepared for the Bicentennial Observation of the American Bar Association and to be presented at the annual meeting of the Association in Atlanta, Georgia, on August 5–12, 1976*, at 35–72. n.i.

Langdon, *Government Corrupted*
> Samuel Langdon. *Government corrupted by Vice, and recovered by Righteousness. A Sermon Preached Before the Honorable Congress of the Colony of the Massachusetts-Bay in New-England, Assembled at Watertown, on Wednesday the 31st Day of May, 1775. Being the Anniversary fixed by Charter for the Election of Counsellors.* 1775. Reprinted in *The Pulpit of American Revolution*, at 227–58.

Langford, *Excise Crisis*
> Paul Langford. *The Excise Crisis: Society and Politics in the Age of Walpole.* Oxford, England, 1975.

Larkin, *Property in Eighteenth Century*
> Paschal Larkin. *Property in the Eighteenth Century with Special Reference to England and Locke.* Dublin and Cork, Ireland, 1930.

Laslett, "Introduction and Notes"
> Peter Laslett. "Introduction" and footnotes to John Locke, *Two Treatises of Government.* 2d ed. Edited by Peter Laslett. Cambridge, England, 1967.

Lediard, *Charge to Westminster Jury*
> Thomas Lediard. *A Charge Delivered to the Grand Jury at the Sessions of the Peace Held for the City and Liberty of Westminster, On Wednesday the 16th of October, 1754.* London, 1754.

[Leslie], *Right of Monarchy*
> [Charles Leslie.] *The Right of Monarchy Asserted; Wherein the Abstract of Dr. King's Book, With the Motives for the Reviving it at this Juncture are fully considered.* London, 1713.

*Letters between Wilkes*
> *Letters between the Duke of Grafton, the Earls of Halifax, Egremont, Chatham, Temple, and Talbot, Baron Bottetourt, Right Hon. Henry Bilson Legge, Right Hon. Sir John Cust, Bart. Mr. Charles Churchill,*

*Monsieur Voltaire, the Abbé Winckelman, &c. &c. and John Wilkes, Esq. With Explanatory Notes*. Vol. I. London, 1769.

Letters of Charles Carroll
  *Unpublished Letters of Charles Carroll of Carrollton, and of his Father, Charles Carroll of Doughoregan*. Edited by Thomas Meagher Field. New York, 1902.

Letters of Delegates to Congress
  *Letters of Delegates to Congress: 1774–1789*. 8 vols. Edited by Paul H. Smith. Washington, 1976–1981.

[Lind], *Letters to Price*
  [John Lind.] *Three Letters to Dr. Price, Containing Remarks on his Observations on the Nature of Civil Liberty, the Principles of Government, and the Justice and Policy of the War with America*. London, 1776.

Locke, *Two Treatises*
  John Locke. *Two Treatises of Government: A Critical Edition with an Introduction and Apparatus Criticus*. 2d ed. Edited by Peter Laslett. Cambridge, England, 1967.

Lockwood, *Worth and Excellence*
  James Lockwood. *The Worth and Excellence of Civil Freedom and Liberty illustrated, and a Public Spirit and the Love of our Country recommended. A Sermon Delivered before the General Assembly of the Colony of Connecticut, at Hartford, on the Day of the Anniversary Election. May 10th 1759*. New London, Conn., 1759.

Lofft, *Observations on Publication*
  Capel Lofft. *Observations on a late Publication, entitled "A Dialogue on the Actual State of Parliament," and also on a Treatise Entitled "Free Parliaments"*. London, 1783.

Lofft, *Observations on Wesley's Address*
  Capel Lofft. *Observations on Mr. Wesley's Second Calm Address, and Incidently on other Writings upon the American Question. Together with Thoughts on Toleration, and on the Point how Far the Conscience of the Subject is Concerned in a War; Remarks on Constitution in General, and that of England in Particular; on the Nature of Colonial Government, and a Recommendation of a Plan of Peace*. London, 1777.

Lofft, *Summary of Treatise*
  Capel Lofft. *A Summary of Treatise by Major Cartwright, entitled the People's Barrier Against Undue Influence: or the Commons' House of Parliament According to the Constitution*. [London], 1780.

London Magazine
  *The London Magazine or Gentleman's Monthly Intelligencer*. London [Monthly magazine].

Lowth, *Durham Assize Sermon*

Robert Lowth. *A Sermon Preached Before the Honourable and Right Reverend Richard, Lord Bishop of Durham, the Honourable Henry Bathurst, One of the Justices of the Court of Common Pleas, and the Honourable Sir Joseph Yates, One of the Justices of the Court of King's Bench; at the Assizes Holden at Durham, August 15, 1764.* 2d ed. Newcastle, England, 1764.

Lucas, *Divelina Libera*

Charles Lucas. *Divelina Libera: An Apology for the Civil Rights and Liberties of the Commons and Citizens of Dublin.* Dublin, 1744.

[Macfarlane], *George the Third*

[Robert Macfarlane.] *The History of the Reign of George the Third King of Great Britain, &c. to the Conclusion of Session of Parliament, ending in May, 1770.* London, 1770.

Maier, *Resistance*

Pauline Maier. *From Resistance to Revolution: Colonial Radicals and the Development of American Opposition to Britain, 1765–1776.* New York, 1973.

[Marat], *Chains of Slavery*

[J. P. Marat.] *The Chains of Slavery. A Work Wherein the Clandestine and Villainous Attempts of Princes to Ruin Liberty are Pointed Out, and the Dreadful Scenes of Despotism Disclosed. To which is prefixed, An Address to the Electors of Great Britain in order to draw their timely Attention to the Choice of proper Representatives in the next Parliament.* London, 1774.

*Massachusetts Gazette*

*The Massachusetts Gazette.* Boston [Weekly newspaper, printed with and generally filed with the *Boston Post-Boy*].

*Massachusetts Gazette & News-Letter*

*Massachusetts Gazette and Boston News-Letter.* Boston [Occasional name for *Boston News-Letter*].

*Massachusetts Provincial Congresses*

*The Journals of Each Provincial Congress of Massachusetts in 1774 and 1775, and of the Committee of Safety, with an Appendix, Containing the Proceedings of the County Conventions—Narratives of the Events of the Nineteenth of April, 1775—Papers Relating to Ticonderoga and Crown Point, and Other Documents, Illustrative of the Early History of the American Revolution.* Boston, 1838.

*Massachusetts Representatives Journal*

*Journal of the Honourable House of Representatives, Of His Majesty's Province of the Massachusetts-Bay, in New-England, Begun and held at Concord, in the County of Middlesex, on Wednesday the Thirtieth Day of May, Annoque Domni, 1764.* Boston, 1764.

*Massacre Orations*

*Orations Delivered at the Request of the Inhabitants of the Town of Boston to Commemorate the Evening of the Fifth of March, 1770; When a Number of Citizens were Killed by a Party of British Troops, Quartered Among them, in a Time of Peace.* Boston, 1785.

[Mather], *America's Appeal*

[Moses Mather.] *America's Appeal to the Impartial World. Wherein the Rights of the Americans, as Men, British Subjects, and as Colonists; the Equity of the Demand, and of the Manner in which it is made upon them by Great-Britain are stated and considered. And the Opposition made by the Colonies to Acts of Parliament, their resorting to Arms in their necessary Defence, against the Military Armaments, employed to enforce them, Vindicated.* Hartford, Conn., 1775.

*Mauduit Letters*

*Jasper Mauduit: Agent in London for the Province of the Massachusetts-Bay 1762–1765.* Massachusetts Historical Society Collections, vol. 74. Boston, 1918.

Mayhew, *Discourse*

Jonathan Mayhew. *A Discourse Concerning Unlimited Submission and Non-Resistance to the Higher Powers.* 1750. Reprinted in Bailyn, *Pamphlets*, at 212–47.

Mayhew, *Discourse Concerning Unlimited Submission*

Jonathan Mayhew. *A Discourse Concerning Unlimited Submission and Non-Resistance to the Higher Powers: With some Reflections on the Resistance made to King Charles I. And on the Anniversary of his Death: In which the Mysterious Doctrine of that Prince's Saintship and Martyrdom is Unriddled.* 1750. Reprinted in *Pulpit of American Revolution*, at 39–104.

Mayhew, *Snare Broken*

Jonathan Mayhew. *The Snare broken. A Thanksgiving-Discourse Preached At the Desire of the West Church in Boston, N.E. Friday May 23, 1766 Occasioned by the Repeal of the Stamp-Act.* Boston, 1766.

Maynard, *Speech in reply to Strafford*

John Maynard. *Mr. Maynards Speech Before Both Houses in Parliament, upon Wednesday the xxiiijth of March, in reply upon the Earle of Straffords Answer to his Articles at the Barre.* [London], 1641.

McDonald, *Novus*

Forrest McDonald. *Novus Ordo Seclorum: The Intellectual Origins of the Constitution.* Lawrence, Ks., 1985.

McIlwain, *Revolution*

Charles Howard McIlwain. *The American Revolution: A Constitutional Interpretation.* Ithaca, N.Y., 1958.

[Meredith], *Question Stated*

[Sir William Meredith.] *The Question Stated, Whether the Freeholders of Middlesex lost their Right, by voting for Mr. Wilkes at the last Election?* London, [1769].

[Meredith], *Remarks on Taxation*
[Sir William Meredith.] *Historical Remarks on the Taxation of Free States, in a Series of Letters to a Friend.* London, 1778.

Millar, *Observations Concerning Ranks*
John Millar. *Observations Concerning the Distinction of Ranks in Society.* 2d ed. London, 1773.

Missing, *Letter to Mansfield on Instructions*
John Missing. *A Letter to the Right Honourable William Lord Mansfield, Lord Chief Justice of the Court of King's Bench: Proving that the Subjects of England, lawfully assembled to Petition their King, or to Elect or Instruct their Representatives, are intitled to Freedom of Debate; and that all Suits and Prosecutions for exerting that Right, are Unconstitutional and Illegal.* London, 1770.

[Moir], *Obedience the best Charter*
[John Moir.] *Obedience the Best Charter; or, Law the Only Sanction of Liberty. In a Letter to the Rev. Dr. Price.* London, 1776.

Molesworth, *Principles of a Real Whig*
*The Principles of a Real Whig; Contained in a Preface to the Famous Hotoman's Franco-Gallia, Written by the late Lord-Viscount Molesworth; And now Reprinted at the Request of the London Association. To which are added their Resolutions and Circular Letter.* London, 1775.

Montesquieu, *Spirit of Laws*
Baron de Montesquieu. *The Spirit of Laws. Translated from the French of M. de Secondat, Baron de Montesquieu, by Mr. Nugent.* 2d ed. 2 vols. London, 1752.

Montgomery, *Sermon at Christiana Bridge*
Joseph Montgomery. *A Sermon Preached at Christiana Bridge and Newcastle, the 10th of July, 1775. Being the Day appointed by the Continental Congress, as a Day of Fasting, Humiliation, and Prayer.* Philadelphia, 1775.

*Monthly Review*
*The Monthly Review; or, Literary Journal: by Several Hands.* London [Monthly magazine].

Montrose, *Precedent in English Law*
James Louis Montrose. *Precedent in English Law and Other Essays.* Edited by Harold Greville Hanbury. Shannon, Ireland, 1968.

Morgan, *Challenge*
Edmund S. Morgan. *The Challenge of the American Revolution.* New York, 1978.

Morgan, *Prologue*
    *Prologue to Revolution: Sources and Documents on the Stamp Act Crisis, 1764–1766.* Edited by Edmund S. Morgan. Chapel Hill, N.C., 1959.
[Mortimer], *National Debt*
    [Thomas Mortimer.] *The National Debt No National Grievance; or the Real State of the Nation, with respect to its civil and religious Liberty, Commerce, Public-Credit, and Finances.* London, 1768.
Moss, *Connecticut Election Sermon*
    Joseph Moss. *An Election Sermon, Preached Before the General Assembly of the Colony of Connecticut, at Hartford, May the 12th. 1715.* New London, Conn., 1715.
Mulford, *Speech to New York Assembly*
    *Samuel Mulford's Speech to the Assembly at New-York, April the Second, 1714.* [New York, 1714.]
[Mulgrave], *Letter from a Member*
    [C. J. Phipps, Lord Mulgrave.] *A Letter from a Member of Parliament to One of his Constituents, on the Late Proceedings of the House of Commons in the Middlesex Elections.* London, 1769.
Mullet, *Fundamental Law*
    Charles F. Mullet. *Fundamental Law and the American Revolution 1760–1776.* New York, 1933.
Munro, *Bristol*
    Wilfred H. Munro. *The History of Bristol, R.I.—The Story of the Mount Hope Lands From the Visit of the Northmen to the Present Time.* Providence, R.I., 1880.
[Nedham], *Excellencie of a Free State*
    [Marchamont Nedham.] *The Excellencie of a Free State.* London, 1767.
Nelson, *American Tory*
    William H. Nelson. *The American Tory.* Boston, 1964.
Nelson, "Eighteenth Century"
    William E. Nelson. "The Eighteenth-Century Background of John Marshall's Constitutional Jurisprudence." 76 *Michigan Law Review* (1978):893–960.
Nelson, "Ideology in Search of Context"
    Jeffrey M. Nelson. "Ideology in Search of Context: Eighteenth-Century British Political Thought and the Loyalists of the American Revolution." 20 *Historical Journal* (1977):741–49.
*New York Journal of Votes*
    *Journal of the Votes and Proceedings of the General Assembly of the Colony of New-York. Began the 8th Day of November, 1743; and Ended the 23th of December, 1765 Vol. II. Published by Order of the General Assembly.* New York, 1766.

Noble, "Lions or Jackals"
Richard L. Noble. "Lions or Jackals? The Independence of the Judges in Rex v. Hampden." 14 *Stanford Law Review* (1962):711–61.

*North Carolina Colonial Records*
*The Colonial Records of North Carolina, Published Under the Supervision of the Trustees of the Public Libraries, By Order of the General Assembly.* Vols. 7–10. Edited by William L. Saunders. Raleigh, N.C., 1890.

Northcote, *Observations on Rights*
Thomas Northcote. *Observations on the Natural and Civil Rights of Mankind, the Prerogatives of Princes, and the Powers of Government.* London, 1781.

Okoye, "Chattel Slavery"
F. Nwabueze Okoye. "Chattel Slavery as the Nightmare of the American Revolutionaries." 37 *William and Mary Quarterly* (1980):3–28.

[Oldfield], *History of the Boroughs*
[J. H. B. Oldfield.] *An Entire and Complete History, Political and Personal, of the Boroughs of Great Britain; to which is Prefixed, an Original Sketch of Constitutional Rights, from the Earliest Period Until the Present Time; and the Principles of our Ancient Representation Traced from the Most Authentic Records, Supported by Undeniable Testimonies, and Illustrated by a Variety of Notes and References, Collected from the Most Respectable, Legal, Political, and Historical Authorities.* 3 vols. London, 1792.

Olson, "Parliamentary Law"
Alison Gilbert Olson. "Parliament, Empire, and Parliamentary Law, 1776." In *Three British Revolutions: 1641, 1688, 1776,* edited by J. G. A. Pocock, at 289–322. Princeton, N.J., 1980.

Paley, *Principles of Philosophy*
William Paley. *The Principles of Moral and Political Philosophy.* London, 1785.

[Parker], *Case of Shipmony*
[Henry Parker.] *The Case of Shipmony briefly discoursed, according to the Grounds of Law, Policy, and Conscience. And Most Humbly Presented to the Censure and Correction of the High Court of Parliament.* n.i., 1640.

[Parker], *Observations upon some Answers*
[Henry Parker.] *Observations upon some of his Majesties late Answers and Expresses.* [London, 1642].

*Parliamentary History*
*The Parliamentary History of England, From the Earliest Period to the Year 1803.* 36 vols. London, 1806–1820.

Parmenter, *Pelham*
> C. O. Parmenter. *History of Pelham, Mass. From 1736 to 1898, Including the Early History of Prescott.* Amherst, Mass., 1898.

Patten, *Discourse at Hallifax*
> William Patten. *A Discourse Delivered at Hallifax in the County of Plymouth, July 24th 1766. On the Day of Thanks-giving to Almighty God, throughout the Province of the Massachusetts-Bay in New England, for the Repeal of the STAMP-ACT.* Boston, 1766.

Payson, *Election Sermon*
> Phillips Payson. *A Sermon Preached before the Honorable Council, and the Honorable House of Representatives, of the State of Massachusetts-Bay, in New-England, at Boston, May 27, 1778. Being the Anniversary for the Election of the Honorable Council.* 1778. Reprinted in *Pulpit of American Revolution*, at 329–53.

Peach, *Richard Price*
> Bernard Peach. *Richard Price and the Ethical Foundations of the American Revolution.* Durham, N.C., 1979.

Peckard, *Nature and Extent of Liberty*
> Peter Peckard. *The Nature and Extent of Civil and Religious Liberty. A Sermon Preached before the University of Cambridge, November the 5th, 1783.* Cambridge, England, 1783.

Peters, *Massachusetts Constitution*
> Ronald M. Peters. *The Massachusetts Constitution of 1780: A Social Compact.* Amherst, Mass., 1978.

*Petition in Favour of Americans*
> *The Address, Petition, and Remonstrance, of the City of London, to the King, in Favour of the Americans, and their Resolves, presented to his Majesty, July 5, 1775.* [Single sheet broadside.] Huntington Library, Cal., rare book no. 55343.

*Petition of Middlesex to King, 24 May 1769*
> *A Petition of the Freeholders of the County of Middlesex, Presented to his Majesty, the 24th of May, 1769.* London, [1769].

[Phelps], *Rights of the Colonies*
> [Richard Phelps.] *The Rights of the Colonies, And the Extent of the Legislative Authority of Great-Britain, Briefly Stated and Considered.* London, 1769.

"Philonomos," *Liberty of the Subject*
> "Philonomos." *The Liberty of the Subject, and Dignity of the Crown, Maintained and Secured Without the Application of a Military, Unconstitutional Force, or the Tyranny of any inconsiderable Minister. Supported By the Opinion of a Lord High Chancellor of England. Inscribed to Sir Richard Perrot, Bart.* London, [1768].

Pitkin, "Obligation and Consent"

Hanna Pitkin. "Obligation and Consent—I." 59 *American Political Science Review* (1965):990–99.

Pocock, *Ancient Constitution*
J. G. A. Pocock. *The Ancient Constitution and the Feudal Law: A Study of English Historical Thought in the Seventeenth Century.* Cambridge, England, 1957.

Pocock, *Machiavellian Moment*
J. G. A. Pocock. *The Machiavellian Moment: Florentine Political Thought and the Atlantic Republican Tradition.* Princeton, N.J., 1975.

Pole, *Paths to Past*
J. R. Pole. *Paths to the American Past.* New York, 1979.

Pole, *Representation*
J. R. Pole. *Political Representation in England and the Origins of the American Republic.* New York, 1966.

*Political Register*
*The Political Register; and Impartial Review of New Books* London [monthly magazine].

*Political Writings of James Otis*
*Some Political Writings of James Otis. Collected with an Introduction by Charles F. Mullett.* The University of Missouri Studies: A Quarterly of Research. Vol. 4 (July–October 1929).

Porteus, *Sermon on Charles I*
Beilby Porteus. *A Sermon Preached before the Honourable House of Commons, at St. Margaret's, Westminster, on Friday, January xxx, 1767.* London, 1767.

Pownall, *Administration Fifth Edition*
Thomas Pownall. *The Administration of the British Colonies. The Fifth Edition. Wherein their Rights and Constitution are discussed and stated.* 2 vols. London, 1774.

Pownall, *Pownall*
Charles A. W. Pownall. *Thomas Pownall M.P., F.R.S., Governor of Massachusetts Bay.* London, 1908.

Price, "Introduction to Two Tracts"
Richard Price. "Introduction," to Price, *Two Tracts.*

Price, *Nature of Civil Liberty*
Richard Price. *Observations on the Nature of Civil Liberty, the Principles of Government, and the Justice and Policy of War with America.* London, 1776.

Price, *Two Tracts*
Richard Price. *Two Tracts on Civil Liberty, the War with America, and the Debts and Finances of the Kingdom: with a General Introduction and Supplement.* London, 1778. Reprint. New York, 1972.

Price, *Two Tracts: Tract One*

Richard Price. *Observations on the Nature of Civil Liberty, the Principles of Government, and the Justice and Policy of the War with America.* 8th ed. London, 1778. Reprinted in Price, *Two Tracts*, at 1–112.

Price, *Two Tracts: Tract Two*

Richard Price. *Additional Observations on the Nature and Value of Civil Liberty, and the War with America: Also Observations on Schemes for raising Money by Public Loans; An Historical Deduction and Analysis of the National Debt; And a brief Account of the Debts and Resources of France.* 3rd ed. 1778. Reprinted in Price, *Two Tracts*, at vii–xiv, 1–216.

[Priestley,] *Address to Dissenters*

[Joseph Priestley.] *An Address to Protestant Dissenters of all Denominations, on the Approaching Election of Members of Parliament With Respect to the State of Public Liberty in General, and of American Affairs in Particular.* Philadelphia, 1774.

Priestley, *First Principles*

Joseph Priestley. *An Essay on the First Principles of Government; and on the Nature of Political, Civil, and Religious Liberty.* London, 1768.

[Priestley], *Present State of Liberty*

[Joseph Priestley.] *The Present State of Liberty in Great Britain and Her Colonies.* London, 1769.

*Prior Documents*

*A Collection of Interesting, Authentic Papers, Relative to the Dispute Between Great Britain and America; Shewing the Causes and Progress of that Misunderstanding From 1764 to 1775.* London, 1777.

*Protests of the Lords*

*A Complete Collection of the Protests of the Lords, with Historical Introductions. Ed. from the Journals of the Lords by James E. Thorold Rogers.* 3 vols. Oxford, 1875.

*Protests of the Lords of Ireland*

*A Collection of the Protests of the Lords of Ireland, From 1634 to 1771.* Dublin, 1772.

*Pulpit of American Revolution*

*The Pulpit of the American Revolution or, The Political Sermons of the Period of 1776.* Edited by John Wingate Thornton. Boston, 1860.

[Pulteney], *Plan of Reunion*

[William Pulteney.] *Plan of Re-Union Between Great Britain and Her Colonies.* London, 1778.

Pulteney, *Thoughts on Present State*

William Pulteney. *Thoughts on the Present State of Affairs with America, and the Means of Conciliation.* 5th ed. London, 1778.

"Putney Debates"
    "The Putney Debates: At the General Council of Officers, 1647."
    Printed in *Puritanism and Liberty Being the Army Debates (1647–9)*
    *from the Clarke Manuscripts with Supplementary Documents,* edited
    by A. S. P. Woodhouse, at 1–124. Chicago, 1938.
Pym, *Declaration of Grievances*
    John Pym. *A Declaration of the Grievances of the Kingdome.* 1642.
    Reprinted in 4 *Somers' Tracts,* at 390–404.
Quincy, *Memoir*
    Josiah Quincy. *Memoir of the Life of Josiah Quincy Jun. of Massachu-*
    *setts.* Boston, 1825.
Quincy, *Reports*
    Josiah Quincy, Jr.. *Reports of Cases Argued and Adjudged in the*
    *Superior Court of Judicature of the Province of Massachusetts Bay.*
    Boston, 1865.
*Records of Rhode Island*
    *Records of the Colony of Rhode Island and Providence Plantations in*
    *New England.* Edited by John Russell Bartlett. 10 vols. 1856.
[Ramsay], *Historical Essay*
    [Allan Ramsay.] *An Historical Essay on the English Constitution: Or,*
    *An Impartial Inquiry into the Elective Power of the People, from the*
    *first Establishment of the Saxons in this Kingdom. Wherein the Right of*
    *Parliament, to Tax our distant Provinces, is explained, and justified,*
    *upon such Constitutional Principles as will afford an equal Security to*
    *the Colonists, as to their Brethren at Home.* London, 1771.
*Remonstrance of Many Thousand*
    *A Remonstrance of Many Thousand Citizens, and other Free-born*
    *People of England, To their owne House of Commons, Occasioned*
    *through the Illegall and Barbarous Imprisonment of that Famous and*
    *Worthy Sufferer for his Countries Freedoms, Lieutenant Col. John*
    *Lilburne.* [London,] 1646.
*Revolution Documents*
    *Documents of the American Revolution 1770–1783.* Edited by K. G.
    Davis. Vols. 1–16. Dublin, 1972–1981.
*Revolutionary Virginia*
    *Revolutionary Virginia: The Road to Independence.* Vol. 1, *Forming*
    *Thunderclouds and the First Convention, 1763–1774. A Documentary*
    *Record.* Compiled by William J. Van Schreeven, edited by Robert L.
    Scribner. Vol. 2, *The Committees and the Second Convention, 1773–*
    *1775. A Documentary Record.* Compiled by William J. Van Schreeven
    and Robert L. Scribner. Vol 3, *The Breaking Storm and the Third*
    *Convention, 1775. A Documentary Record.* Compiled and edited by

Robert L. Scribner. Vol. 4, *The Committee of Safety and the Balance of Forces, 1775. A Documentary Record.* Compiled and edited by Robert L. Scribner and Brent Tarter. Vol. 5, *The Clash of Arms and the Fourth Convention, 1775–1776. A Documentary Record.* Compiled and edited by Robert L. Scribner and Brent Tarter. Vol. 6, *The Time for Decision, 1776. A Documentary Record.* Compiled and edited by Robert L. Scribner and Brent Tarter. [Charlottesville, Va.,] 1973–81.

Richard, Bishop of Peterborough, *Sermon on King Charles*
Richard, Lord Bishop of Peterborough. *A Sermon Preached before the House of Lords, In the Abbey-Church of Westminster, on Monday, January 30, 1758. Being the Day appointed to be observed as the Day of the Martyrdom of King Charles I.* London, 1758.

Ritcheson, *British Politics*
Charles R. Ritcheson. *British Politics and the American Revolution.* Norman, Okla., 1954.

Robbins, *Commonwealthman*
Caroline Robbins. *The Eighteenth-Century Commonwealthman: Studies in the Transmission, Development and Circumstance of English Liberal Thought from the Restoration of Charles II until the War with the Thirteen Colonies.* Cambridge, Mass., 1959.

Robert, Bishop of Peterborough, *Sermon to Lords*
Robert, Lord Bishop of Peterborough. *A Sermon Preached before the Lords Spiritual and Temporal, in the Abbey-Church Westminster: on Saturday, January 30, 1768: Being the Day Appointed to be observed as the Day of the Martyrdom of King Charles I.* London, 1768.

Robertson, *Chatham*
Sir Charles Grant Robertson. *Chatham and the British Empire.* Collier ed. New York, 1962.

[Robertson], *Liberty, Property, and Religion*
[William Robertson.] *The Liberty, Property, and Religion of the Whigs.* London, 1713.

Rogers, *Empire and Liberty*
Alan Rogers. *Empire and Liberty: American Resistance to British Authority 1755–1763.* Berkeley, Cal., 1974.

Rokeby, *Further Examination*
Matthew Robinson-Morris, Second Baron Rokeby. *A Further Examination of our Present American Measures and of the Reasons and the Principles on which they are founded.* Bath, England, 1776.

Rossiter, *Political Thought*
Clinton Rossiter. *The Political Thought of the American Revolution.* New York, 1963.

[Rous], *Claim of the Commons*
[George Rous.] *The Claim of the House of Commons, to a Negative on*

*the Appointment of Ministers by the Crown, Examined and Confuted.* London, 1784.

[Rous], *Letter to Jurors*

[George Rous.] *A Letter to the Jurors of Great-Britain. Occasioned by an Opinion of the Court of King's Bench, read by Lord Chief Justice Mansfield in the Case of the King and Woodfall; and said to have been left by his Lordship with the Clerk of Parliament.* London, 1771.

Rude, "London Mob"

George Rude. "The London 'Mob' of the Eighteenth Century." 2 *Historical Journal* (1959):1–18.

Rude, *Wilkes and Liberty*

George Rude. *Wilkes and Liberty: A Social Study of 1763 to 1774.* New York, 1962.

[Ruffhead], *Considerations*

[Owen Ruffhead.] *Considerations on the Present Dangerous Crisis.* Edinburgh, 1763.

Rushworth, *Historical Collections: Third Part*

John Rushworth. *Historical Collections: The Third Part; in Two Volumes.* Vol. 1. London, 1692.

Rusticus, *Good of Community*

Rusticus. *The Good of the Community Impartially Considered.* Boston, 1754.

Rutherforth, *Natural Law*

T. Rutherforth. *Institutes of Natural Law Being the substance of a Course of Lectures on Grotius de Jure Belli et Pacis Read in S. Johns College Cambridge.* 2 vols. Cambridge, England, 1754.

Ryder, "Parliamentary Diaries"

"Parliamentary Diaries of Nathaniel Ryder, 1764–7." Edited by P. D. G. Thomas. *Camden Miscellany,* vol. 23. Camden Society Fourth Series, vol. 7, at 229–351. London, [1969].

[Saint-John], *Speech or Declaration*

[Oliver St. John.] *The Speech or Declaration of Mr. St. John, His Majesties Solicitor-Generall. Delivered at a Conference of both Houses of Parlament, held 16. Caroli, 1640. Concerning Ship-Money. As it is revised, and allowed according to order.* London, 1641.

*St. Patrick's Anti-Stamp Chronicle*

*St. Patrick's Anti-Stamp Chronicle: Or, Independent Magazine, of News, Politics, and Literary Entertainment.* Dublin.

Samson, *Sermon at Roxbury-Camp*

Ezra Samson. *A Sermon Preached at Roxbury-Camp, Before Col. Cotton's Regiment; On the 20th of July, P.M. 1775. Being a Day set apart for Fasting and Prayer, throughout all the United Colonies in America.* Watertown, 1775.

Samuel, Bishop of St. David's, *Sermon on Charles I*
> Samuel, Lord Bishop of St. David's. *A Sermon Preached before the Lords Spiritual and Temporal in the Abbey Church, Westminster, On Saturday, January 30, 1762, Being the Anniversary of the Martyrdom of King Charles I.* London, 1762.

Savelle, "Nationalism in the Revolution"
> Max Savelle. "Nationalism and other Loyalties in the American Revolution." 67 *American Historical Review* (1962):901–23. Reprinted in Max Savelle, *Is Liberalism Dead? and other Essays.* Seattle, Wash., 1967, at 97–126.

[Sayre], *Englishman Deceived*
> [Stephen Sayre.] *The Englishman Deceived; A Political Piece: Wherein Some very Important Secrets of State are briefly recited, And offered to the Consideration of the Public.* New York, 1768.

Schutz, "Galloway"
> John A. Schutz. "Joseph Galloway's *Historical and Political Reflections.*" In *The Colonial Legacy: Volume I, Loyalist Historians,* edited by Lawrence H. Leder, at 59–88. New York, 1971.

Schuyler, *Empire*
> Robert Livingston Schuyler. *Parliament and the British Empire: Some Constitutional Controversies Concerning Imperial Legislative Jurisdiction.* New York, 1929.

*Scots Magazine*
> *The Scots Magazine* Edinburgh [monthly magazine].

*Select Collection of Letters*
> *A Select Collection of the Most Interesting Letters on the Government, Liberty and Constitution of England; Which have appeared in the different News-papers from the elevation of Lord Bute, to the death of the Earl of Egremont.* 2d ed. 3 vols. London, 1763–1764.

[Sharp], *Defence of Strictures*
> [William Sharp.] *A Defence of Strictures on Dr. Lowth, Respecting Liberty. With Observations on Other Men and Things.* 2d ed. London, 1767.

Sharp, *Law of Nature*
> Granville Sharp. *A Tract on the Law of Nature, and Principles of Action in Man.* London, 1777.

Shebbeare, *Essay on National Society*
> J. Shebbeare. *An Essay on the Origin, Progress and Establishment of National Society; in which the Principles of Government, the Definitions of physicial, moral, civil, and religious Liberty, contained in Dr. Price's Observations, &c. are fairly examined and fully refuted: Together with a Justification of the Legislature, in reducing America to Obedience by Force.* London, 1776.

[Shebbeare], *Third Letter*

    [John Shebbeare.] *A Third Letter to the People of England, on Liberty, Taxes, and the Application of Public Money.* 4th ed. London, 1756.

[Sheridan], *Observations on the Doctrine*

    [Charles Francis Sheridan.] *Observations on the Doctrine laid down by Sir William Blackstone, Respecting the extent of the Power of the British Parliament, Particularly with relation to Ireland. In a letter to Sir William Blackstone, with a Postcript Addressed to Lord North.* 2d ed. London, 1779.

[Sheridan], *Review of Three Questions*

    [Charles Francis Sheridan.] *A Review of the Three Great National Questions Relative to the Declaration of Right, Poynings' Law, and the Mutiny Bill.* London, 1781.

[Shipley], *Intended Speech*

    [Jonathan Shipley.] *A Speech, Intended to have been Spoken on the Bill, for Altering the Charters of the Colony of Massachusett's Bay.* London, [1774].

Shute, *Election Sermon*

    Daniel Shute. *A Sermon Preached before his Excellency Francis Bernard, Esq; Governor, his Honour Thomas Hutchinson. Esq; Lieutenant-Governor, the Honourable His Majestay's Council, and the Honourable House of Representatives, of the Province of the Massachusets-Bay in New-England, May 25th, 1768.* Boston, 1768.

Smith, "John Adams"

    James Morton Smith. "John Adams and the Coming of the Revolution." In *Perspectives on the American Revolution: A Bicentennial Contribution,* edited by George G. Suggs, Jr., at 75–98. Carbondale, Ill., 1977.

Smith, "1758 Pennsylvania Brief"

    William Smith. "Brief in Matter of Smith" in "Law and Liberty: In the Matter of Provost William Smith of Philadelphia, 1758." 38 *William and Mary Quarterly* (1981):681–701.

*Society for Constitutional Information*

    Two Publications distributed by the Society for Constitutional Information without title, imprint, or binding. The copies at the Huntington Library, San Marino, Cal. are numbered: for 1782, rare book no. 310802; for 1783, rare book no. 305204.

*Somers' Tracts*

    *A Collection of Scarce and Valuable Tracts, on the Most Interesting and Entertaining Subjects: But Chiefly such as Relate to the History and Constitution of these Kingdoms. Selected from an Infinite Number in Print and Manuscript, in the Royal, Cotton, Sion, and other Public, as well as Private, Libraries; Particularly that of the Late Lord Somers.* Edited by Walter Scott. 2d ed. Vols. 4 and 5. London, 1809–1815.

*South-Carolina Gazette*
    Charles Town, S.C. [weekly newspaper].
*Speech upon the Scaffold*
    King Charles. *His Speech Made upon the Scaffold at Whitehall-Gate,*
    *Immediately before his Execution, On Tuesday the 30 of Jan. 1648. With*
    *a Relation of the manner of his going to Execution.* London, 1649.
[Squire], *Historical Essay on Ballance*
    [Samuel Squire.] *An Historical Essay Upon the Ballance of Civil Power*
    *in England, From its first Conquest by the Anglo-Saxons, to the Time of*
    *the Revolution; in which is introduced a new Dissertation upon Parties:*
    *With a proper Dedication to the Freeholders and Burgesses of Great*
    *Britain.* London, 1748.
"Stamp Act Debates"
    "Debates on the Declaratory Act and the Repeal of the Stamp Act,
    1766," 17 *American Historical Review* (1912):563–86.
Stark, *Loyalists*
    James H. Stark. *The Loyalists of Massachusetts and the Other Side of*
    *the American Revolution.* Boston, Mass., 1910.
*State Trials*
    *A Complete Collection of State Trials and Proceedings for High Treason*
    *and Other Crimes and Misdemeanors From the Earliest Period to the*
    *Year 1783, With Notes and Other Illustrations.* Compiled by T. B.
    Howell. 34 vols. London, 1816–1828.
Stearns, *View of the Controversy*
    William Stearns. *A View of the Controversy subsisting between Great-*
    *Britain and the American Colonies. A Sermon Preached at a Fast in*
    *Marlborough in Massachusetts-Bay. On Thursday May 11, 1775.*
    *Agreeable to a Recommendation of the Provincial Congress.*
    Watertown, Mass., 1775.
[Stevens], *Discourse on Constitution*
    [William Stevens.] *A Discourse on the English Constitution; Extracted*
    *from a Late Eminent Writer and Applicable to the Present Times.*
    London, 1776.
Stevens, *Election Sermon*
    Benjamin Stevens. *A Sermon Preached at Boston, Before the Great and*
    *General Court or Assembly of the Province of the Massachusetts Bay in*
    *New England, May 27. 1761. Being the Day appointed by Royal*
    *Charter for the Election of his Majesty's Council for the said Province.*
    Boston, 1761.
[Stevens], *Revolution Vindicated*
    [William Stevens.] *The Revolution Vindicated, and Constitutional*
    *Liberty Asserted. In Answer to the Reverend Dr. Watson's Accession*

*Sermon, Preached before the University of Cambridge, on October 25th, 1776.* Cambridge, England, 1777.

[Stewart], *Letter to Dr. Price*

[James Stewart.] *A Letter to the Rev. Dr. Price, F.R.S. Wherein his Observations on the Nature of Civil Liberty, the Principles of Government, &c. Are Candidly Examined; His Fundamental Principles refuted, and the Fallacy of his Reasoning from these Principles detected. Also the True Principles of Liberty, Explained and Demonstrated; the Constitutional Authority of the Supreme Legislature of Great Britain, Over every Part of the British Dominions, Both in the Matter of Legislation and Taxation, and in every Act of Legal Authority, Asserted and Fully Vindicated.* London, 1776.

Stout, *Perfect Crisis*

Neil R. Stout. *The Perfect Crisis: The Beginning of the Revolutionary War.* New York, 1976.

[Strafford], *Brief and Perfect Relation*

[Thomas Wentworth, earl of Strafford.] *A Briefe and Perfect Relation, of the Answeres and Replies of Thomas Earle of Strafford; To the Articles exhibited against him, by the House of Commons on the thirteenth of April, An. Dom. 1641.* London, 1647.

Sullivan, *Lectures on the Constitution*

Francis Stoughton Sullivan. *Lectures on the Constitution and Laws of England: With a Commentary on Magna Carta, and Illustrations of Many of the English Statutes. To which Authorities are added, and a Discourse is prefixed, concerning the Laws and Government of England by Gilbert Stuart, LL.D.* 2d ed. London, 1776.

Sydney, *Discourses Concerning Government*

Algernon Sydney. *Discourses Concerning Government.* Reprinted in *The Works of Algernon Sydney.* Revised by J. Robertson. London, 1772, at 1–542.

*The Crisis*

*The Crisis.* London, January 1775 to 6 October 1776. [Newspaper "Printed and published for the Authors by T. W. Shaw."]

*They Preached Liberty*

*They Preached Liberty: With an Introductory Essay and Biographical Sketches by Franklin P. Cole.* New York, 1941.

Thomas, *British Politics*

P. D. G. Thomas. *British Politics and the Stamp Act Crisis: The First Phase of the American Revolution, 1763–1767.* Oxford, England, 1975.

Thompson, *African Trade*

Tho. Thompson. *The African Trade for Negro Slaves, Shewn to be*

*Consistent with Principles of Humanity, and with the Laws of Revealed Religion*. Canterbury, England, [1772].

Thompson, *Whigs and Hunters*
E. P. Thompson. *Whigs and Hunters: The Origin of the Black Act*. New York, 1975.

Thornton, "Introduction and Notes"
John Wingate Thornton. "Introduction and Notes" to *Pulpit of American Revolution*.

*Three Speeches Against Army*
*Three Speeches Against Continuing the Army, &c. As they were Spoken in the House of Commons the Last Session of Parliament. To which are Added the Reasons given by the Lords, who Protested against the Bill for Punishing Mutiny and Desertion*. London, 1718.

Throop, *Thanksgiving Sermon*
Benjamin Throop. *A Thanksgiving Sermon, Upon the Occasion, of the glorious News of the repeal of the Stamp Act; Preached in New-Concord, in Norwich, June 26, 1766*. New London, Conn., 1766.

Toohey, *Liberty and Empire*
Robert E. Toohey. *Liberty and Empire: British Radical Solutions to the American Problem 1774–1776*. Lexington, Ky., 1978.

[Towers], *Letter to Samuel Johnson*
[Joseph Towers.] *A Letter to Dr. Samuel Johnson: Occasioned by his late Political Publications. With an Appendix, Containing Some Observations on a Pamphlet Lately Published by Dr. Shebbeare*. London, 1775.

[Towers], *Letter to Wesley*
[Joseph Towers.] *A Letter to the Rev. Mr. John Wesley; In Answer to his late Pamphlet, Entitled, "Free Thoughts on the Present State of Public Affairs."* London, 1771.

*Town and County Magazine*
*The Town and Country Magazine; or Universal Repository of Knowledge, Instruction, and Entertainment* London [monthly magazine].

*True Copy*
*A True Copy of the Journal of the High Court of Justice for the Tryal of K. Charles I. As it was Read in the House of Commons, and attested under the hand of Phelps, Clerk to that Infamous Court*. Edited by J. Nalson. London, 1684.

Trumbull, *Discourse at New Haven*
Benjamin Trumbull. *Discourse, Delivered at the Anniversary Meeting of the Freemen of the Town of New-Haven, April 12, 1773*. New Haven, Conn., 1773.

Tuck, *Natural Rights Theories*
Richard Tuck. *Natural Rights Theories: Their Origin and Develop-ment*. Cambridge, England, 1979.

Tucker, *Election Sermon*
John Tucker. *A Sermon Preached at Cambridge, Before his Excellency Thomas Hutchinson, Esq; Governor; His Honor Andrew Oliver, Esq; Lieutenant-Governor, the Honorable His Majesty's Council, and the Honorable House of Representatives, of the Province of the Massachusetts-Bay in New England, May 29th, 1771. Being the Anniversary for the Election of His Majesty's Council for the Province*. Boston, 1771.

Tucker, *Treatise*
Josiah Tucker. *A Treatise Concerning Civil Government, In Three Parts*. London, 1781.

Tully, *Discourse on Property*
James Tully. *A Discourse on Property: John Locke and his Adversaries*. Cambridge, England, 1980.

Valentine, *Lord North*
Alan Valentine. *Lord North*. 2 vols. Norman, Okla., 1967.

Vyse, *Sermon Preached before Commons*
William Vyse. *A Sermon Preached Before the Honourable House of Commons, at the Church of St. Margaret's, Westminster, on Friday, February 27, 1778, Being the Day appointed by His Majesty's Royal Proclamation, to be observed as a Day of Solemn Fasting and Humiliation*. London, 1778.

Walpole, *Memoirs*
Horace Walpole. *Memoirs of the Reign of King George the Third First Published by Sir Denis Le Marchant Bart. and now Re-Edited by G. F. Russell Barker*. 4 vols. New York, 1894.

Warrington, *Grand Jury Charge*
Henry Booth, 2d Baron Delamere. *The Charge of the Right Honourable Henry Earl of Warrington, to the Grand Jury at the Quarter Sessions Held for the County of Chester, On the 25th Day of April, 1693*. London, 1694.

Welles, *Patriotism Described*
Noah Welles. *Patriotism Described and Recommended, in a Sermon Preached before the General Assembly of the Colony of Connecticut, at Hartford, on the Day of the Anniversary Election, May 10th, 1764*. New London, Conn., 1764.

Welsteed, *Dignity and Duty*
William Welsteed. *The Dignity and Duty of the Civil Magistrate. A Sermon Preached in the Audience of His Honour Spencer Phips, Esq;*

*Lieutenant Governour and Commander in Chief, the Honourable His Majesty's Council, and the Honourable House of Representatives, of the Province of the Massachusetts-Bay, in New-England, May 29th 1751. Being the Anniversary for the Election of His Majesty's Council for the said Province.* Boston, 1751.

Wesley, *Some Observations on Liberty*

John Wesley. *Some Observations on Liberty: Occasioned by a late Tract.* London, 1776.

West, *Election Sermon*

Samuel West. *A Sermon Preached Before the Honorable Council, and the Honorable House of Representatives, of the Colony of the Massachusetts-Bay, in New-England. May 29th, 1776. Being the Anniversary for the Election of the Honorable Council for the Colony.* Boston, 1776, reprinted in *Pulpit of American Revolution*, at 259–322.

White, *Connecticut Election Sermon*

Stephen White. *Civil Rulers Gods by Office, and the Duties of such Considered and Enforced. A Sermon Preached before the General Assembly of the Colony of Connecticut, at Hartford, on the Day of their Anniversary Election, May the 12th, 1763.* New London, Conn., 1763.

Wilkes, *Arms of Liberty and Slavery*

John Wilkes. *Arms of Liberty and Slavery (a Letter to the Gentlemen, Clergy, and Freeholders of the County of Middlesex, 18 June 1768).* Cambridge University Library Broadsides B. 76.5.

Wilkes, *English Liberty*

John Wilkes. *English Liberty: Being a Collection of Interesting Tracts, From the Year 1762 to 1769. Containing the Private Correspondence, Public Letters, Speeches, and Addresses, of John Wilkes, Esq. Humbly Dedicated to the King.* London, [1770].

[Wilkes], *Letter to Johnson*

[John Wilkes.] *A Letter to Samuel Johnson, L.L.D.* London, 1770.

Willcox, *Age of Aristocracy*

William B. Willcox. *The Age of Aristocracy 1688–1830.* Lexington, Mass., 1966.

Williams, *Election Sermon*

Abraham Williams. *A Sermon Preach'd at Boston, Before the Great and General Court or Assembly of the Province of the Massachusetts-Bay in New-England, May 26, 1762. Being the Day appointed by Royal Charter, for the Election of His Majesty's Council for the said Province.* Boston, 1762.

[Williams], *Essential Rights*

[Elisha Williams.] *The Essential Rights and Liberties of Protestants. A Seasonable Plea for the Liberty of Conscience, and the Right of private Judgment, In Matters of Religion, Without any Controul from human*

*Authority. Being a Letter from a Gentleman in the Massachusetts-Bay to his Friend in Connecticut.* Boston, 1744.

[Williams], *Letters on Liberty*
[David Williams.] *Letters on Political Liberty. Addressed to a Member of the English House of Commons, on his being Chosen into the Committee of an Associating County.* London, 1782.

Wills, *Inventing America*
Garry Wills. *Inventing America: Jefferson's Declaration of Independence.* Garden City, N.Y., 1978.

Wilson, "Speech in the Pennsylvania Convention"
James Wilson. "Speech in the Pennsylvania Convention, January 1775." In *The Debate on the American Revolution 1761–1783.* Edited by Max Beloff, at 178–79. London, 1949.

Wilson, "Speech of 1775"
James Wilson. "Speech Delivered in the Convention for the Province of Pennsylvania." In 2 *The Works of James Wilson,* edited by Robert Green McCloskey, at 747–58. Cambridge, Mass., 1967.

Wood, *Creation*
Gordon S. Wood. *The Creation of the American Republic 1776–1787.* Chapel Hill, N.C., 1969.

Wooddeson, *Jurisprudence*
Richard Wooddeson. *Elements of Jurisprudence Treated of in the Preliminary Part of a Course of Lectures on the Law of England.* Dublin, 1792.

Wright, *Grand Jury Speech*
John Wright. *The Speech of John Wright, Esq; One of the Magistrates of Lancaster County, to the Court and Grand-Jury, on his Removal from the Commission of the Peace at the Quarter-Sessions held at Lancaster for the said County in May 1741.* [Philadelphia, 1741.]

Wynne, *Eunomus*
Edward Wynne. *Eunomus: or, Dialogues Concerning the Law and Constitution of England. With an Essay on Dialogue.* 2d ed. 4 vols. London, 1785.

*York Address of January 1781*
*An Address From the Committee of Association of the County of York, to the Electors of Great-Britain. To which are prefixed the Resolutions of that Committee, at their Meetings, Held on the 3rd and 4th of January, 1781, and the Instrument of Instructions to their Deputies.* n.i., n.d.

Yorke, *Reason against Precedent*
Henry Yorke. *Reason Urged against Precedent, in a Letter to the People of Derby.* London, 1793.

Young, *Constitution Safe*

Arthur Young. *The Constitution Safe without Reform: Containing Some Remarks on a Book Entitled the Commonwealth in Danger, by John Cartwright, Esq.* Bury St. Edmund's, England, 1795.

Young, *Political Arithmetic*

Arthur Young. *Political Arithmetic. Containing Observations on the Present State of Great Britain; and the Principles of her Policy in the Encouragement of Agriculture.* London, 1774.

[Young], *Political Essays*

[Arthur Young.] *Political Essays Concerning the Present State of the British Empire.* London, 1772.

Zubly, *Stamp-Act Repealed*

J. J. Zubly. *The Stamp-Act Repealed; a Sermon Preached in the Meeting at Savannah in Georgia, June 25th, 1766.* 2d ed. Savannah, Ga., 1766.

# Index

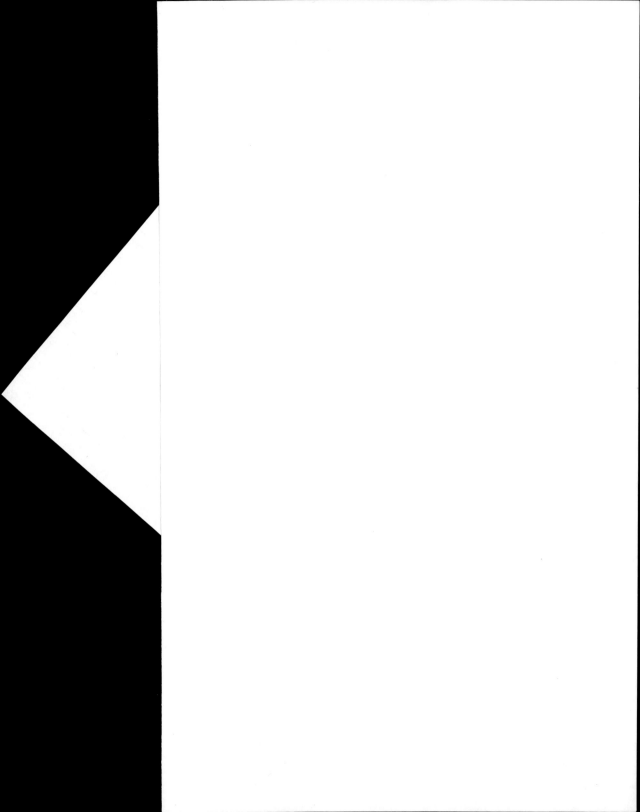

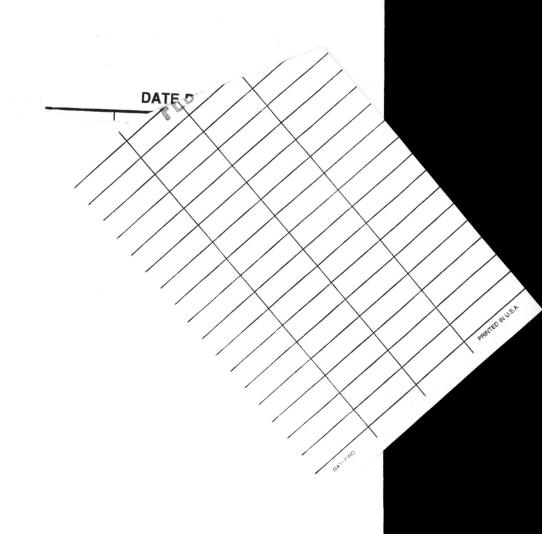

DATE D

PRINTED IN U.S.A.

GAYLORD